MUCK CITY

WINNING AND LOSING
IN FOOTBALL'S
FORGOTTEN TOWN

BRYAN MEALER

CROWN ARCHETYPE

NEW YORK

Library of Congress Cataloging-in-Publication Data
Mealer, Bryan.
Muck city / by Bryan Mealer.
     p.   cm.
1. Football—Florida—Belle Glade—History. 2. High school football players—Florida—Belle
Glade—History. 3. Belle Glade (Fla.)—History. 4. Belle Glade (Fla.)—Social conditions.
5. Belle Glade (Fla.)—Economic conditions. I. Title.
GV959.52.B45 2012
796.332'620975932—dc23
2012011275

ISBN: 978-0-307-88862-4
eISBN: 978-0-307-88864-8

Printed in the United States of America

Book design by Maria Elias
Jacket design by Michael Nagin
Jacket photograph: Gary Coronado/Palm Beach Post

10   9   8   7   6   5   4   3   2   1

First Edition

To Nolan,
Evelyn, and
Ann Marie

Do or die!
Better not cry!
We shall win!
They shall die!
Kill! Kill! Kill! Kill!

—Raider pregame chant

PROLOGUE

If there was ever a moment to look back upon and remember the love of a town, it was tonight under the lights of Effie C. Grear Field, when all of Belle Glade came out for the Jet.

In a halftime ceremony on homecoming night, Jessie Lee Hester stood on the fifty-yard line and gazed into a familiar crowd. His team, the Glades Central Raiders, was already ahead by thirty-four points—a throwaway game in a march toward another winning season. But tonight's ceremony wasn't about winning and losing. It was about honoring a man who'd come home himself and, long before doing so, had returned some dignity to this blighted lakeside town.

To everyone in the stands, he was known as Jet, the local kid who'd found his way into one of the most elite fraternities in the world, leaving an opening for hundreds of others. And as with many cheering from the bleachers tonight, his history was their own.

He'd grown up among poor migrants: the Jamaicans, Haitians, and African Americans who worked the black muck in one of the most fertile corners of the earth. He'd lived alongside them in the teeming boarding-houses in Belle Glade's "Colored Town," one of six children piled atop one another in a two-room apartment that lacked its own toilet. His mother, Zara, left her brood each morning at four thirty for whatever field was in harvest, and didn't return until late, bent-backed and exhausted, her heavy sleep filling the soupy darkness. Two siblings had been born with autism, and with no father in the house, their care had fallen on Jessie and his older brother Roger. Back in those days there was never enough food, and Jessie remembers once having awakened at school surrounded by his peers after falling out of his desk from hunger. His willowy arms still bore the scars where his field knife had missed the stalk, his mind so hazy from fatigue during long hours in the vegetable rows. To the surprise of many, he would insist that his childhood had been happy, simply because in Belle Glade he'd seen nothing better.

As a high school track star and wide receiver, he could sprint forty yards in 4.2 seconds. Roger was even faster, but he played in the band. And if you believed everything you heard in Belle Glade, neither boy could be called the *fastest ever*. For the graveyards were filled with the bones of all those who'd ever been christened *the greatest*—Friday-night legends such as James Otis Benjamin, Rosailious Hughley, C. W. Haynes—their destinies cut short by common fallibility and a childhood not likely described as happy.

In addition to speed, Hester was blessed with shrewdness. He'd avoided pitfalls: He never smoked or drank or chased women he knew he couldn't outrun. Decades later, his former teammate and future Hall of Famer Isaac Bruce would describe him as one of the most intuitive route runners he'd ever seen play the game. As a young man in Belle Glade, Hester had spied the hidden lanes in the canefields and slipped quietly into the light.

Everyone still remembers the crowd of recruiters and coaches that used to camp outside Zara's house. They remember when Bobby Bowden marched through the front door, grabbed a Coke from the fridge, and announced to the other coaches seated in the living room that "Jessie's *my* boy." He was All-American at Florida State, then, to the shock of everyone back home, taken in the first round of the 1985 draft, number twenty-three, just south of Jerry Rice and William "the Refrigerator" Perry.

It was the first time that Belle Glade had been associated with anything more than sugarcane, black poverty, or disease—the same month as the draft, the town made international headlines when researchers discovered it had the highest rate of AIDS in the world. When Jessie Hester declared himself a Los Angeles Raider, Belle Glade felt a cool wash of redemption. Then the floodgates opened.

In the years that followed, there would be scores of others to enter the league from Belle Glade and Pahokee, the rival town just eight miles across the canefields. Over time it would be hard to watch a game on Sunday and not find a player from the muck. But out of all the young men who made it, who tasted the cream in the faraway places where money and education could now take them, very few came home. Judging from the term papers Jessie composed in college describing his room in Zara's house ("My room at home is sunflower yellow. My mother made me matching curtains and a spread . . ."), to the way he'd suddenly appear during off-seasons, parting Avenue E like Moses in a red Mercedes—it was as if he'd spent his whole career just waiting to get back.

"After ten years in the NFL," the announcer said over the public-address system, "he returned to give back to the youth of his hometown, which he loves."

A statue in the shape of a football helmet was revealed atop the press box, emblazoned with Hester's legendary number, 42, now being retired. Cheers erupted from the stands. Flanked by his wife, Lena, and two of their three sons, he stared back through the familiar light, returning the love with the smile the town had come to know. It was the smile he'd given every woman who'd ever fed him as a child, to every man not his father who'd ever praised him in the form of advice—*watch that middle gap, Jet, you know how you do it.* And it was the smile the few whites left in Belle Glade would remember when later asked to describe him.

"He was the best those folks ever had," one man said, then added, "It's a shame what they did to him."

Looking closely now at that smile, there was nothing behind the eyes that seemed to betray it, nothing that resembled distrust. The Jet was still running his routes, unaware the lanes were slowly closing around him.

MUCK
CITY

CHAPTER

1

One of the greatest high school football programs in America, one that has supplied the NFL with an average of one prospect per year, does not have a booster club. There is no team bus or multimillion-dollar stadium in which they play. There are no parents who volunteer their time for raffle drawings and car washes, or to decorate the windows of Main Street on game days. There are no steak nights or bumper stickers, and no water tower or welcome sign along the highway that boasts of their achievements.

So it was little surprise that on a sweltering football field in Tallahassee, Florida, where the temperature soared above a hundred degrees, the Glades Central Raiders did not even have their own water.

It was early August, and the Raiders had traveled six hours north to the campus of Florida State University for an off-season "seven-on-seven" tournament against some of the best high school teams in the South. The glorified touch football games—usually twenty minutes long and played without pads—were primarily a showcase for passing offenses, which were a specialty in a state that consistently produced speedy skill players. In recent years they'd also become one of the chief exhibitions for college coaches and recruiters to eyeball the current crop of talent. For elite teams such as the Raiders, the invitations to such tournaments now filled the summer months.

That afternoon at Florida State, twelve games were scheduled in a round robin. During a lull between matchups, the boys from Belle Glade appeared exhausted. At the motel the night before, most had stayed up until dawn playing video games. They'd overslept, missed breakfast, and forced the team to arrive late, barely escaping disqualification. They'd also arrived without enough uniforms, forcing players to strip off their sweat-soaked jerseys and share.

Now, along the sidelines, they were wilted and starving. As other teams rested under giant tents bearing their school logos, enjoying sandwiches and cold Gatorade, about ten Raiders squeezed under the skinny shadow of a light pole—the only shade they could find—and split a bag of M&Ms.

For the Raiders, the tournament at FSU was only their second appearance since suffering a humiliating loss the previous season in the state 2A championship, a defeat that still hung like swamp gas over the Glades. Worse, at the end of the school year they'd graduated twenty-two seniors off the title-seeking roster, and twenty-eight the year before. For most teams, it would take years to recover a loss of that many starters. By all estimates, the Raiders entered Tallahassee a team looking for direction, testing whatever talents remained in hopes of a decent season.

But, as the saying went in Belle Glade, "The Raiders don't rebuild, they just reload."

That afternoon, under a cloudless sky with the sun burning white hot, the arsenal was on full display. The Raiders had entered two teams in the tournament, one of starters and one of reserves. By the end of the afternoon, the two squads were undefeated and barely missed meeting each other in the championship round.

As the Raiders' starting seven dominated Miami's Booker T. Washington High School, crowds of parents, coaches, and recruiters soon formed to watch the electrifying show and, in particular, a blue-chip wide receiver who'd arrived that morning one of the most heavily recruited high school athletes in the nation. Reporters had nicknamed him "Treetop." The recruiters who routinely crowded the Glades Central practice field had their own term:

Kelvin Benjamin was a "beautiful freak."

"KB," as he was known in Belle Glade, stood six foot six in bare feet and weighed 220 pounds. He was half Jamaican, and his mixed blood gave his skin a light, feverish complexion. He was broad-chested and wrapped in muscle and carried a curvy, feline frame like a dancer. His face had the delicate bone structure of a woman's, so that whenever he pulled off his helmet and tied back his long braids, lips parting to reveal a mouthful of gold teeth, he evoked the picture of an androgynous warrior. The girls in Belle Glade called him "pretty."

The official team roster inflated Benjamin's size to six foot eight, which is basketball territory. At first glance at the numbers, many recruiting coaches pegged him as a tight end, bulky enough to block and break tackles and snatch up short, first-down yardage. Hearing that he ran the forty in 4.5 seconds put the glimmer in their eye, but it needed seeing to believe. Once they played the film, or watched the snap from the perimeter, they beheld a rare kind of athlete, a dream wide receiver that appeared only so often.

The paradox of Benjamin's size and quickness shattered once he burst off the line. Your eyes followed the legs, which were massive and covered nearly two yards of field with every powerful, arching stride. As with a distant, approaching train, it was difficult to determine his true speed until he broke on a dime and was gone. But his true gift revealed itself in coverage, the heavier the better.

Since KB towered over most receivers at his position, the same held true for the cornerbacks and safeties sent to cover him. A spry, high-flying defender could compensate for the mismatch in height. But what usually beat the coverage were KB's hands: two mitts over nine inches long from fingertip to wrist, yet nimble and delicate instruments. The hands added to a wingspan stretching eighty inches—a mere three inches shy of Michael Jordan's. In thick coverage, a leaping grab—usually one-handed—was enough to leave most defenders staring straight into his numbers.

"Just put it up," he'd tell the quarterback.

"KB's hands are his best thing," said a coach who was relentlessly pursuing him for one of Florida's top universities. "He can catch like a smaller receiver. He's big, but he plays like a little man. There aint many like him in the country."

That afternoon in Tallahassee, a cluster of assistant coaches from FSU and Auburn gathered along the sideline. Play after play, Benjamin executed cross routes and hook patterns with defensive backs trailing his hulking body like pilot fish. He'd dash to the corners of the end zone with two of them pounding at his heels, turn, leap, and reach one arm toward the sky like a giant cat stretching in the sun. With defenders swatting dead air around him, the ball would land gently in his hand, as if delivered on a velvet rope.

Touchdown!

The coaches on the sidelines puckered their lips in awe.

"He's a goddamn superman," said one.

One FSU assistant whipped out his cell phone and dialed his boss, Seminoles head coach Jimbo Fisher, who was sitting in his office across campus. Fisher had already sent offers to KB on the basis of film alone, yet had never seen him up close.

"You gotta get over here right now," the coach beckoned. "The second coming of Randy Moss has arrived."

For Benjamin, the comparisons to NFL greats and the college letters that now filled two entire dressers at his home seemed a lifetime away from where he'd stood two years before. Raised by a mother who'd struggled to raise three children on her own and a father who was deported when Kelvin was three, the boy had fluttered like an aimless moth against the tantalizing fire of street life.

By the time he turned sixteen, he'd already served a term in juvenile prison and was searching for his way. A chance discovery by a Raider coach at a Saturday pickup game had carried him back into football, a game he'd once played and hated, but one that suddenly provided a structure for living and success. Awkward and out of shape, but seemingly born to play, he received his first college offer after only four weeks on the team.

His sophomore and junior seasons were impressive, but not chart-topping: nearly two thousand yards receiving and seventeen touchdowns. In both years, the Raiders' roster was loaded for bear with signature Glades receivers, so much so that a reporter once likened Benjamin to "a Lamborghini in a garage full of Ferraris."

Now a senior, Benjamin was finally entering his crowded hour. He was the premier receiver on the Raider squad and captain of the team. Polls ranked him the number-eight receiver in the country and his name appeared on every major recruiting list, including that of gridiron oracle Tom Lemming.

Coaches from Florida, FSU, Auburn, Michigan, Notre Dame, and Miami sent upward of two letters a week to his house. They also bombarded him with text messages, faxes, phone calls, and visits to the school, to assure him of the singular threat he would pose on their teams before blowing the doors off the NFL draft. ("Definitely a first-rounder," a recruiter told him. "Right now, if they'd let you.")

Barring any injury or misstep, Benjamin had the physique and natural talent to be one of the biggest sensations ever to rise from the muck. Entering his final season as a Raider, he would have to prove to his town, his team, and especially his coach that all the commotion over the big, beautiful freak wasn't just hype when it came down to hard work and winning.

• • •

THAT AFTERNOON THE facilitator of the Kelvin Benjamin Show did not fit the mold of the tall, strapping Raider quarterbacks of yesteryear, guys who'd left Glades Central to become college heroes and Heisman Trophy contenders. Nor was he one of two second-string QBs off the roster, both standing six feet with rocket-fire arms.

The quarterback here stood five foot nine in cleats with short legs, a bulging behind, and a gut that spilled over his shorts. In their quest for redemption, the mighty, title-seeking Raiders were now under the helm of an undersized, overweight linebacker.

But Jamarious Rowley, aka Mario, was Hester's secret weapon. As a middle linebacker his junior year, he'd recorded a hundred tackles, six sacks, and four interceptions to earn the honor of first team all-state. He had quick instincts and deceptive speed. But most of all, Mario was driven by a dark and pressing desire to win.

When he was eight years old, in a space of five months, both Mario's mother and father suddenly passed away, leaving a bottomless well of sadness the boy would often tumble down.

His mother, Mary, was a schoolteacher who'd always dreamed of having a big family. But her heart was weak, and bearing six children had only made it weaker, so much so that the doctor had warned that a seventh child might kill her. She'd borne Mario anyway, then flatlined a month after leaving the hospital. Doctors had kept her alive long enough for the boy to grow and love her, and then died before he could understand that it wasn't his fault. Mario's grieving father followed five months later, suffering a fatal stroke.

"Mary gave her life to Mario," Mary's sister Gail would say. "The boy has purpose. He is here for a reason."

For Mario, that reason was to play football, something he'd discovered to fill the gaping emptiness inside. And now in his senior year, it was to deliver his father's dream: having a son win a championship as a Raider, a wish his three older brothers were unable to deliver.

The linebacker had been the last person to leave the field after the Raiders lost the title game the previous year. Sitting alone in the end zone, tears streaking his face, he'd looked up at Hester and told him, "We'll be back. I'll bring us here."

Hester sensed a leader in his midst. When the quarterback position came open, he chose Mario, not caring that physically he was hardly quarterback material.

Like Gail, the coach had seen something undeniable.

"The will drives him," he said.

But for Mario, leading the Raiders and fulfilling his father's desire would take both an emotional and physical toll. And the spotlights that so often found young men in the Glades and bestowed them with opportunity and fame would prove elusive for the unlikely quarterback.

• • •

IF DAVONTE ALLEN had a nickname, it would be "Clean."

For him, Belle Glade symbolized the great valley of the shadow of death that he steeled himself against each morning in prayer. But his feet had never walked its menacing streets, something that Deacon Julius Hamilton would credit as one of his greatest achievements in life.

Davonte was raised in his grandparents' tiny church overlooking the canal, where regal men still donned bowler hats in the Everglades summer. Growing up, he'd followed a rigid course of schoolwork, Bible study, athletics, and weekend chores. Crossing these lines guaranteed swift rebuke, "for the wrath of God shall fall upon the disobedient child," Julius liked to warn.

In a region where many children never traveled as far as the coast, Davonte's grandparents had shown him the country and introduced him to a bigger world. They'd enrolled him at Glades Day School, a private, mostly white institution on the opposite end of town that opened in the 1960s, before integration, and boasted six state football titles of its own.

After two years as a standout receiver for the Glades Day Gators, Davonte transferred into Glades Central already a champion. The diamond-studded ring from that winning season now sat on a shelf in his room next to his old Bible, a display that provided both daily nourishment and inspiration. For Davonte, the move to a lesser school was the only way to prove himself on a bigger stage, where the rewards of a righteous servant—college and a career in the NFL—lie waiting under those prime-time lights. But to reach them, he would first have to escape the long, imposing shadow of Kelvin Benjamin.

•　,　•　•

FOR THE 96 PERCENT of Glades Central students who did not wear the maroon and gold on Friday nights, there were no weekly faxes by way of the Crimson Tide or Hurricanes. There were no photo spreads in the *Palm Beach Post*, no middle-aged men in performance wear sending texts laced with promise; no eleventh-hour home visits by the head coach to seal the deal, and certainly no expenses-paid tours of universities across the nation, replete with restaurant dinners, hotel rooms, and eager coed escorts.

For the other 96 percent left in the shadow of football—and especially teenage girls, who accounted for 31 percent of all pregnancies in the Glades—getting a college scholarship was a hard-fought slog up a mountain, one whose peak was reached by only the most focused and diligent students. Luck could carry you only some of the way. For students like Jonteria Williams, it also helped to be fearless and never forget how to smile.

The smile was the first thing to radiate from her tiny, muscular frame, like a single pinhole pouring light through the darkness, her message to the world that said, *I have chosen to shine, thank you.*

The smile was front and center—on the sidelines of Effie C. Grear Field as she led the Raider cheerleaders through their chants; through the coursework of senior year and two college courses she attended each week to get ahead; through the corridors of the local hospital where she did her internship; through debutante practice, meetings of the Twenty Pearls sorority, National Honors Society, and the planning committee for the prom. And the impulse to smile kept her eyes open another twenty hours each week at Winn-Dixie, where she stood over a cash register to help her mother pay the bills.

"Her smile is the smile," said Theresa Williams. "Everyone always asks, 'Is that your little girl in Winn-Dixie? She smiles *all the time.*'"

When Jonteria was eleven years old, Theresa sat her two daughters down and explained that their father was not coming home. John Williams, the competent, hardworking provider, had been arrested in Georgia and was serving a ten-year sentence. The man was gone in an instant. The girls were on their own.

That same year, watching her mother work two jobs to fill the gap, Jonteria announced she would become a doctor. Right away, mother and daughter formed an alliance in pursuit of this goal, because if Theresa knew anything, it was this: for a girl to make it out of the Glades and into medical school—poor, black, with a single parent and nary a connection— she would need a long and running start.

• • •

TO UNDERSTAND WHERE our characters and story begin, to feel the isolation of the far-flung Glades, first you must drive.

You begin in Palm Beach along Worth Avenue, "the Rodeo Drive of Florida," where a parakeet caws from a coconut palm outside the Hermès store and a woman in tea-saucer shades keeps a limousine waiting. After three quick turns, you enter Southern Boulevard and keep your wheels pointed west, past Donald Trump's Mar-a-Lago Club and the shopping malls of Wellington, until the land unfurls into a green carpet of sawgrass and sugarcane, and heat waves dance along the bend of the earth. The plunge into wilderness is so sudden it brings to mind what you know about that road: how gators can cross at night and send a car careening into the canal, how the cane fires in autumn can jump the blacktop, and how, every spring, swarms of mating flies crossing the plain explode against the windshield like fat, yellow rain.

Forty minutes after leaving one of the wealthiest enclaves in America, you enter one of the poorest. The welcome sign that greets visitors to Belle Glade reads, HER SOIL IS HER FORTUNE, but any profits produced by the black, loamy muck have long eluded most of those still living there. The region was once known as the "Winter Vegetable Capital of the World." But many of those fields and the jobs they produced were engulfed long ago by Big Sugar and the machines that now turned its fortunes. In 2009, the per-capita income in Belle Glade was just $14,018. Official unemployment stood at 25 percent, although city officials estimated it was closer to 40. The crumbling, sun-blasted apartment blocks in the migrant ghetto more resembled the outskirts of Kampala or Nairobi than any rural American town. It was a place so removed from modern society that some families had resorted to catching rainwater to survive.

In a farming town of 17,467 people, there were more than a dozen gangs that preyed on young men and saturated the downtown streets with cocaine. In 2003, Belle Glade had the second-highest violent crime rate in the country. Shootings remained near-weekly occurrences. AIDS had left its indelible scar and lingering stigma. If you stayed long enough, there came a time when you felt as if everyone you spoke with had been touched by some sort of tragic episode—so that even along Main Street, with its fast-food restaurants and sleek Bank of America branch, and within the quiet, middle-class neighborhoods, Belle Glade carried the aura of a trauma zone.

Yet somehow from this crush of poverty and tragedy came one of the country's greatest concentrations of raw football talent. After Jessie Hester went to the Los Angeles Raiders, thirty players from Glades Central reached the NFL, while more found their way into Canada and other professional leagues (Pahokee's numbers were even greater). For a school of only 1,037 students, it was a staggering rate of success, considering that only eight out of every ten thousand high school football players (or .08 percent) are ever drafted into the NFL.

In recent years, Glades Central has sent an average of eight players to NCAA Division I programs. It is said that in any given year, one hundred former Raiders are playing football somewhere in North America. Glades Central also boasts six state titles and twenty-five district championships.

With such numbers, one might think, *It's a town obsessed with football*, and tick down the other places that come to mind: Aliquippa, Pennsylvania, Odessa, Texas, or perhaps even Long Beach, California, where Polytechnic High School alone has sent more than fifty players to the NFL since 1927. Or it could be one of a hundred other places in Texas, Pennsylvania, Ohio, or Michigan that inform Hollywood's treatment of the Friday-night game—the story of bighearted kids winning it all behind a coach's tough love in a town where football is like religion.

But this is not that story.

In Belle Glade, where the risk of joblessness, prison, or early death followed each boy like a toxic cloud, high school football was more than religion, it was like salvation itself—the raft by which to flee a ship that kept drifting back in time. Football offered an education, a chance at life. As for the town, the relationship with the game went beyond fandom. It was something deeper, more psychological, like a weekly remembrance of lost, unblemished youth. Glades Central had to be one of the only high schools in America where its students were largely absent from football games. Watching from the bleachers were the uncles, fathers, and old gridiron kings whose own escape had eluded them. For a town with trouble on its mind, the Friday-night lights were the closest things to a catharsis, or at least a fleeting escape.

"Down here," one player said, "there's so much trouble that winning is the only thing to look forward to. It's the only thing we're good at. For that moment, all our problems go away."

Belle Glade was like no other football town in America. There was no Hollywood treatment of the Muck City game. What follows instead is the messy and chaotic pursuit of a title-seeking team, a story about home, loyalty, and the pressure to win in a town whose identity lay rooted in a game. It is a tale of great escapes, a story of survival.

CHAPTER

2

The city of Belle Glade was born in the watery wake of Manifest Destiny, a settlement hacked and forged from America's last wild frontier. Like most of South Florida today, Belle Glade emerged as the result of one of the most ingenious and cataclysmic feats of modern engineering, the draining of the Florida Everglades.

For thousands of years, summer storms over Florida had caused water to spill naturally over the southern rim of Lake Okeechobee. A vast, shallow sheet of water crept hundreds of miles from the Atlantic shoreline to the Gulf of Mexico, feeding swamp and sawgrass marshes along the way. This "River of Grass" was the sustaining blood of an extraordinary ecosystem and the chief obstacle for an American dream pushing southward.

Beginning in 1906, the first of six canals was dredged from the lake to the Atlantic, draining the Glades into the sea. And once the lake and swamp began to recede, they left behind a nearly magical black soil that has since come to build empires and define a region and its people.

Glades muck is silty, the texture of talcum powder or finely ground espresso, and streaks the skin like powdered ink. When you walk in a field, it explodes in fine clouds beneath your shoes and seeps into your socks and under toenails. In the motels in Belle Glade that cater to migrants and construction workers, it's not uncommon to find the shower walls stained with black handprints. Drive your car down a canefield road and the black dust will appear in every crevice of the vehicle for months, no matter how many washings.

The muck is also flammable, its organic matter so rich that fields have been known to catch fire underground and smolder for years. These properties also make it some of the most fertile soil in America.

The first settlers in the Glades arrived before the First World War and found the much-promised black gold under a watery bog. The rest remained covered under an armor of impenetrable sawgrass that stretched beyond the imagination. When the water receded enough to plant, the boggy muck swallowed tractor tires and the sawgrass tangled plows. Snakes and flying insects covered the land and helped purge all but the strong and determined.

As war drove the demand for food, the region became a major producer of string beans and potatoes, which thrived in the muck. By 1928 the southern shores of Lake Okeechobee produced more string beans than anywhere else in the country. Since beans were a labor-intensive crop requiring many hands, thousands of black migrants from the South and the West Indies flooded into the Glades, where they could earn as much as twenty dollars a day in the fields.

Belle Glade began to boom, and much of the town that emerged during the 1920s was as wild and untamed as the swamps pressing in around it. This "Catfish Row" atmosphere of juke joints, bonfire dances, and lonely men far from home provided the backdrop for Zora Neale Hurston's 1937 novel, *Their Eyes Were Watching God*.

"Saturday afternoon when the work tickets were turned into cash everybody began to buy coon-dick and get drunk," Hurston wrote. "By dusk dark Belle Glade was full of loud-talking, staggering men. Plenty of women had gotten their knots charged too."

On the morning of Sunday, September 18, 1928, a storm blew in. The newspaper from the day before, fetched from nearby West Palm Beach, reported that a hurricane had hit Puerto Rico, killing hundreds, and was now headed for southern Florida. But radio reports picked up Sunday morning said the storm would miss the lake region, leaving residents confused and apprehensive. There was reason to fear: Two years earlier, during the Great Miami Hurricane, a section of the mostly muck dikes that formed a half circle around the lake had crumbled above the nearby town of Moore Haven, drowning 150 people.

As the wind and rain began whipping hard, Belle Glade's mayor, Walter Greer, ventured out into the weather to inspect the dikes. Greer returned soaking wet and said the water was indeed high, but he didn't believe it would breach. People chose to stay.

"The people felt uncomfortable but safe because there were the seawalls to chain the senseless monster in his bed," Hurston wrote of the encroaching storm. "The folks let the people do the thinking. If the castles thought themselves secure, the cabins needn't worry."

What was later determined to be a Category Four hurricane hit shortly thereafter, bringing winds of over 150 miles per hour. It came in from the Gulf side, then swung across and pounded the lake.

"The wind, like a thousand devils, howled its hollow roar," Glades historian Lawrence E. Will wrote in *Okeechobee Hurricane*, a riveting firsthand account of the storm.

As the eye of the hurricane moved over the town, people quickly regrouped to search for those lost in the wind and rain. Amid the confusion, the dikes began to burst, releasing a wave of water thirty-five miles long that wiped clean the settlements in its path.

When the surge hit Belle Glade, the water rose at a rate of an inch per minute, cresting at eleven feet in areas nearest the shore. The town quickly disappeared beneath the moving tide, and entire houses were swept down the canal with people clinging to rooftops and from windowsills. Looking out, Will spotted a kitten, a rabbit, and a water moccasin all huddled on the same piece of floating garbage, paralyzed with fear. On two branches of the same tree, a man and a wildcat clung for life, eyeing each other with caution.

When the storm finally calmed, settlers in boats rescued dozens from treetops and floating debris, but most perished under the flood. Search parties were dispatched along the lakeshore to look for the dead or the few survivors who had drifted and become lost in the swamp. Small boats, remembered Will, "brought in the corpses half a dozen at a time, each secured with a turn of rope around its neck, like a ghastly bunch of grapes. Arrived at the bridge, a crew of negroes, their cotton gloves soaked in disinfectant, hauled the bodies out and laid them in rows."

An estimated 2,500 people perished in the flood. Later estimates ventured as high as six thousand dead. What is known is that three-quarters of those killed were black sharecroppers and fieldworkers who'd been as surprised and unprepared for the storm as the whites who'd employed them. Because of their migrant status, and because so many were known to friends and employers only by first names or nicknames, it will never be known exactly how many died that day.

The frenzied weeks following the hurricane read like a chapter pulled from ancient days of plague and fever, rather than twentieth-century America. In the first days after the storm the muck was still too saturated for burials, so corpses were stacked like cordwood along the banks. Trucks then carried them to West Palm Beach and elsewhere along the coast, "trailing slime all the way," as Will wrote. Whites that could be identified were buried in cemeteries, but the number of black victims soon overwhelmed officials, and few were given proper burial. Fearing the spread of disease, workers soon began piling bodies in ditches, black and white skin now undistinguishable due to decay, covering them in fuel oil, and setting them ablaze. Search crews combing through the swamps would find decaying corpses and simply cover them with lime and move on. For decades afterward, farmers breaking ground in the Glades would uncover skeletons of those left behind or never discovered at all, their bones having been swallowed by the sawgrass.

Today there are few traces remaining of those who perished in the storm. The trucks that carried the dead to West Palm Beach first stopped at Woodlawn Cemetery, where sixty-nine bodies were laid in a common hole, sixty-one of them white. A short distance away, in what was then the black paupers' cemetery, the bodies of nearly seven hundred unidentified blacks were dumped into a mass grave.

Hurston recounted this macabre ordeal, in which white lawmen pressed blacks into unloading the trucks by gunpoint. Don't toss any whites into the holes by mistake, they said. Bury the blacks in the rough with lime, instead of pine-box caskets.

"Look at they hair when you cain't tell no other way," they instructed. "And don't lemme ketch none uh yall dumpin' white folks, and don't be wastin' no boxes on colored. They's too hard tuh git holt of right now."

A marble plaque memorialized the sixty-nine buried at Woodlawn Cemetery. But it took seventy-four years for the mass grave containing 674 black victims to receive any recognition. It wasn't until 2002, after a dogged campaign by community activists, that the city of West Palm Beach purchased the land and finally marked the grave site.

The entire city of Belle Glade was in ruins, most of its inhabitants dead or missing. Only one hotel still stood. Taking even the lowest estimates of those killed, the hurricane of 1928 ranks as the second most deadly natural disaster in American history, next to the 1900 storm that struck Galveston, Texas, and killed six thousand. It's also been called by black scholars the single most deadly natural disaster to strike African Americans, even worse than Hurricane Katrina in 2005.

• • •

THE STAGGERING DAMAGE and loss of life from the 1926 and '28 storms incited an uproar across the country, exacerbated in part by near-biblical flooding along the Mississippi River in 1927 that left more than a million people homeless. The floods had overwhelmed man-made dikes and levees and debunked any notion that modern engineering could bridle nature in her full fury. But in the decade that followed, the U.S. Army Corps of Engineers set out to prove that indeed it could be done, at least in the Everglades. The response was not only to tame the giant beast, but to chain it forever behind a ring of prison walls.

Built during the height of the Depression, the Herbert Hoover Dike, named after the president who commissioned the project, stands more than thirty feet above sea level and nearly wraps the entire lake. Whereas the old dike was mostly muck, the new structure was given a core of stone and covered in grass, trees, and bamboo to control erosion, and hurricane gates to maintain balance when severe storms struck. And while the dike has never failed, it also concealed much of the lake completely from view. It left the towns along its shores butted against a giant mound of grass that appeared more like a covered landfill than the nation's seventh-largest lake. Today, any unsuspecting traveler passing through Belle Glade or Pahokee could come and go without ever knowing it existed.

With the dike rising up around the lake, the final act of strangling the great River of Grass was nearly complete. As more and more land began to dry, South Florida continued to boom. The population of Belle Glade tripled, making it the largest city in the Glades. It was during this heady time that a second industry rose from the black, fertile muck, one that would define the region and render it forever notorious.

As it turned out, the muck was ideal for producing sugar. Cane is planted not by seeds, but with shoots that mature and can return over five successive seasons, much like grass. There are no branches or stems to mess with, only long, narrow leaves that can grow as tall as twenty feet. Sugarcane doesn't require as much fertilizer as vegetables. It's also more durable. After a heavy rain, farmers must scramble to drain their fields holding spinach or sweet corn, whereas sugarcane can sit underwater for two days.

But while sugarcane was a hardy crop, harvesting it was a costly undertaking. The wheels of mechanical harvesters sank in the muck, and their blades ripped the delicate root systems from the soft soil. As with beans, sweet corn, and celery, the harvesting of sugarcane had to be done by hand and with a machete.

Cutting cane was arguably the most grueling fieldwork performed on American soil: exhausting, repetitive, and prone to serious injury as blades swung toward feet and legs, venomous snakes and insects coursed through the fields, and cane tops impaled skin like green daggers under a broiling subtropical sun.

In 1931 the U.S. Sugar Corporation opened its mill in Clewiston, just fifteen miles up the Hoover Dike from Belle Glade. In its first year of operation, the company posted ads in black neighborhoods across the South seeking labor for the harvest. "Enjoy Florida Sunshine During the Winter Months," the handbills read.

Applicants were promised good wages in cash, plus free room and board, transportation, and medical care. But after the buses traveled through the night and reached Clewiston, canefields stretching in each direction like an ominous sea, the men were charged eight dollars for the ride. They were then told they'd have to buy their own blankets, machetes, and files. Some were even charged for clean drinking water.

In his book *Big Sugar,* which exposed the working and living conditions of cane cutters in the Glades, *New Yorker* writer Alec Wilkinson detailed how men in those early years essentially found themselves property of the sugar bosses. Wages were never as promised, but a pittance designed to keep each man in perpetual debt to the company store. Workers were forbidden to leave. Some were beaten, others told they would be whipped or shot if they tried to escape. Those caught out on the roads or trying to hop a train were charged with hitchhiking and thrown in jail. In the fields, white supervisors lorded over workers with rifles and blackjacks like horseback deputies on a chain gang. Other reports claimed that men were shackled to their beds as punishment for attempted escape. Many fled under cover of darkness, more destitute than when they'd arrived.

In early 1942, as the nation entered the Second World War, the FBI began interviewing workers across the South who'd returned and complained about the treatment by U.S. Sugar. The U.S. attorney general later issued a grand-jury indictment against the company on charges of peonage and conspiracy to commit slavery.

Four men were arrested—guards and lawmen whose names commonly surfaced in the interviews. However, the judge threw out the case before it could ever progress, citing a flaw in the way the grand jury had been picked.

By 1945, U.S. Sugar operated the largest sugar mill in the nation, spread across 100,000 acres around Okeechobee. But its growth was greatly constrained by federal limits on domestic sugar production, allowing Florida to produce only nine-tenths of one percent of the country's overall crop. Everything changed in 1959, when Fidel Castro's Communist-leaning rebels in Cuba overthrew the government of Fulgencio Batista. The U.S. government responded by issuing an embargo on Cuban sugar imports. It temporarily repealed the restrictions and allowed a free-for-all on planting sugarcane.

In the Glades, the rush was on. Two additional sugar companies would emerge in the coming months, giving rise to Florida's super-industry.

For years, Bahamians had been a fixture in the Glades during vegetable harvests, and even more so during the war as the draft diminished the availability of American men. So, starting in 1943, in the midst of the FBI investigation, U.S. Sugar started turning to the Caribbean for its field labor, and the industry as a whole followed suit. For the next fifty years, half the sugarcane grown in the United States was harvested by as many as ten thousand workers from Jamaica, Barbados, St. Kitts, the Bahamas, and elsewhere in the Caribbean. They were known as "offshores" or "H-2s" for the government worker program that brought them here. Most people simply referred to them collectively as "the Jamaicans."

Each morning before dawn, buses would be waiting to carry the men to the fields. The cutters wore hats and long pants and long-sleeved shirts, both to protect them from the sun and to keep the gritty muck from irritating their skin. Slicing one's toe or hand was common, so cutters outfitted themselves with aluminum guards that fit over their arms, legs, and boots, giving them the appearance of jousting knights or storm troopers. The camps they returned to each evening were drab, airless structures made of concrete, with few amenities. There were common toilets and showers, and dorms often featured a single sink where workers could get water for cooking and scrub the black dust from their clothes.

Even as the sugar industry grew, the muck around Belle Glade was producing bumper crops of produce. Each harvest brought its own groups of people: Jamaicans for cane, while Haitians, Mexicans, migrants from the South, and local "mucksteppers" all flooded in for sweet corn, celery, oranges, and beans. From September through May, more than fifty thousand migrants would move through town. They arrived in old buses and jalopies packed to the roof, squeezing under whatever shelter they could find in Belle Glade's black quarter.

Whereas the housing provided to cane cutters was stark and gloomy, the rooms and hotels available to migrants were wholly abysmal, operated by slumlords who saw an easy buck in the desperation of the moving masses.

"Thousands sleep packed together in sordid rooms, hallways, tar-paper shacks, filthy barracks with one central faucet and toilet, sheds, lean-tos, old garages, condemned and shaky buildings," wrote Marjory Stoneman Douglas in her landmark 1947 book, *The Everglades: River of Grass*. "The patched and peeling walls seem saturated with their heavy smell of dirt and fatigue and disease and misery."

In the early 1930s, Eleanor Roosevelt had been appalled by an article in *Collier's* magazine that described the conditions of migrants in the Glades as worse than anything in the Dust Bowl. The plight of farmworkers became her cause, and on April 24, 1940, the First Lady visited Belle Glade and christened the Okeechobee and Osceola labor housing projects. With war in Europe dominating the news, the event had merited only a small, bottom-of-the-fold story in the *Belle Glade Herald*. Twenty years later, how-ever, these same tin shelters, now tumbledown and rank, would appear on televisions across America, with Belle Glade once again depicted as a cauldron of human suffering.

The day before Thanksgiving 1960, the documentary "Harvest of Shame" aired on the TV series *CBS Reports*, and indicted an entire industry. Narrated by Edward R. Murrow, the opening scene of the film takes place in Belle Glade at an early-morning call for farmworkers. We see crowds of thin, wan-looking blacks pressed around the toothless hawkers who barked the daily picking rate, before being crowded like livestock into belching open-bed trucks and taken to the fields.

"This is not taking place in the Congo," Murrow said. "It has noth-ing to do with Johannesburg or Cape Town. . . . This is Florida. These are citizens of the United States, 1960. . . . This is the way the humans who harvest the food for the best-fed people in the world get hired. . . . They are migrants. Workers in the sweatshops of the soil." A farmer who saw Murrow's footage of Belle Glade commented, "At one time we owned our slaves. Now we just rent them."

The documentary was scathing. American families gathering for the holiday were shown the human toll for the Thanksgiving spread: migrants dragging their families across thousands of miles to pick the produce bound for supermarket shelves, their children filthy and largely unedu-cated, living off rancid-looking beans in one-room shanties with beds eaten by rats.

The living conditions for migrants were certainly deplorable, even hazardous. But those who traveled the circuit all agree that good money could be made in the process, depending on the fields and the farmers who owned them. A more truthful portrait of Belle Glade probably fell some-where in between Murrow's exposé and what Johnny Davis described:

"It was a rich poor town," said Davis, who arrived in 1963 from Woodbine, Georgia, to coach football. "You had migrants living in these stilt houses. But they had some of the most beautiful cars you've ever seen. Buicks, Cadillacs. It's what they spent their money on, and I thought that was so strange. They'd be living better in their cars than their houses."

Amid this fleeting cycle of coming and going, boom and bust, a football tradition was born in the Glades. Included in the masses of migrants who moved up and down America each year were the thousands of blacks who called Belle Glade home. Most had arrived from towns and cities across the South looking for work and settled in, gotten married, had children, laid down roots. Once the muck got in your toes, the saying went, it was too damned hard to leave. Some bought homes in the densely packed quarter, while most cut deals with landlords for year-round leases, then went "up the road" once the money seasons began.

Buried in the boot heel of the Deep South, Belle Glade was racially segregated at every level of society, with the canal providing a watery, gator-infested divide between the black and white sections of town. Whites attended Belle Glade High School, located behind a grove of trees on the canal's northern edge, while blacks attended Lake Shore High, out toward the railroad tracks where the sugarcane thickened at the lake's approach.

Since it opened in 1943, Belle Glade High had showcased a football program stacked with scrappy farm kids and coaches from small towns across the South drawn to the Glades for its community and good fishing. By the 1960s, the Golden Rams had won three championships in the Suncoast Conference, which stretched east to Fort Lauderdale on the coast. Its Friday-night games drew hundreds and became an imperative on any social calendar, especially if the opposing team was rival Pahokee.

For the fans of Lake Shore, it wasn't so easy. Each May when the school season came to a close, most black families in Belle Glade would pack up and chase the harvests. They'd gather in the community center of the Okeechobee housing project or along a giant parking lot known as the "Ramp" that bordered Southwest Fifth Street in the heart of the black neighborhood. Here, as Murrow's film depicted, they'd find the contractor that paid the highest rates or offered the best living arrangements, then squeeze into buses or covered trucks and head north.

There were beans to pick in North Carolina, sweet corn in Georgia, then more beans and apples in upstate New York and New Jersey. The trucks were covered with tarps, with one bench down the center for kids and two along the sides for adults. Pressed shoulder to shoulder, they often traveled two and three days at a stretch, stopping only for the needs of the driver.

"We slept sitting up, leaning against one another's backs. And if you had to use the bathroom, you had to wait till everyone went," said James Johnson, Lake Shore Class of 1959. "Once we got to the farms, we usually slept in a barn. Someone gave you a mattress and told you to fill it with hay."

By the time school started again, many families were still finishing seasons up north. Some even enrolled kids at schools in Utica or Waterville, New York, and points along the way as they returned south. At Lake Shore, the children of migrants trickled in throughout the fall, with their own woeful and fantastic tales of rocky bean fields, sore knees, and the towns and people they'd encountered along the way. For teachers, it was a yearly hurdle. For football coaches, it was plain maddening.

"My first two games of the season I didn't even have half my players," said Antoine Russell, who coached in Pahokee. "Here you had a 250-pound boy you can't even use as a tackle because his mama's making him work. Until the third game, we used what we could get."

With no preseason conditioning or time to foster chemistry, black teams in the Glades were often left playing catch-up against those along the coast. Even worse, the schools were too poor to provide training equipment. Cast-off sleds were fitted with old tires in place of padding. Tackle dummies were handmade and hung from chain hoists otherwise used to pull engines from vehicles. Few players even had shoes.

"When guys would come off the field in a game, they'd toss you their shoes," said Elsie Dawson, who played for the Lake Shore Bobcats. "We'd keep a cardboard box in the locker room that was full of shoes. First come, first served. Maybe you got one size nine and another size eleven and then have to trade."

Being migrants also gave the boys a reputation throughout Palm Beach County. "Down on the field, other teams would tease us by calling us 'bean-pickers,'" Dawson said.

In 1959 the Lake Shore Bobcats managed to defy the odds by going undefeated with the help of now-mythical players who stand as pillars for the storied tradition. Rosailious Hughley was a head-busting lineman who'd been raised in an Everglades boys' home. He conditioned himself by ramming his forearms into cinder-block walls until they dripped blood and the skin hardened like elephant hide. Later on, those forearms became weapons, once splitting a boy's helmet and sending him out on a stretcher.

The team also had C. W. Haynes, a quarterback in the mold of Randall Cunningham or Vince Young: six foot six and powerful enough to launch eighty-yard bullets with either arm, while also running for eighteen touchdowns in a season. Teammates called him "the Mummy" from his insistence on wrapping his arms and legs entirely with brown tape, even when playing basketball.

The Bobcats of the early 1960s also had Lawrence Chester, a topflight receiver who later became the first black player from Belle Glade to go to the NFL (the first white player was Marvin Davis from Belle Glade High, drafted by the L.A. Rams in 1965). In 1967, after playing four years at Allen University in South Carolina, Chester was drafted by the newly formed Atlanta Falcons. When he arrived at camp, he was informed of a quota on black players—they could keep only five, he said. After spending a season on Atlanta's minor-league team in Huntsville, Chester tried to play in Detroit. He ended up leaving football and spent the next twenty years as a manager at Ford.

In later years, without playmakers such as Chester, Haynes, and Hughley, the Bobcats struggled.

The team had ended the 1964 season with a dismal 5–6 record; the year before, they'd lost every game, partly due to increased academic standards that made certain players ineligible. Heading into the 1965 season and facing yet another autumn of incomplete rosters, head coach Willie Irvin had an idea. That year the H.J. Heinz Company—unable to find enough migrants to work its vegetable fields in the North—had started recruiting high school students in black neighborhoods across the South, offering attractive pay and a little adventure. Hearing this, Irvin contacted the company and signed up the entire Bobcat team. If his boys were going to leave town anyway, he reasoned, they might as well go together.

With defensive coach Alonzo Vereen serving as chaperone, twenty-seven members of the Bobcat squad squeezed aboard a bus in late May and headed up to Bay City, Michigan, where Heinz grew cucumbers for its pickles. Gazing out the bus windows were young Ronald Cook, a defensive end who was sixteen years old, Dawson, and a host of players with colorful nicknames such as Poochie, Scuffle, and Gatemouth, this last given the boy because he had no teeth.

In Michigan, the wooden bunkhouses the farmer provided were crude and sparse. Seven boys squeezed into one room. The toilets were ripe, stifling outhouses, while showers were taken cold in a barn. The workdays were long and hot, spent mostly on hands and knees dragging bulging hampers of vegetables down the rows.

To the boys, it was absolutely exhilarating. Not only were they earning $175 a week to work with their friends, but for once they could finally play some real football.

"You wake up at five thirty and eat breakfast, then go to the fields and do laps," said Cook. "All day, nothing but work and practice until you dropped. But we was gung ho, excited to be there."

Coach Vereen, a former soldier, cut the boys no slack. After lunch, he'd run the team through one-on-one pick drills in a dirt courtyard outside their dorms. A weight program was fashioned using rebar and concrete blocks. And when work was finished in the afternoons, the serious practicing commenced.

"We had no proper field. We were on a pickle farm," said Cook. "There was no boundaries. You had twenty yards of cucumbers this way and twenty yards that way. Out of bounds was that fifth row. We'd just run and dart between those rows."

"We had no pads and played barefoot, but we tackled," remembered Dawson. "Coach Vereen was hard. He'd stand there picking the hair bumps on his face and shout, *'Hey hamfat, the hell you thinkin, bwah?'* The man demanded respect and you gave it to him."

On weekends the team would travel to nearby Bay City or Saginaw to play softball, compete in fishing tournaments, or go clothes shopping with their pay; once they all bought matching mohair sweaters to wear on the first day back to school. During the week they conditioned their bodies with fieldwork and weights, the cucumber rows providing a natural obstacle course for agility. They developed such plays as "Coconuts," "Sugarcane," and of course "Pickle," learned formations, and built the mechanics of a team.

"We were in sync," said Cook. "We bonded and got to know what each man was capable of doing. And when we finally got back to Belle Glade, we were unstoppable."

The teams on the Bobcat schedule were probably expecting just another rusty squad of beanpickers. What they got instead was four quarters of humiliation. That season the Bobcats went 9–0 before crushing the Pahokee East Lake Hawks 28–0 to become Southeast Atlantic Conference champions. Lake Shore would suffer no more losing seasons, but little did they know the program they'd worked so hard to resurrect would soon come to a contentious end.

By the time the Bobcats staked their place as champs, the civil rights movement in the South had reached unstoppable momentum. Surprisingly enough, the roiling violence, murders, and intimidation happening in places such as Selma and Birmingham never manifested in the backwaters of the Glades.

In 1961, Lawrence Chester and friends had staged a sit-in at the Rexall drugstore in Belle Glade, which ended without violence or arrests. There had been trouble in Pahokee following the passage of the Civil Rights Act in 1964. A white movie house downtown closed rather than open for blacks, sparking a riot in the streets with boys throwing rocks and bottles through shop windows. Sheriff's deputies then found themselves pressed between a group of black desegregationists marching downtown and the whites who raced to stop them, many clutching machetes and rifles and threatening war.

Pahokee had integrated its schools in 1965 without great incident, but Belle Glade remained stubbornly defiant. Many whites simply pulled their kids out of Belle Glade High and enrolled them in the newly opened Glades Day School, which was private and solidly white. Others moved out altogether, relocating to predominantly white Clewiston and Okeechobee, or to West Palm Beach and its lure of gated communities and better services.

In terms of day-to-day life, both blacks and whites in Belle Glade seemed to fear any grand upheaval or change. Blacks maintained their own city within a city, and rarely ever mixed with whites. Each side had its own groceries, restaurants, juke joints, churches, and beauty parlors. Black police officers patrolled the black neighborhoods, while whites saw to their own. Aside from the drugstore, one of the few places where athletes remember ever having to use a separate doorway was in the office of a local doctor who served as the team physician.

If there was one institution in which blacks took the most pride, it was their schools. Their equipment and teaching materials were largely secondhand and tattered, textbooks arrived from the state missing covers and held together with tape and rubber bands, yet administrators could still boast of the many graduates—the kids of poor, uneducated migrants—who'd become doctors, lawyers, and teachers. In 1954, the U.S. Supreme Court had cleared the way for black students to attend the better white schools, but it wasn't until the Civil Rights Act of 1964—and the threat of losing federal funding—that Palm Beach County began to comply. Integration was mainly voluntary, and in Belle Glade only a handful of parents dared take advantage. Johnnie Ruth Williams was one, and her decision was pivotal in the way Belle Glade would handle the sea change barreling its way.

A cafeteria cook at Lake Shore High and the daughter of Georgia migrants, Johnnie Ruth wanted more enlightenment for her children. In 1968, when her three oldest reached junior high, she sat them down and took a vote. "Who wants to go to the white school?" she asked. Only Anthony, the youngest of the group, kept his hand down. Anthony, whom everyone called "Pearl," wanted to go nowhere else but Lake Shore. His father, Herman, a World War II vet who worked as a school custodian, would often bring him onto the practice field to watch Poochie, Gatemouth, and the Mummy. The scene was always one of violence and shouting, with players running headlong into bare metal sleds, and coaches clearing the field for two-on-one gladiator drills that drew fists and blood.

"I was so intimidated, but I got the big picture," he said. "If you could fight your friend in the trenches, no telling what you could do in a game."

Anthony wanted to be a Bobcat, but he'd lost the vote. That fall, he and his brother and sister walked across the Fifth Street bridge, out of the familiar arms of Belle Glade's black quarter, and into a cruel, unwelcoming world. At the time, Williams remembered only half a dozen black students attended Belle Glade Junior High, and their numbers provided no safety. Harassment was constant. Students stole Anthony's textbooks and returned them with the word "NIGGER" scrawled through the pages. They painted it across his locker and reminded him at lunch, adding, "We just don't want you here."

The harassment was more pointed in the afternoons once they crossed back over the bridge. Black kids lashed them with "Uncle Tom" and "honky lover" and shouted, "What, our school aint good enough for ya?" Back at junior high, white teachers were slow to defend them, only asking politely, "Weren't yall happy in your own place?" And when her kids would come home wounded and crying, Johnnie Ruth would always preach the high road, reminding them, "There's meanness in every race."

Around this time, Johnnie Ruth discovered she had cancer.

She'd been feeling sick for months and was growing concerned about a knot that had hardened under her arm near her breast. But with Herman's pay as a custodian, and hers as a cook, there was no affording a doctor. Finally, one morning while she was taking a shower, the tumor burst. Anthony and his siblings stood frozen with fear as Herman helped Johnnie Ruth to the car, a bloody towel under her arm, then sped off to the hospital. Doctors immediately removed her breast and started her on crippling rounds of radiation.

The treatment ravaged Johnnie Ruth's body. She lost weight and became weak, and her skin developed large black spots. At night the children would hear her retching in the bathroom. Yet she was up every morning to make breakfast and send the kids to school, never lacking the energy to fetch a switch if homework wasn't finished.

Not wanting to add more stress, the children started keeping quiet about the problems at school. In fact, Anthony and his brother Lawrence used their mother's resolve to stage their own little insurgency into the heart of the white institution. They tried out for the football team.

"I wanted to play sports so bad I wasn't going to let the local blacks who called me Uncle Tom stop me from my little dream," he said. "Nor was I going to let the whites who hated me keep me from participating."

His first season, Anthony remembered, coaches referred to him and his brother only as "niggras." One afternoon in practice, a coach kicked Lawrence so hard in the backside it sent him to the hospital. Johnnie Ruth, when urged by black leaders in Belle Glade to press charges, took the high road and asked only that the coach be dismissed.

By season's end, Williams had earned a spot in the starting lineup and a little compassion from the coaches, who were at least calling him by his name. It helped that he'd become pals with the team quarterback, a tall, skinny kid named Mark Newman, who'd eased his entry into white circles.

The two had established a quick rapport on the football field, mainly because Williams could catch just about anything Mark threw at him. Later, an invitation to Newman's birthday party acted as a blessing. "When he started talking to me, it opened the doors for others to talk to me," Williams said. Before long, Newman was just like one of the family, sitting down in Johnnie Ruth's tiny kitchen and putting away three plates of chicken.

As the boys prepared to enter Belle Glade High, determined to make the varsity cuts, they began meeting each afternoon for drills and conditioning. With Williams acting as receiver, a tight chemistry developed. Later, when the starting quarterback of the Rams came down with an injury, Newman was called to take his spot. Not long afterward, a receiver broke his ribs and coaches pulled up Williams.

Coaching the Rams was a Mississippian named Eulas "Red" Jenkins. Like others at Belle Glade High, Jenkins was a quiet and deeply religious man, probably most content floating across Lake Okeechobee in a johnboat, fishing for bass and perch.

Jenkins didn't seem to have a problem with having a few black players on his team. Williams even remembered the coach reminding the squad one afternoon that God had created everyone equally, and on the Rams, the only difference came down to each boy's assignment on the field.

"There were still some problems with some of the white kids," Williams said. "But by addressing it directly early on, Jenkins really made our lives easier. I felt like we could finally play football."

The Rams were coming off a dreadful season and ranked last in the area standings. Whatever animosity existed seemed to fade away once Newman and Williams began connecting for touchdowns. To the surprise of many, the team went 10–1 in the regular season. After beating Pahokee in the season finale, Williams looked up into the stands and saw whites hugging one another. Even after the team lost in the playoff game to Leesburg, strangers still cheered his name. When Williams went for his checkup at the team doctor's office, he was shown the door for white patrons and assured it would never be a problem.

"After that season, the town just seemed to love us. They seemed to understand we were just young men who loved to play football," he said. "But then integration happened, and all that came tumbling down."

In 1970, court-ordered desegregation came to Palm Beach County. Chaos and violence ripped through the coastal schools that were forced to comply. Bombs were discovered at Twin Lakes and Suncoast High Schools. Bus boycotts, riots, and mass arrests plagued the system throughout September. As Lake Shore and Belle Glade High merged into one, black students staged walkouts in protest of beloved teachers and administrators being relocated or replaced. Fights between blacks and whites took place in the school's parking lots and at popular hangouts, such as the Royal Castle hamburger joint on Main Street. White families were moving out of town and hostility was high. As the month unfolded, people held their breath and waited, and one thing they seemed to be waiting for was football.

Gone were the beloved Golden Rams and Bobcats, their fight songs swept into the dustbin of dark history. The new integrated school was named Glades Central Community High, and Jenkins was selected to lead its new football team, the Raiders.

The school was now predominantly black. On the first day of tryouts for the new Raider squad, many of the Rams' former starters were absent, having transferred or just refused to take part. "They'd played with a few blacks like myself," Williams said, "but this was just too many."

Even so, about seventy-five players now stood on the sidewalk because the locker room was too small to hold them all. Two sides of town, two storied programs, two radically different histories, now stood facing each other, chests puffed, eyeballing.

"Yeah, we here," someone said. "It don't mean we gonna like you crackers."

One of the Bobcats turned to Williams. "I know you been playin this light football with these boys," he said. "But we about to see what kind of real men yall are."

"Both sides felt they were being forced," said Newman. "No one had made us party to the decision-making process. There was a lot of tension that day."

The Lake Shore boys had brought with them a giant chip on their shoulder. The Rams had always had the better equipment, the better schedule that allowed them to play the bigger teams in bigger venues along the coast. For years they'd tried to schedule a public game against the Rams, but with no luck. They'd played only once in the mid-sixties, when the two teams met in secret on a muck patch near the fire station, but the police had broken it up. It was now the Bobcats' chance to prove something they'd felt all along.

"We knew we could beat them," said Wayne Stanley, the Bobcat starting quarterback. "Our attitude was that we were going to come in and take all the positions. We were going to take that team."

In the first days, fistfights broke out between the two sides. A favorite target of black players was a leathernecked lineman named Dan Griffin. The son of a sod farmer and local businessman, Griffin had grown up working alongside blacks in the fields and at his father's grocery store, the Chicken Shack, located in the heart of the migrant neighborhood. Now among the few whites on the Raiders, Griffin was not intimidated by his new teammates.

"I wasn't but 180 pounds," he remembered, "but I was strong."

When Jenkins commenced one-on-one drills, the biggest black players lined up to challenge Griffin. One by one, they found themselves flat on their backs and staring into the sun.

"To Dan, it was just football," said Williams. "He never backed off and the black guys loved him for it. After that, they started calling him 'Wildlife.' "

If the new arrangement was to work, Jenkins's biggest test was choosing a starting quarterback. Wayne Stanley was already a superstar across the canal. He was handsome, bright, and exceptionally athletic. His father was the foreman of a 4,600-acre farm outside of Belle Glade, a position that offered the family status and a life of relative comfort. During the summers, Wayne helped his father turn the soil on the farm for a daily wage, but he'd never had to endure the rigors of the migrant road.

Wayne drove around Belle Glade in a souped-up metallic '56 Chevy, so slick it had its own name, "the Rooster," on account of its tail fins. As a player, Stanley was blessed with a superb arm, but he was even better at running the ball. At Lake Shore, he'd doubled as a tailback.

Newman stood six foot five and weighed 165 pounds. "If you can imagine a stick, that was me," he said. But his height allowed him to scan the entire field, then drop back and launch bullets. Both quarterbacks had only two losses between them and, more important, the loyalty of their teammates and communities.

Both white and black players remembered Jenkins being quick to address racial tension early on. At the same time, players said that Jenkins's Mississippian upbringing, plus pressure from the white community, may have prevented him from fully embracing equality on the football field. When it came time to choose a starting quarterback, Jenkins went with Newman.

"I started most of that year," said Newman. "I feel that was because Coach Jenkins probably felt like a black quarterback couldn't do it. If that was the case, he was really wrong. Wayne was an unbelievable quarterback. No one on the team was happy about it."

Black students at Glades Central were definitely not happy. Dan Griffin remembered a group of students, led by a local black activist group, interrupting a team film meeting one afternoon to inquire why Stanley was not getting more playing time. "Jenkins pretty much let them have it," Griffin said.

The disharmony in the locker room and hallways of Glades Central was also reflected in the home crowd, which was starkly divided down the color line. It even manifested in the Raider uniform. The new maroon and gold outfits had yet to arrive, so players dressed in a raggedy patchwork of purple, blue, and gold from both the Rams and Bobcats. Despite these problems, the sheer athleticism of the combined forces made the Raiders fierce contenders.

By Thanksgiving the team was undefeated and headed into the playoffs. After victories in the district and regionals, Glades Central met Hollywood Chaminade for a berth in the state finals. But here the experiment finally fell short; the Raiders dropped the game 28–13.

In February, a race riot rocked the campus of Glades Central. What began as a protest led by dozens of black youth—many of them non-students—erupted into a massive brawl that spread throughout the school. White teachers and students were pulled out of classrooms and beaten. Police were called en masse. In the midst of the chaos, someone even phoned in a bomb threat.

The explosive atmosphere of race and politics seemed too much for Jenkins. That April, the coach resigned.

The *Palm Beach Post* later reported that intimidation may also have played a factor. At one of the games, Jenkins's daughter had been pushed by a group of black teenagers. Others said whites had threatened his family if the team dared to win a championship. Whatever the reason, Jenkins soon took a job as an assistant football coach at Cocoa Beach High School.

Taking his place was a man they called Shorty Red.

Al Werneke was built like a triangle, with a broad chest and stumpy legs. As his nickname suggested, he was small. A native of Terre Haute, Indiana, Werneke had played basketball and football at Indiana State, then, for the next decade, had coached high school football in small midwestern towns with names like Dugger, Oblong, Flora, and Brazil. When he arrived in Belle Glade in August 1971, he found a school still brimming with racial tension. On his first day of practice, the coach was greeted by another idiosyncrasy of the Glades: many of his players were still in the vegetable fields.

"This is the first time in my experience all the squad hasn't been on hand for opening practice," an exasperated Werneke told the *Belle Glade Herald*. "They keep telling me, 'They're up north—in Georgia—working.' I am at a loss."

For Johnnie Ruth Williams, that summer had marked the first time she didn't require her children to travel for the harvests. The living conditions in the northern labor camps had become too unsuitable for families, she felt. There was too much drinking and fighting, and on their last trip up north, someone had been shot and killed. That same summer, her father had suffered a stroke while driving a truck and died in a Georgia hospital.

With his summer now free, Williams devoted the time to conditioning his body with one goal on his mind. Each morning, he and his teammate Dan Brown, a white running back, would lace up in army boots and run the three miles to the lake marina, then sprint up and down the thirty-foot Hoover Dike until their knees could no longer hold them.

"We ran that dike and ran that dike," Williams said, "talking about a championship and nothing else." That summer, he even began sleeping with a football in his bed. "I've never wanted anything more," he added.

That same kind of resolve was evident once Werneke finally assembled his new team and stood before them. Unlike his predecessor, Werneke hailed from the North and didn't carry the same racial baggage. "All he saw was this phenomenal group of football players," said Newman.

To avoid conflict, Werneke broke the Raiders into four groups: Red Team offense and defense, and Blue Team offense and defense. He also realized what a gifted quarterback he had in Wayne Stanley. Not wanting to choose between him and Newman, Werneke made the decision to start both players. Stanley and Newman would simply alternate halves.

"Each team was mixed black and white, all based on talent, attitude, and ability," said Williams. "And with this setup, the black players bought into the system. It was fair."

For any coach, it was a dream team.

"We just didn't have a weakness," said Stanley. "We had strength and we had it two and three deep in every spot. For other teams, it was just ugly."

The Raiders tore through their regular-season schedule with little resistance, the victories so lopsided that Werneke started ordering his starters to shower and dress at halftime and sit in the bleachers. By midseason the intimidation factor was enough to wilt teams before the whistle even blew.

"We'd play some of these all-white schools and they'd get this deer-in-the-headlights look when we walked onto the field," said Mark Maynor, a running back who was white. "The black guys would stand together and do this chant to get us all going. I'm sure it looked and sounded ferocious."

As the Raiders rolled from victory to victory, they were propelled by a force that had been largely missing the previous season: the town. The harmony and camaraderie between black and white players was now starkly evident on the field. Stepping back from the lens of race and politics, the only thing visible under the football lights was a group of kids playing a game they both loved. On Friday nights, at least for a few hours, the town understood this and was united.

"The full thrust of the stands cheered for both black and white," said Williams. "When you looked into the crowd, you saw it was now all mixed. Maybe they saw the brotherhood on the field. That must have been the reason."

In the playoffs, the Raider dream of a rematch against Hollywood Chaminade was realized. Except in this matchup, the Raider defense held the Lions to only five first downs in a 31–0 rout. The next week, Tampa Catholic fell 35–0, catapulting Shorty Red's Raiders into the state championship.

The title game was against the Haines City Hornets. Located forty miles south of Orlando, Haines City was predominantly white and just as rabid about its football as any mucksteppers in Belle Glade. The Hornets were known for their powerful defensive line and a wishbone offense that pounded opponents while mercilessly chewing the clock. But the Raiders were also coming into the game with one of the toughest defenses in the state.

Dan Brown received the opening kickoff, and there before a crowd of ten thousand people, his summer mornings running the Hoover Dike paid off with a ninety-one-yard return for a touchdown. The rest of the game was a defensive battle. The giant Hornet line blitzed the Raider quarterbacks nearly every play and wrangled them in their own distant territory. Newman and Stanley managed only two completions, while the Raider running game gained a mere fifty-two total yards. Likewise, the only two passes thrown by Haines City quarterback Steve Wilkinson were intercepted. With no passing attack, the Hornets resorted to a game of hammer-and-nail. On four different occasions they managed to get inside the Raider ten-yard line, but only accomplished one touchdown and a field goal.

By the fourth quarter, the Raiders were losing 10–7. With three minutes remaining, the Hornets mustered a final sustained drive and were perched on the Raider seventeen-yard line, ready for the kill. Werneke called a time-out. The game was all but over.

Playing both receiver and defensive end, Williams had hardly left the field all game. Now he shouted to his line, "Hold your man up," and to his linebackers, "Plug them holes and leave no space. Aint nothing getting through."

Wilkinson snapped the ball. The Hornets' play call was a lateral option pass, but when Wilkinson turned to flip the ball to his running back, there was no one there. The back somehow misread the play and sprinted ahead, leaving the ball bouncing on the naked grass.

"I watched it fly out," Williams said. "And I took it."

The instant shot of adrenaline caused Williams to juggle the ball, as if it were a thousand degrees in his hands. But once he had control, he began to run. Reaching the fifty-yard line, he felt his tired body begin to falter. Glancing back, he saw a Hornet defender quickly slicing toward him, gaining ground. *I'll never make it*, he thought. *I'll just lie down*. It was then that teammate John Banks suddenly appeared between them like an attending angel, following Williams step for step, shouting, "Come on, Pearl. Don't stop, Pearl. Keep going, keep going."

At the twenty-yard line, Banks turned and stuck his helmet in the numbers of the Hornet pursuer and cleared the path. When Williams crossed the end zone for the winning touchdown, he crumpled like a sack of rocks.

"There was no air in the atmosphere," he said. "My lungs were burning. I just collapsed and lay there. All I could hear was the crowd going crazy."

Raiders win the championship, 13–10.

One of those voices cheering in the stands was Johnnie Ruth's, but she was not well. Her cancer had returned just before the playoffs, and both the disease and the aggressive treatment had whittled her down to half. Her cheeks were now sunken, and her body thin from the nausea and vomiting that plagued her days and kept her indoors. But she'd gathered enough strength to make the three-hour drive to Haines City. For she was the one who'd set this whole thing into motion, who'd challenged her children to be fearless and grab hold of dreams no matter what side of the canal.

As the fans lifted Williams and his teammates onto their shoulders in celebration, he saw his mother walk onto the field. He knew right away that she'd probably never see him play football again.

"I didn't break down until I saw her walking to meet me," Williams said. "She asked, '*Anthony, why are you crying?*' And I didn't want to tell her it was because I'd seen her and knew the cancer was winning. 'I'm just crying, Mom,' I said. 'I'm just crying.'"

Afterward, Williams walked to the locker room and wept in the showers, the victory not as sweet as he'd long imagined. Six months later, as he prepared to play in the all-star game, Johnnie Ruth passed away. She was thirty-nine.

The following season, with Stanley, Williams, Newman, and most of the starters graduated, the Raiders continued to win. The team was led by Byron Walker, a junior quarterback who "couldn't hit a bull in the butt with a bass fiddle" by his own admission. But with a solid team of athletes behind him—and guided by Werneke's deft coaching—the Raiders won back-to-back championships.

In Belle Glade, the great experiment had not only prevailed, but given birth to what was known as "the tradition." It realigned the world that held the tiny town, moved the North Star from its perch above the migrant road to its place between two yellow posts, and gave young boys in the muck a new kind of beacon.

One of those boys was Jessie Hester.

CHAPTER

3

When Hester was growing up in the mid-1970s, little had changed from the days of Gatemouth and Poochie. For the most part, Belle Glade remained a place of toil and hard lessons, where children were sent to the fields and little came for free.

The people who lived there back then like to say it was a simpler time, when kids had to learn how to be tough. And it was for this reason, apart from most others, that so many of them became great athletes.

The ten-block section of downtown still hummed with migrant families on the move. Calypso poured from the Jamaican clubs, along with the smells of jerk chicken and roasted breadfruit. On weekend mornings after the clubs had emptied, Jessie and his brother Roger would scan the downtown sidewalks, picking up the bills and loose change the drunks had dropped in their merrymaking.

By the 1970s, little had improved since the days when Marjory Stoneman Douglas was so struck by its misery. The migrant quarter remained a warren of mostly flat-roofed, two-story concrete rooming houses. Built in the 1930s, few of the buildings had ever been renovated or given a fresh coat of paint. They sat bleached and faded under the sun, festooned with fluttering laundry and beset with idle men between harvests.

By the time Zara and her children rented a one-bedroom on Seventh Street and Avenue E (now MLK Boulevard), the neighborhood held over 40 percent of the town's population. A consultant hired by the city in the 1970s reported the area housed as many as one thousand people per acre. By contrast, the Haitian capital, Port-au-Prince, had only 284 people squeezed into the same amount of space.

Jessie and his siblings slept on bunk beds, stacked atop one another like Lincoln Logs. The walls were made of cardboard and carried every sound. The entire building shared a few common toilets and a shower. In the evenings, Jessie or Roger would have to stand guard at the door while their sister Agnes bathed.

"There were big spiders in those showers," Roger remembered. "And walking into the toilet some mornings, you'd find feces smeared everywhere."

One block away, their grandparents' apartment offered a respite from the crowded dinginess. Jessie's grandmother Eva was the grand matriarch of the family, a big woman who kept her daughter's children in step. "My mom worked and my grandma raised us," said Roger. "She did the discipline and didn't run after you. She made you go and get the switch."

Like her daughter, Eva and her husband, Willie, made their living in the fields. But on Sundays, Eva would preach. The revivals held in her tiny apartment were legendary, a crush of sweaty bodies speaking in tongues and dancing, so drunk on the spirit that the building would rattle on its foundation. In addition to the Holy Ghost, Eva was guided by old superstitions that would find their way into her grandson Jessie. The strangest things would set her off, such as sweeping near her feet.

"Boy, get that broom away from me," she would shout. "You gonna cause me to go to jail."

• • •

WHEN JESSIE WAS in sixth grade, the family moved into a bigger, two-bedroom house a few blocks away. By then Anthony and Cora had been born. Even as babies, both children behaved oddly, but it wasn't until much later that they were diagnosed with autism.

For Anthony, the condition first manifested itself when he was six years old and fell into seizures. Jessie remembers seeing Zara one morning before work, the boy bent and contorted in her arms. When she put him down to walk, all he did was limp and mumble as though something had broken inside him. Zara went hysterical.

His sister Cora had always been special, exhibiting a brilliance that hid behind her quiet brown eyes and revealed itself in her artwork. Cora's notebooks read like illustrated soap operas of the street life and family dramas surrounding her. But that brilliance had a dark riptide that would turn the lights out while it dragged her under. When this happened, Jessie and Roger would have to hide sharp objects in the house because Cora liked to cut herself. Some afternoons they'd come home and find her sitting on the floor covered in blood, ramming her forehead into a wall.

To keep his mind off problems at home, Jessie, like most boys in Belle Glade, turned to sports. On weekends and after school, the neighborhood kids would gather for pickup games of football. For kids whose parents labored in the fields, there was barely enough money to cover food and clothes, much less an actual ball. So, to compensate, the boys filled socks with dirt and tied them off at one end. They used Coke bottles, old shoes, and, when nothing else could be found, a wad of newspaper—whatever could be tucked, thrown, and caught in the land of make-believe.

The games were played in empty lots and outside the bars and rooming houses. The boys wore no pads and tackled on streets covered in gravel and shattered glass, leaving knees and elbows chewed and bloody. Cars ran over them, but most often it was the other way around.

"Some of the hardest hits I've ever seen in football were from parked cars," Hester said.

The street games instilled an essential fearlessness that formed the bedrock to their becoming good football players. And for Hester, they laid the foundation that in later years would make him a great receiver. Aside from speed, courage was the one true requirement for the position, an understanding that your head could be taken off at any moment—yet still you ran for the ball.

"Everything else can be taught," he said. "You can teach a guy to run a route. But you cannot teach a guy to run out and catch a ball in traffic. It's got to be something he already possesses. And most of us got that early on as kids."

Summer days were spent diving off the Torry Island bridge into the canal infested with alligators. Ray McDonald, one of Hester's childhood friends, remembered watching Jessie and Roger drag old mattresses in front of a two-story boardinghouse, then jump off the roof.

"They'd hit those mattresses and flip," said McDonald. "I'm not talking about a single flip, but spinning and twisting in midair. Greg Louganis kind of stuff."

Zara started bringing her kids into the fields when Jessie was ten. The older kids would work weekends and holidays picking corn, celery, and leafy stuff like cabbage and lettuce. In the orange groves north of Pahokee, Jessie would earn five dollars for every bucket he filled, sometimes tumbling from tree limbs whenever a snake dropped from the branches. Summers were spent piled into various relatives' cars to work the fields in Delaware, Pennsylvania, and Georgia.

Early on, Jessie was vigilant about saving money because he knew if his mother ran out, as she often did, she would need help keeping the lights on. She would also need help buying school supplies and clothes. Jessie's wardobe was nothing high fashion, just sensibly stylish: white Converse sneakers and blue jeans heavily starched, with a razor crease down the middle.

"And whatever you did, always color-coordinate," he said.

But the snappy clothes couldn't cover the blisters that opened in class, or the scars that zigzagged down his arms. All scars told a story, and the thick, fleshy ridge that ran down Jessie's hand, thumb to wrist, reminded him of the life that must never be.

He'd acquired the scar one morning when he was twelve. His family was working a field of romaine, with Jessie cutting the leaves from their roots and laying them down for Roger to box behind him. Taking his eyes off his work, he missed and dug the blade into his hand. The wound was jagged and deep and needed stitches. But it was too close to Christmas and his mother was broke. Instead of asking to leave, he took off his shirt and dipped it into the icy water from the coolers, wrapped his hand, then kept cutting.

As the knife handle pressed into the wound, he'd had a revelation: *This won't be me*. It was the first time he'd ever seen himself as separate from the rows that bound his mother and the town, from the poverty that squeezed them so tightly atop one another it had driven the whole place crazy.

By then, Wayne Stanley was quarterback at Iowa State and would later sign with the Browns. Anthony Williams was playing at Middle Tennessee State and would go to the Buffalo Bills in the fourteenth round. Newman was a Florida Gator. This was basic knowledge to every young boy in town. If you played for the Raiders, you could go to college, even beyond. As Jessie moved down the row, blood soaking through the wrap, he decided there was a better way to help his mother. But at twelve years old, he was no intimidating presence. Jessie was puny, like a pretzel with a mouthful of teeth.

He wouldn't realize how skinny he actually was until a few months later, when he'd wake up on the floor of his sixth-grade classroom, dizzy and confused, with a huddle of faces staring over him, murmuring, "Jessie, what's wrong wit you? Someone call the ambulance!" The doctor would take one look at his drawn belly and ribs grinning out of his chest and use that word *malnourish*. Oh Lord, was Zara embarrassed! "People gonna think I'm too busy to feed my child," she said.

They both knew it was because Anthony always ate all the supper. It was Anthony who raided the stove top and left them nothing, licking the pots so clean they could comb their hair by their reflection.

"You waste no time getting home," Zara would warn them in the mornings, putting down a pot of beans or oxtails before heading to work. "Anthony gonna eat all this." And he did.

Anthony could *eat*. Even Grandma called him the Human Trash Compactor.

• • •

"FOOTBALL?" ZARA SAID to Jessie when he asked, not even giving it a thought. "Baby, you too scrawny to be playing football. Them boys'll hurt you up."

So, like his brother, Jessie joined the middle-school band. He practiced his trumpet long enough at night in his room to convince Zara that he was still dedicated, even long after he'd told the band director, "Don't look for me here no more," and made the football team. Since the band always traveled with the team, the plan worked for a while. Until the day in practice when one of his teammates looked out toward the parking lot, frowned, and said, "Jessie, is that your mama comin?"

Zara was blazing a hot streak across the football field with the devil in her eyes. "I thought I told you you can't be playing no football," she screamed, then jerked Jessie by the neck and dragged him all the way home. It took his uncles a week to persuade her to let Jessie play.

"The boy's an athlete," they told her. "You got yourself a Raider."

Jessie was so small that he would enter high school weighing barely 150 pounds. But his uncles had been right, he was an athlete—proficient in anything won and lost with speed. Athletics gave him a quiet confidence. He got to where he could watch people, the way they moved, and immediately know if he was faster.

When he was a freshman at Glades Central, coaches put him on the junior varsity football team to let him grow, then reconsidered one afternoon at the school's annual field day. Jessie had casually approached the fastest seniors on the Raider track team and doubled down.

"I'll give you five yards," he told them.

"You crazy" was the response.

"Okay, I'll give you ten."

Then *boom*, he was gone.

By senior year, Jessie was the fastest kid in the Glades. He and McDonald were on the same 4x100 relay team that won the Raiders a state championship. McDonald also remembered the crowds that started gathering at the city pool when Jessie would step on the diving board, executing triple gainers with hardly any effort. Or the afternoons in the school gym playing basketball when Jessie would stand motionless under the rim, then jump up and dunk.

"Jessie didn't say a lot, but he dominated every sport," said Louis Oliver, a former safety for the Miami Dolphins who grew up idolizing Hester. "He was just more focused than anyone else. He knew where he wanted to go and how to get there, and he applied himself."

• • •

BY HIGH SCHOOL, Jessie had also come to live by an ironclad discipline that he observed with almost neurotic diligence. His resolve was driven by a desire to "become somebody," but also, surprisingly, by not wanting to embarrass his mother.

He stayed away from alcohol and drugs and boys with chips on their shoulders. It wasn't the acts themselves he strayed from, but the fear of getting caught. Getting caught meant admitting that someone else had forced his hand, that he was weak and no longer in control. Even worse would be the look of disappointment on his mother's face. That look would be devastating, he thought, "simply unbearable to take."

A famous story about Jessie concerns the time in high school when he was riding in a car with friends and one of the boys lit up a joint. As the car filled with smoke, Jessie realized with sudden horror, *I'm breathing this stuff*, then demanded they pull over and let him out. They were in Pahokee, near the marina, some eight miles from Belle Glade. Jessie got out and walked all the way home.

He also didn't touch caffeine. "I don't like that sudden jolt of energy it gives you," he'd later say. A former college tutor remembered how once he even refused to eat cookies baked for the football team because he hated to feel the sugar "shoot up his jaw." A teammate explained to her, "You know how careful Jessie is of his ownself."

• • •

THE RAIDER VARSITY team that Jessie joined in 1978 was nothing like the one he'd grown up watching. In 1974, two years after winning back-to-back championships, Werneke's Raiders were once again undefeated and playing their arch-nemesis Hollywood Chaminade in the first round of the playoffs.

The Raiders were hit with penalties the entire game, leading many fans to suspect the officials were putting in the fix. In the final seconds of the fourth quarter, after a pass interference call against the Raiders set up a winning Chaminade field goal, the fans rioted. Spectators jumped onto the field and attacked referees, then players got involved. When it was all over, four policemen were hospitalized after being beaten with rocks and football helmets. One officer was dragged unconscious from the field.

The state threatened the death penalty for the entire Glades Central football program, then suspended the team from postseason contention. Several players were arrested. "After a game like last night," Werneke told a reporter the following morning, "you do a lot of soul-searching. You ask youself, 'Is it worth it?' You preach to the kids about sportsmanship and try and set an example, then you see adults go and behave like that."

The betrayal by the adults in the community was too much for Werneke; he resigned before the next season and took the head coaching job at Titusville High School, where he would win two more titles and become one of the great legends of Florida high school football. Vice-principal and junior varsity coach Willie McDonald, a former Lake Shore Bobcat (and father of Jessie's friend Ray), took over the Raider team.

McDonald's first move was to fire every player who'd been involved in the riot. "I'd rather have a team of disciplined athletes than any team at all," he said. For the next three seasons, the Raiders went 13–17, one year winning only a single game.

In Jessie's sophomore year, under new coach Ben McCoy, the Raiders finally had the semblance of a championship squad. Led by Hester and running backs Johnny Rowe and Greg Bain, the Raiders put up their first winning season before scandal plagued them again. The state athletics board determined that Rowe, whose father was stationed in Stuttgart, Germany, hadn't lived with his grandmother in Belle Glade longer than a calendar year, which was the required period of residency to play sports. The team was forced to forfeit two games, one of which was a victory over a division rival, which pushed them out of the playoffs.

In Jessie's junior year, the Raiders advanced to their third state championship game, this time against Milton High School, whose team was bigger, faster, and in much better health. Under the lights of Booster Stadium in Ocala, the Panthers drubbed Glades Central in a 35–6 rout. Hester scored the Raiders' only touchdown.

By his senior year, Jet had come into his own, well known for his blazing acrobatics and out-of-nowhere catches as both a receiver and a bandit safety. We see him in the pages of the *Belle Glade Herald*, midflight up the open lane, with a caption that reads, "Speedy Alka-Seltzer didn't have anything on Glades Central Raider Jessie Hester on Friday night."

He'd grown up hearing the stories of the fabled '71 and '72 teams, championship squads who, despite the racial division and hatred all around them, had bonded as a team and a family and found a way to win. Those stories had inspired Jessie. And now, in his senior year, it was his last chance to experience it himself. With Jessie nominated for All-American, the Raiders advanced to the semifinals, where ironically they came face-to-face with Titusville High, coached by Al Werneke. The game was held in Belle Glade. The Terriers were blessed with a hulking defensive line and Werneke's unshakable coaching. All night they blitzed Raider quarterback Leonard Camel relentlessly, while shutting down Hester with double coverage.

With seconds left on the clock, the Raiders found themselves down by five points. There was time for one final play. Having been smothered most of the night, Hester had mainly run decoy for his friend and fellow wideout Ray McDonald. Now, with the game and his Raider legacy in jeopardy, Jet drew up the last play with Camel.

"Leonard," he told him, "they don't expect me. So as soon as you get the ball, buy some time. I'm going straight to the post. Just hang it up."

Camel snapped the ball and scrambled, giving Jet a few precious seconds, then cocked back to throw. But the ball never left his hands. He was hit from behind and went down in a heap as the clock hammered zero. In Hester's final game as a Raider, he stood alone in the end zone, having never brought home a ring.

• • •

IN JESSIE'S QUEST for a title, Bobby Bowden's Seminoles seemed the best possible option. After the appearance in the championship game the previous year, the Raiders had begun attracting the attention of college scouts. They'd mainly come to Belle Glade to see Greg Bain, who by then was running over defenses in South Florida like John Henry through the mountain, sometimes scoring half a dozen touchdowns a game. Bain was Big Time, bigger than Wayne Stanley, Anthony Williams, Newman, all of those boys combined. When the scouts had come looking for Bain, they'd also seen Hester. But sadly for Bain, he'd snapped his ankle senior year in a playoff game against Fort Pierce Westwood. That same night, Hester put up five TDs and the scouts didn't have to waste a trip.

Hester would later describe the recruiting process that followed as "a nightmare." For a person who'd always moved to the back of the picture, who savored privacy and sought to keep his family's problems out of public view, the experience was debilitating.

"There would be guys lined up outside Jessie's house in their cars waiting their turn," remembered McDonald, who was also being heavily recruited at the time.

The Ohio State recruiter actually slept out front, remembered Roger. They'd already found Jessie hiding at his girlfriend's, so to avoid them he started staying at his grandmother's and wearing whatever clothes were there.

Bowden's relentless pursuit of Hester finally broke him, but he'd been comfortable in that decision. The Seminoles were a serious bowl contender, but most important, after carefully studying campus maps of FSU, the University of Miami, and the University of Florida, he'd determined that FSU was "compacted together" enough to feel the most like Belle Glade.

In his freshman year in Tallahassee, Jessie did all he could to transport the little world of Zara's tiny two-bedroom. He called home every other day and found rides on weekends back to Belle Glade. Home became the theme of every term paper Jessie would write. "How Much I Miss Home," by Jessie Hester; "How Much I Miss Home Cooking," by Jessie Hester; "How Much I Miss My Room at Home," and so on.

"Looking at him, one saw the product of a lifetime of adoring women," wrote Caroline Alexander, a former tutor at FSU who later profiled several of her student athletes in the book *Battle's End*. "He was extremely good-looking, with the even, clean-cut features of a matinee idol. . . . His were the playful, unthreatening good looks of a best friend's older brother."

In Tallahassee, Hester clocked the fastest forty on the Seminole squad, along with the fastest one hundred. We see him as an eager freshman receiver, shortly after catching his first touchdown in a 17–0 victory over Louisville. In front of fifty thousand fans at Doak Campbell Stadium, with a late-summer mist shimmering off the lights above, Hester shot from the eleven-yard line on a fade route, but was bumped by cornerback Roger Clay just as the ball was thrown. Off balance, he leaped into the end zone, curling his body around Clay's legs, and came up with the catch.

"I thought I was in a dream," Hester told the *Lakeland Ledger*. "Coach Bowden has always told us that once your number is called, you have to drive to the top."

"When he made that diving catch," joked Bowden, who was standing nearby, "I became a better coach."

In his four years at Florida State, Hester caught 107 passes for 2,100 yards, leaving behind electrifying memories, such as running a seventy-seven-yard reverse for a touchdown in a victory against number-one-ranked Miami, and against South Carolina making ten catches for 170 yards. But despite lofty predictions during the early eighties that Bowden's Seminoles had the bones to be national champions, the team never went farther than the Orange Bowl.

At the end of his senior season, Hester was standing with friends at a fraternity party when somebody pinched his butt. Whipping around, he saw Lena Derouen, whose friend had committed the offense and dashed away, leaving her alone. The two instantly clicked.

Lena was just a freshman, eighteen, beautiful, with light mocha skin that she'd inherited from her Creole father, a career naval officer who'd settled his family in Jacksonville. Lena could be loud and sassy, and her bubbly confidence perfectly offset Jessie's stoic shyness. Probably more appealing to Hester was that Lena knew nothing of football, or of Jessie the Jet.

"I had no idea who he was," she said. "He never even talked about football. He was a homebody. Most of the time we'd just stay at his apartment and watch TV."

It wasn't until weeks after meeting Lena, during her first trip to Belle Glade, that Jessie even allowed her a glimpse of the athlete he was. Standing in the backyard, dressed in tight jeans, he'd started executing double backflips off the wooden fence, leaving her in stitches. So it was an even bigger surprise a month later when he told her he was going to the NFL.

At the end of his junior season, Hester had first realized he could possibly be draft material, but he didn't know how high. Running back Greg Allen had always been the superstar on the Seminoles squad, and everyone predicted he would go early in the first round.

On draft day, Jessie called Lena, who was at her parents' house in Jacksonville, and suggested she might want to come back to Tallahassee in case he got picked. Teams had already started calling: first Buffalo, who said they'd love to have him if he was still available in the second round. Same with Dallas, Chicago, and Denver. Incredibly superstitious, Hester had scheduled no parties; he watched the draft on television at his apartment with roommate and fellow Seminole Cletus Jones. Shortly after Mississippi Valley State wideout Jerry Rice was picked number sixteen by the 49ers, Jessie got a phone call.

"Are you ready to become an L.A. Raider?" the voice asked.

"Am I ever," he said.

The Raiders had chosen him number twenty-three. Greg Allen went number thirty-five to Cleveland in the second round. The 1984 Super Bowl championship team of Howie Long, Cliff Branch, and Jim Plunkett would soon offer Hester a million-dollar contract, a $605,000 signing bonus, and $400,000 in other bonuses. His life, and the lives of his family, had just been forever altered. After years of careful attention to his ownself and the little things, Jet was finally seeing the reward. He was finally the provider he'd always dreamed of becoming. But if there was any excitement, he did his best to hide it.

"Me and Greg gotta do an interview," he told Lena once the draft was over.

"It didn't hit me what had just happened," she said. "Because when he came back, we didn't celebrate or anything. We just sat around with Cletus and watched *Batman*."

• • •

THE FIRST-ROUND SELECTION of Jessie Hester was more symbolic than anything; colleges had been pouring into Glades Central ever since Jet's high school days. And four years earlier, Pahokee's Rickey Jackson, a future Hall of Famer, had been drafted in the third round by the Saints. Like the cane and vegetables that grew in the silty soil, Hester's selection simply solidified the muck as a football land of plenty.

The following year, New England would draft Hester's high school teammate Ray McDonald. Before the decade was out, Louis Oliver would go first round to the Dolphins. Jimmy Spencer to the Saints. Rhondy Weston would be drafted by the Cowboys, Willie Snead by the Jets, and John Ford would go to Detroit.

The rise of Jessie the Jet seemed to coincide perfectly with the decline of the home he knew and loved. In April 1985, two weeks before Hester declared himself an L.A. Raider, Belle Glade was once again the focus of national embarrassment.

At the first International AIDS Conference, held in Atlanta, tropical disease doctors Mark Whiteside and Carolyn MacLeod presented research about a small agricultural town in the Everglades that was defying what doctors understood about the transmission of the deadly virus.

Until then, it was agreed that AIDS was confined mainly to homosexuals and intravenous drug users. But in Belle Glade, they discovered, it had also infected heterosexual men living predominantly in the town's migrant ghetto. Whiteside and MacLeod suspected that environmental conditions—the cramped living quarters, leaky pipes, communal bathrooms, drugs, casual sex, prostitutes, and mosquitoes that fed on the population—all contributed to Belle Glade's staggering rate of infection.

At the time of their presentation, there were thirty-seven confirmed cases—giving Belle Glade an infection rate fifty-one times the national average. The fallout was immediate. The *New York Times* ran the headline POVERTY-SCARRED TOWN NOW STRICKEN BY AIDS, and a deluge of negative media coverage ensued.

Local papers in South Florida had long reported the conditions in the migrant quarter. In 1979, five years after Palm Beach County produced a record-setting $680 million in vegetables and sugarcane, a survey found that nearly half of the city's housing was substandard, while 16 percent was "dilapidated and unfit for human habitation." In 1984 the city accounted for half of the black households in the county without bathrooms. A report by the *Miami Herald* that same year found that a large number of these substandard buildings were actually owned by Belle Glade city commissioners.

Add the concrete bodegas surrounding these apartments, painted bright colors with elaborate hand-painted signs; the vacant lots filled with garbage and weeds, chickens scratching in the dirt, traces of Spanish, Creole, and French on the breeze, and blackness in every direction, and downtown Belle Glade took on the appearance of another country.

Reporters arrived from as far as Sweden to write the AIDS story, and while in town they also found the sex, crime, and tales of drug dealers directing traffic along Avenue E. The new label "AIDS Capital of the World" was all Belle Glade needed to continue its journey to the bottom.

Most damning about MacLeod and Whiteside's presentation was the misconception that mosquitoes could possibly transmit the virus. That fear turned Belle Glade into a leper colony overnight. Businesses began closing and moving away. A major retail store withdrew plans for an opening, along with a developer ready to build a large subdivision. Belle Glade residents shopping in Miami and Fort Lauderdale were stunned when merchants sprayed their checks with Lysol. Teams canceled games scheduled for Belle Glade, and after an away match, cheerleaders returned upset when other girls refused to shake hands or share refreshments. Visitors were seen driving though town wearing surgical masks. And guests at the Belle Glade Motor Inn began calling ahead seeking guarantees they wouldn't catch the virus and die.

"What's the first sign of AIDS?" the joke went.

"Belle Glade: 5 miles."

But behind the jokes and sensational stories, the disaster was indeed real. AIDS ravaged Belle Glade, particularly downtown, where sex and drugs were readily available. Entire families disappeared. Houses went empty. The *Miami Herald* reported that one girl had lost both her parents twenty-four hours apart. Even today, the city carries a staggering number of cases (434 living with HIV/AIDS in 2010), and most everyone you met had a friend or a relative who'd died of the disease in the past decade.

If the stigma and fallout of AIDS weren't bad enough for the Glades economy, Big Sugar dealt an even greater blow. In the early 1990s, the region's sugar companies found themselves mired in lawsuits filed by H-2 cane cutters, who claimed they were being cheated on wages. For the growers, the lawsuits ran up millions in legal fees and caused a public-relations fiasco for an industry already reviled as one of the "evil empires" alongside Big Tobacco and Big Oil. With the recent advent of mechanical harvesters that could now travel atop the soft muck, growers decided to end the worker program altogether.

"From a public-relations standpoint," said Barbara Miedema, spokesperson for the Sugar Cane Growers Cooperative of Florida, "there was no way you could put a pretty face on importing people to do a job that people of America wouldn't do, who are black as coal, work in black muck in shin guards in the heat, swinging a machete. I don't care what you do. It just doesn't look great."

In 1993, H-2 workers harvested the last sugarcane in Florida, and when these men left, so did their money. Businesses along Avenue A and Main Street slowly began to vanish. The rapidly expanding coastal suburbs such as Wellington—now just a half-hour drive east along state route 80—began pulling away many of the remaining white and middle-class black families, lured by shopping centers, gated communities, and better schools. The city's tax revenue plummeted. By 2006 the county had taken over most public services in Belle Glade, including the city's fire and police departments.

Many now feel that Big Sugar's only lasting legacy in the Glades is the chronic joblessness and underemployment that soon gripped the region. Much of the old land that once made Muck City the winter vegetable capital of the world and employed tens of thousands now sits under cane, which is harvested by machines. Perpetuating this system, critics say, is the archaic U.S. sugar program that continues to prop up growers despite the collateral damage done to the local economy.

United States sugar policy, which is wrapped inside every farm bill passed by Congress, guarantees American sugar growers 85 percent of the domestic market, which in turn drives up prices for consumers and businesses. As of May 2011, Americans paid thirty-six cents a pound for sugar—about 50 percent higher than the world market price. The high price of sugar has proven hurtful to small businesses that depend on it to function. In 2000, the Government Accountability Office reported the sugar program had cost refiners, manufacturers, and consumers about $2 billion per year. More recently, economists put that figure at around $4 billion. Because of this, food and beverage conglomerates largely did away with sugar years ago in favor of cheaper corn-based sweeteners.

Today, most of the top jobs in the Glades-area sugar mills are held by Cubans, whites, or those with advanced education or connections, while local blacks are left with mostly low-paying jobs such as janitors and truck drivers. U.S. Sugar's citrus division near Clewiston even came under recent criticism for importing more than four hundred Mexican workers to pick oranges at $9.20 per hour.

Greg Schell, the labor lawyer who challenged them, was told the younger generation of local African Americans were unwilling to work as hard.

"We've encouraged the sugar industry to supplant all the vegetable land to grow sugar, a crop we don't even need to produce domestically. But it's profitable for a few people, and these guys can't lose money the way the sugar program is set up," said Schell, the managing attorney at the Florida Legal Services' Migrant Farmworker Justice Project, based in Lake Worth.

What few jobs remain in agriculture are now divided among local African Americans, Haitians, and a relatively recent influx of Latinos, who now make up over one-third of Belle Glade's and Pahokee's citizens. (In Belle Glade alone, Hispanics were solely responsible for a 17 percent jump in population over the last decade.) These migrants plant sugarcane from August through December, but mostly they pick corn. Belle Glade produces nearly one-third of the sweet corn grown in America, which is harvested each spring and early fall. But come late fall and winter, when sugar is being harvested as far as the eye can see, very few locals are involved.

"People simply cannot make a decent living, and our sugar program is central to that," said Schell. "It creates this distorted model that encourages production of this crop which is run by companies who choose to segregate all the good jobs by race, leaving very little, if anything, for the African Americans and Haitians. So what you've got is just chronically poor people. And it's hard to see how that pattern changes."

The nature of migrant work had historically made for an ever-shifting employment rate. With the jobless rate consistenly high (city officials estimated it was around 40 percent), crime flourished.

Already a nuisance in Belle Glade, crime began spiking in the mid-1990s to levels unprecedented for a small rural town. In 2003, Belle Glade made the FBI's list of top-three most violent cities in the country, its crime rate fueled by nearly a dozen gangs that saturated the downtown streets with drugs. In Palm Beach County, the sale of marijuana or cocaine within a thousand feet of a church or school carried a higher felony rap than the sale of it elsewhere. And in downtown Belle Glade, a church seemed to rise up every three blocks.

These days, according to Schell, most criminal defendants in drug cases are urged by their public defenders to plead guilty, rather than run the risk if scheduling a trial on the coast and not getting witnesses. "So they walk out with time served," said Schell, "but now they have a criminal conviction." In 2010 the Palm Beach County Sheriff's office estimated that over half of all young men in Belle Glade between the ages of eighteen and twenty-five had felony convictions that barred them from getting well-paying jobs. These days, even the Burger King on Main Street requires a background check for management positions.

For the many kids who avoided trouble, finding a career path in the Glades was daunting. Aside from seasonal labor, the only remaining jobs were with the sheriff's department and two prisons that shimmered in the outlying cane like dark omens. "In the Glades, either you pick it or you guard it," said Schell.

Which is why, more so than anywhere else in America, the game of football carried such profound importance that it held near-magical properties. It seemed as though the worse things became, the more athletes the Glades produced. The 1994 and '95 Raider teams yielded nine NFL players, including Fred Taylor of the Jacksonville Jaguars and Reidel Anthony of the Tampa Bay Buccaneers, both first-round draft selections. In 2001, Glades Central had seven former players in the NFL—more than any other high school in the nation.

Eight players from the Raiders' 2001 team went on to play at Division I universities and two later advanced to the NFL, including New York Jets wide receiver Santonio Holmes. As a Pittsburgh Steeler, Holmes was MVP of Super Bowl XLIII for his stunning last-second grab in the corner of the end zone to give the Steelers the victory. Standing on the opposite sideline that night was Arizona's Anquan Boldin, his old rival from Pahokee.

"The special thing about Glades Central is that kids love to play," said Willie Bueno, who coached the Raiders in the 2000 championship. "It's important to them. They're born to compete and they give great effort. For a coach, the carrot you give at Glades Central is you do good and you'll get out of here and go to school. You go to some of these other schools on the coast, and that's just not the motivator. A lot of times their daddy can pay for school."

The only memorial to these men and their tradition is a wall at Glades Central's Effie C. Grear Field containing a list of title seasons and the former players who have gone pro. Although the list is outdated, its positioning makes it the first thing you see as you enter the field.

Looking at the wall, one would be wrong to assume it is a celebration. Rather, it could be read as a statement of expectation, a warning to all who enter with the title head coach.

CHAPTER

The season began on a sweltering August morning with dark, low-hanging clouds that seemed to snag along the cane tops in the distance. At one end of the practice field, head coach Jessie Hester leaned against his gray Ram pickup and surveyed the land. He was dressed in standard attire: a matching T-shirt and shorts, and a cap turned backward on his head. A gold nameplate with the word JET hung around his neck. Every few minutes, he'd tip a bag of sunflower seeds into his mouth and reveal the scars of his trade. Apart from the dark rows of turf burn along his arms, both pinky fingers had been permanently deformed, the result of being broken and dislocated dozens of times by incoming passes. Hester would work the seeds with his teeth, then crane his neck to spit. Each time, he'd glance up at the gathering of fresh recruits and appear to wince.

For the Glades Central Raiders, the 2010 season was kicking off with all the familiar signs. The sugarcane was high and green and shimmered in the breeze like a whispering sea. The summer air was like breathing through cotton. And Glades Central, still the poorest high school in the state of Florida, had one of the best-ranked football teams in America. It was this last part that filled Hester's stomach with dread.

The national ranking in *USA Today*, published that morning, came despite what had happened the previous season, when Hester's team, once again ranked among the country's most elite, had dropped the state championship game.

The loss had been a colossal disappointment, especially since the season had been so glorious, so near perfect. As in so many seasons past, the Raiders had won their division undefeated, then coasted through the playoffs. In late November, after a blowout win against Tampa Robinson, they'd sealed a date with Cocoa High School in the state 2A title game, which was held in the Orlando Citrus Bowl.

The Cocoa Tigers were the reigning champs and had everything under the hood: a pounding running game that took victories by attrition, a fleet of DI receivers, and a swarming defense that held opponents to double-digit yardage.

They'd ended the regular season with a stunning come-from-behind victory against Jacksonville's Bolles School in a clash of defending champions. Bolles had won ten state titles, nine of them under Charles "Corky" Rogers, who was the winningest coach in Florida high school history. Rogers and the Bulldogs were riding a forty-two-game winning streak. They'd not lost a game at home in four years, until Cocoa rallied from a two-touchdown deficit to beat them 44–37 in overtime.

Still, the Raiders entered the game the favorites, mainly due to their star-studded roster full of skill players. Nearly all of Belle Glade had turned out, eager to launch a new dynasty in the Glades. Fox Sports Florida had broadcast the game live. And there before seven thousand in attendance and all the Sunshine State, the mighty Raiders, those uncatchable, seen-on-Sunday Raiders, had gone and laid a giant egg.

The Raider offense tacked up thirteen easy points before the half, then spectacularly fell apart in the third quarter, dismantled by a team whose greatest strength was its unflashy discipline and attention to the little things. The Tigers won the game by a score of 27–13, mainly by seizing on interceptions and a litany of mindless penalties. It was like watching eleven ants take apart a Porsche in under half an hour.

After Cocoa's quarterback took a knee to end it, Hester had to run halfway onto the field shouting, "Lose with dignity!" because his players were flinging their helmets to the ground while others crumpled to the turf and sobbed. The ride home to Belle Glade seemed to last days.

• • •

HESTER'S HIRING TWO years earlier had caused enormous excitement. Jessie the Jet, the most celebrated player in Raider history, had returned to his embattled hometown *to give something back*. But Belle Glade was different from most small towns, in that Hester was not actually the first former legend to return. That was Willie Snead, whose abrupt departure had left an opening for Hester in the first place. Snead, the former wide receiver for the New York Jets, had also been compelled to give something back, which he did in 2006, bringing Glades Central its sixth state title and golden rings as fat as walnuts for his team.

That season, Snead had been blessed with one of the best Raider teams in years, with two NFL-bound receivers on his wings in Deonte Thompson and Travis Benjamin (no relation to Kelvin). But the Raiders still dropped three games, including the one that arguably mattered most, the annual matchup against rival Pahokee.

Snead's coaching and motives came into question. People started talking, the way they do. Maybe Snead was just career-obsessed, looking to leverage a bigger job on the back of his famous alma mater. It didn't take long before Snead was plain "anti-community" and the town was boycotting his home games. Even after he won the championship, Snead was a pariah.

The Raiders lost again to Pahokee the following season before being eliminated in the semifinals by three points. A month later, Snead seemed to confirm everyone's wisdom by accepting a high-paying job at a private school in Michigan, where he won another title. His coaches parlayed their stints in Belle Glade for assistant jobs at LSU and the University of Miami.

"The opportunity I got to come back to my alma mater and give to the community, and then to face the ridicule that you face, it was really disturbing," Snead told the *Palm Beach Post* upon his resignation. "It really bothered me and I think it bothered the other coaches too."

Once Snead was gone, fans and players petitioned the school to offer the job to Hester. By that time, Jet was in his twelfth year of retirement, two years longer than he'd even played, living quietly between Belle Glade and his home in Wellington, a suburb of West Palm Beach. During his career, as his hometown had started its slow decline, he'd invested in devalued real estate, buying and refurbishing apartment blocks in and around the quarter. He'd also built a house for Zara in a new development on Belle Glade's south side, then bought a small meat market and Laundromat for her to manage.

He was spending his days engrossed in the puttering routine of family life: getting kids ready for school, sending Lena off to her job at the sheriff's department, then driving thirty miles to his properties to paint, lay carpet, and wait for plumbers.

His connection with his alma mater had remained solid. During the years in the league, Hester had paid for football cleats and jerseys, and bought the Raiders' mascot costume. For his old track team, he'd covered the cost of shoes and plane tickets for out-of-state meets. Once he'd retired, his face was a familiar one at Raider home games, especially during years when his eldest son, Jessie junior, played wide receiver.

To the fans, there had been no need to question allegiances. Jessie had kept his roots deep. Even if his wife did make him live in Wellington, Jet's home was in Belle Glade. He was a muckstepper to the bone.

During those years, whenever one coach would fall out of favor, the school and fans would lobby Hester to take the job. But he always declined.

The game had already kept him away from his family for a decade; he'd even missed Jessie's birth while playing in Los Angeles. But after the latest petition and subsequent offer, Hester was driving downtown, near his old apartment, when he saw something that made him reconsider.

The sight was nothing extraordinary: two men in sagging jeans standing on the corner of Southwest Sixth Street and Avenue A. The corner was a known drug market, and if Hester had to guess, they were most likely dealers or lookouts. But as he drove past, he recognized them as old teammates of his son Jessie. The men had not only been Raiders, but they'd also sat in his kitchen and eaten his groceries. Now here they were on the corner, just two more jitterbugs caught in the swirl.

All day, the question nagged at him: *Could I have helped those guys?*

Hester accepted the job and the meager $3,600 salary, the annual pay for a head football coach in Palm Beach County. He announced to friends and family, "I'm not here to win championships, I'm here to win kids," and was quickly put to the test.

The first thing he realized was that half his team were affiliated with gangs. Some were actual members, but most had simply been intimidated into vowing allegiance. The gangs and cliques pitted neighborhood against neighborhood, town against town: trailer park versus South Bay; Pahokee versus Belle Glade. The rivalries had also infected the harmony of his team.

No wonder they're losing games, he thought. *Most of these kids hate each other.* Linemen would flat-out refuse to block for a running back, fights would break out during practice, and kids were beaten while walking home.

After the realization, Hester and his coaches called a team meeting. "We got one gang on this team," he told them. "One family."

By midseason, two of his players had been shot. In September, cornerback Byron Blake was shot in the hand while exchanging gunfire with another man. A month later, linebacker Robert Hardnett was hit in the chest and arm during a gang-related drive-by shooting, which also wounded junior varsity linebacker Carl Vereen—the bullet passing less than half an inch from his spine.

The same week Blake was shot, Pahokee captain Norman "Pooh" Griffith was murdered at a dance in downtown Belle Glade. It was hours after the Blue Devils' homecoming victory over Jupiter. As Griffith tried to leave that evening, two men blocked his truck while one opened fire through the window, then reached in and snatched his gold chain. A simple robbery, the sheriff concluded.

Griffith had done everything right: he was a decent student, a disciplined player, a regular "house boy," as people endearingly described children who chose to stay indoors rather than risk going outside. With offers already from Iowa State and Buffalo, Pooh was on his way out.

Hester was quickly overwhelmed, naïve about the new realities of coaching in Belle Glade. He and his assistants were now arranging grief counseling because so many players had been friends with Pooh. His assistants were buying groceries, paying light bills, waiting for the next phone call. So little of the job had anything to do with football. And it dragged Hester out of his comfort zone, put him in a funk.

"Jet's first year, he didn't even talk," said one assistant coach. "He'd say maybe three words to you all practice. You had to get inside that dude's head to know what was going on."

Amazingly, the Raiders still went undefeated through twelve games, only to lose in the regional playoffs. For Jet, the love affair with fans endured despite the loss; most agreed it was because Miami Pace had soaked their grass just hours before the game, thus robbing Raider receivers of their God-given ability to separate and explode.

At the outset of Hester's second season, another scandal befell the team. A local minister named Richard Harris was arrested for sexually assaulting young boys in Belle Glade, several of whom were identified as football players. For years, Reverend Harris had been a fixture on the sidelines and in the locker room, an overeager booster who provided the team with Gatorade, bought shoes and clothes for players, and persuaded parents to let him pick their boys up from practice. Little did anyone know he was also luring kids into his home with promises of college connections, then pressuring them into sex.

In March 2009, burglars robbed Harris's home and made off with stacks of homemade videotapes showing him with various students and former players. The tapes made their way around Belle Glade before police were able to confiscate them and make an arrest. One fifteen-year-old former player told detectives that Harris asked him, "What would you do to go to college?" before pressing him to perform sex acts.

Despite these distractions, Hester and his staff still managed to pull off their own private victories. Byron Blake, the kid who was shot through the hand, got a scholarship to Arkansas State. Greg Dent, a versatile athlete who coaches had worried would slip into the void, got picked up by the Seminoles. They'd also managed to pull from the brink one of their youngest, most promising linemen.

Robert Way was so bashful that one would assume he had never learned to speak. And with the nickname "Joon-Joon," the boy's sweet nature seemed to drip out like honey whenever his mother, Shawanna, would call it. But trouble had wooed and beguiled Robert, and often his mother would have to pull him close when the siren song of country hood life became overbearing. In that world, he was an actor trying on deadly poses.

During his sophomore year, his best friend, Willie "Gene" Thomas, was shot and killed inside the trailer park next door to Glades Central, another bloody chapter in the long-standing feud between rival gangs. Months later, a car full of gang members pulled up on Robert and some friends. When the boys jumped out to fight, one of them bobbled and dropped a pistol. Robert's younger brother later found the gun buried in Robert's laundry hamper. Shawanna turned it over to the sheriff, explaining that her son had discovered it on the road.

Later, when Robert beat a kid in school and stole his iPod, the kid's mother called the police and threatened to press charges. The school had Robert on a surveillance camera, they said. At her wits' end, Shawanna tried sending her son to live with his father in Georgia, who refused to take him. The only man who seemed to know how to speak to him was his coach. Having just pulled Robert onto the varsity squad, Hester staged an intervention, along with Shawanna and his coaching staff.

"The rest of your life can be decided today," Hester told him. "You can either choose to be great, or become just another dead jitterbug on the street that nobody remembers."

The confrontation broke Way down into tears; then he chose to be great. Within months, his GPA rose to 3.0. The next season, Way recorded 146 tackles, thirty-nine for negative yardage, and twenty-seven sacks. The last was a school record previously held by Ray McDonald Jr., now a defensive tackle with the San Francisco 49ers, who phoned Robert to congratulate him. As Way excelled on the field, the *Post* published a story about the great transformation of the Raiders' young lineman. The scholarship offers came trickling in.

But certain fans—the most vocal ones anyway—did not register such victories. After the Raiders lost to Cocoa later that year under the lights of the Citrus Bowl, before God and the Glades, the relationship quickly soured. Hester, the hometown legend, became just another stupid coach. Within hours of Hester leaving Orlando, someone rang his phone, drunk, saying, *"Jet, if I ever see you on Fifth Street, I'm gon' shoot yo ass."* Other callers threatened to burn his cars, his home.

It was all money talking, lost and gone money. Gamblers had always frittered away their Friday paychecks in the bleachers, eyes dancing with gin, wagering on everything from point spreads to total receiving yards before the half. A bookie named Pie ran numbers on Raider games from a cinderblock social club across the street from the school. Hurricane Wilma had blown the roof off the club's upper floor, which still sat gaping under the Florida sun. At home games, there could easily be hundreds of dollars on the line. For a championship, tens of thousands.

The Raider fans had always filled that symbolic "twelfth man" position, yet to great extremes. At Effie C. Grear Field, so went the joke, the bleachers were merely a place to fit the fifteen hundred assistant coaches. But even that implied a kind of playfulness. The fans were more of a variable, ever-shifting force, like weather over the ocean. As Jenkins, Werneke, and Snead could attest, they were a force that could both carry you and bury you, one that could undermine your authority and render you powerless.

• • •

HESTER SAW DARK forces in every direction. On this soupy August afternoon, he sensed them along the fenceline where a group of fans gathered to watch the first week of practice. They were fathers and uncles and men from the club across the street, many of them former players or those whose circumstances had never allowed them such status.

A lineman named Gator had failed to produce sixty-five dollars for his equipment and physical, and now trotted out to where they stood. Helmet in hand, he slowly made his way down the line collecting bills and small change. As Gator counted his loot by the fence, the men gathered around, jabbing the air with their fingers. Coaching.

"I tell the kids one thing, and these guys tell 'em another," Hester said. "Somebody's always in their ear. Come game time, they can't remember nothin.'"

Subversion had infected his own coaching staff, which he'd been forced to purge. Over the past two seasons he'd fired two assistants who were reversing play calls, thwarting his control, going above the program. One had even screamed at the boys after the loss to Cocoa, calling them quitters.

"Some of those guys didn't see it like I did," he said, "like a high school game. It was too big to them and I had to let them go."

The coaches had been former Bobcats and Raiders, men who'd been part of the program for decades. Their dismissal had caused a backlash among many fans, due partly to the men Hester hired to replace them. Out of his twelve assistant coaches, four had never worn the maroon and gold. Even worse, one was from Connecticut. In fact, the only person to carry over from Snead's staff was assistant head coach Sam King, who'd overseen special teams for Glade Central for thirty-one years. Nobody fired Sam, especially someone as superstitious as Jet. Sam King *was* the Raiders. The man came with the field.

As for the other coaches, Hester felt the Raiders needed more than just hard-nosed football guys. Given the kinds of problems affecting his team, what the kids needed most of all were mentors.

"The coaches I chose are guys who worked well with kids, guys who kids would respond to," Hester said. "You want people who are there for the right reasons."

Kids responded to defensive line coach Sherman Adams, the interloper from Hartford, especially when he'd load his SUV with linemen after practice and spring for fried chicken. Sherm stood six foot seven and worked for Geek Squad in West Palm Beach installing televisions. Despite Sherm's Yankee roots, Hester and the others had accepted him as a born-again muckstepper. He even spoke of "sprinkling some of that in your food" for strength and magic. Until Sherm started eating muck, he said, he and his wife had been unable to have children. "Now we got a beautiful baby girl. There's power in this ground."

During summers, the boys pumped iron with strength coach JD Patrick, who was another assistant who'd never been a Raider. In fact, JD had been so small in high school that his nickname was "Squeaky." A sharp mind for numbers and electronics had later served him well in the army, where he'd worked at Fort Bliss preparing the Hawk missile for deployment. Once out, he'd gotten through a nasty divorce by embracing weightlifting, which added bulk and kept him lean and strong in his later years. He was now a youthful man of fifty-five, with a new wife and a two-year-old daughter at home. And despite a bald patch on top, JD let his salt-and-pepper hair grow long in back, almost to his shoulders. Aside from coaching, he worked as Belle Glade's director of parks and recreation. His office was inside the community recreational center off MLK Boulevard where the team did their summer workouts.

The kids responded to Randy Williams, the running backs coach. He'd played on the fabled Raider teams of the mid 1990s that had produced so many pros. After graduation, he ran the football on a scholarship at Savannah State before a broken ankle and tibia ended his career. He now worked as an officer at Glades Correctional Institution, transporting inmates to trials and appointments. At school he spoke the kids' language and often dished hard advice to any potential "danks and jitterbugs" who'd show up bleary-eyed and loiter on the sidelines.

"Stop being a dank," he would tell them.

But out of Hester's coaches, Greg Moreland was the most beloved. He was two years older than Hester, with a shiny bald dome and a sculpted goatee that he kept dyed jet black. His job as a counselor at a youth mental-health facility in Jupiter had given him an easy, natural rapport with players, many of whom he'd given nicknames such as "Standstill," "Little Hands," and "Muscle Mutt."

His own nickname was "Q," which was short for "GQ," which he'd earned after spending some time once as a male model. For a football coach, Q had personal style to spare, from the fifty-six pairs of shoes in his closet to the white convertible Sebring he drove to practice with late-seventies-era Isley Brothers playing softly in the deck.

What kids loved most was Coach Q's bawdy humor, which was irresistible. On a road game later that season, he would leave the team weeping with laughter after complimenting a woman on her eyes, then asking, "If God forbid anything ever happened to you, could I take them things out and keep 'em in a pickle jar?"

His conquests in the bedroom were also public information. "I'm taking my Cialis early," he announced once at the end of practice. "I told my wife to get ready, 'cause tonight I'm puttin on the cape and jumpin off the dresser."

Another time he confided, "Cats and midgets terrify me."

• • •

AS PRACTICE GOT under way, the coaches busied themselves dragging bags of footballs and water, reading excuse notes from doctors and mothers, organizing warm-ups—squats and high knees, lunges and jumping jacks. They downloaded football apps on each other's phones. They ate candy.

Coach Q and a few others stood around Greg Hall, the heavyset receivers coach whom they called Minute. Hall was one of Hester's oldest friends and now worked as a sheriff's deputy. He also struggled with diabetes.

"Minute don't carry a gun 'cause they know he got the sugar," Q said. "When they send Minute out, all they give him is a flashlight and a roll of quarters."

He straightened his face, all serious. "They know he could go at any time."

Hester, behind dark sunglasses, paid no attention. He was busy watching his young squad slowly trickle onto the field while trying to ignore the newspaper article he held in his hand. Mario was already loosening up. Robert Way and Davonte Allen were getting dressed. But there was no sign of Benjamin. In fact, half the team was already late.

"Let's go," he said. "You jitterbugs done wasted enough time."

"Hey, Coach Hester," one player yelled. "You seen us in the papers?"

The coach just scowled.

After the team gathered for prayer and fell into laps around the field, Hester finally looked down at the *USA Today* cinched under his clipboard. The paper's preseason Top 25 poll listed Glades Central at number twenty-one in the nation.

Hester hated national rankings. The way he saw it, of all the outside forces working against him and his coaches, a national ranking only gave them footing. Rankings were a distraction that built false hope and ratcheted expectations. They also gave life to a growing sense of entitlement that many believed had infected the program for years.

As far as expectations, the Raiders' dominating performance at the seven-on-seven in Tallahassee had certainly fed the community's hopes of another title run. Several weeks later in Tampa, the NFL had hosted its annual seven-on-seven with elite teams from all over the country. Already the reigning champions, the Raiders clinched the title again.

But these tournaments were deceiving because they were merely a showcase for the flyboys who came a dime a dozen in the Glades. They provided no window into the health of the team's interior core, which was the offensive and defensive lines. And like rankings, they told you little about the character and chemistry of the squad.

Standing at practice, Hester looked out at the group of kids crowned one of the best teams in the nation. As much as he loathed the rankings, it was something he desperately wanted to believe. After two years of trying to weed out the bad elements, instill discipline, and buffer the outside forces, this was the crew he'd been waiting on. This was the squad he and his coaches had groomed since they were freshmen and sophomores, the ones they'd hoped to inspire into believing in themselves and the program. These were the guys who'd come together as "one gang, one family" and deliver Glades Central its seventh title. And for Hester, his very first.

But now, taking inventory, he began to wonder.

It was already clear his offensive line was a disaster. The few precious linemen who weighed over 250 pounds were slow and out of shape. Realizing their value in the land of cheetahs, many of them had blown off the mandatory summer workouts.

"They don't show up 'cause they know I need 'em," Hester had complained at the time. "These boys got my hands tied."

His two centers—Travis Salter and Kevin Edourd, a soft-spoken Haitian whom everyone called Cubby—now gasped during sprints and wobbled in the heat. Cubby couldn't even make it twice without taking a knee. Corey Graham and Brandon Rodriguez, the two guards, looked on the verge of needing an ambulance.

The OL had been the weak link in the previous year's squad, especially against Cocoa. The Tigers had sliced them apart and hammered away at the quarterback, Leron Thomas, rattling his focus and forcing the key interception that turned the game.

The crushing loss in Orlando seemed to have provided little motivation. Only Gator, whose real name was Tavious Bridges, appeared hardy and fit. He ran his sprints with the same crazed smile that greeted his opposing defenders, one that jacked his eyes open wide and revealed a mouthful of giant white teeth.

"Is that why they call you Gator?" someone asked him.

"Nah," he said, "I'm just physical in everything I do."

The same could be said for Jatavis "Jaja" Brown, the junior linebacker now running shuffle drills. Last season, it had been Jaja and the tight Raider secondary that had largely carried the team. Now that Hester was seeing the shape of the OL, he hoped Brown and his boys could do it again.

He loved watching Jaja play football. The kid was a throwback to a bygone era, with straight-backed posture and a body sculpted by milk, push-ups, and mornings on the dikes. Even the way he tucked his sweats down into his socks was reminiscent of C. W. Haynes and the ironmen from the proud old days. At six foot one and two hundred pounds, he was blessed with blazing muck speed and ferocious power. Running backs remembered him the next morning. So did college recruiters who saw his film. Jaja already had multiple offers from Division I programs.

But his ferocity on the field was betrayed by a terrible shyness. He rarely spoke in public, and when he did, the words came out soft and measured.

"The boy don't say much," said Hester. "But he shows up for work." Of the players on the Raiders who reminded Hester of himself, one was Jaja.

The other was Jaime Wilson, the Raiders' number-two receiver, who now practiced hand drills with the rest of the corps. One by one, the flyboys burst off the line and hooked in front of Coach Hall, who fired footballs straight into their faces. In such drills, Jaime's hands were a thing to behold, trapping the hurtling projectile with a graceful, gentle touch.

Although he was skinny and not very tall, it was Jaime whom coaches considered to be the best overall athlete on the team. He had breakaway speed, instant separation, and those sturdy hands. And he was versatile. Jaime doubled as the team's punter, and during the summer tournaments, he even played quarterback and displayed nimble feet and a rifle arm. As a junior, Jaime was already getting attention from the Hurricanes and Gators. He was also ranked one of the top twenty-five receivers in the state. And to Hester, that's what made Jaime vulnerable to the forces—the uncles and cousins and family friends—that assured him of his singular talent. Hester knew what all coaches knew, that for an athlete with that kind of gift, the worst kind of calamity, aside from injury, death, or prison, was believing your own hype.

As much as Hester feared to admit it, he was already losing Benjamin.

The team captain and figurehead, the playmaker upon whom the Raiders would hang their season's dreams, was now refusing to work out. After arriving late to practice, Benjamin ignored orders to do push-ups. When Coach JD yelled, "Let's go, KB," the nation's number-eight receiver mimicked the motions, then stretched out in the grass. On the first morning of two-a-days, Benjamin had also refused to wear his helmet on account of fresh ear piercings.

"I don't want titties," he protested, referring to lumps of scar tissue left behind by the closed holes.

"Where are your priorities at, KB?" Hester said. "Put your helmet on and get out there."

"Just burn both ends of a broom straw and stick 'em through," Coach Randy said. "That way they won't close. That's how we used to do it."

Hester glared at him. "I said get out there, KB."

Benjamin trotted onto the field bareheaded, the studs in his ears glistening in the sun.

Before the month was out, sportswriters along the coast would pick the boys from Glades Central to rally back to Orlando. Despite what Hester saw, he dared to believe that could be true. The only question remained: *How bad did they really want it?* For any coach, that was something you simply could not teach.

The season started in a week.

If the pressures of maintaining tradition weren't great enough, the Raiders' season openers thrust upon them the burden of state pride. The first two games of the season would be played against nationally ranked teams from Texas, part of a showcase designed to give bragging rights to the true national powerhouse—at least for a year. The first matchup was Saturday against Skyline High School of Dallas, a noon game under the sun at Daytona Beach's Municipal Stadium.

There was no questioning both states' obsession with Friday-night football and the talent each had produced. Before the showcase began, the *Sun Sentinel* even ran a chart showing how the most recent NFL roster was dominated by players from Texas and Florida, with 179 and 176, respectively. Florida's major college programs (Florida, FSU, and Miami) had captured ten national titles, while the Lone Star State's big three (Texas, Texas A&M, and TCU) had won seven.

On the high school level, however, the numbers told a diverging story. Approximately 165,000 students played football in Texas, compared to just 38,291 in Florida—a huge disparity, even when accounting for Texas's size and population difference. But perhaps the greatest difference was money.

Michael Irvin, the Hall of Famer and Fort Lauderdale native, summed it up for a *Sentinal* reporter. "Florida has better players," he said, "and Texas has better facilities."

Texas, where the state capitol in Austin reached fourteen feet higher than the one in Washington by design, carried a similar attitude toward the school gridiron. Multimillion-dollar stadiums dotted the flat Texas land- scape like totems to the gods, replete with indoor practice fields, harems of student trainers, paid assistants, and head coaches who earned upward of six figures to lead boys into championships like lion-hearted generals.

At Glades Central and throughout Palm Beach County, the salary for Hester and his three paid assistants (the others volunteered their time) was just enough to cover the gas to practice and a PlayStation for the kids at Christmas, maybe a new phone. Despite being one of the most elite football programs in the state, it took the school board years to approve $10,000 for a simple press box for Effie C. Grear Field. The track coaches practically had to go to battle to get an eight-lane course. The school board wanted to give them six, which would have made them ineligible to hold regional and district championship meets. Coach Willie McDonald had to remind them that between the boys' and girls' track teams, Glades Central held seventeen state titles.

Pahokee had recently won a string of Class 2B championships, along with an endorsement from Nike that paid for uniforms and equipment. But to hear the coaches at Glades Central grumble, a fistful of rings and famous alumni were worth as much as the paint on the welcoming wall. Couldn't buy you a tent or even a jug of Gatorade.

Grit, discipline, and God-given athleticism were all Glades Central had ever needed to win. So Hester hoped his players could at least draw upon their genetics after looking at Dallas Skyline's roster. They were big boys, bigger than any team the Raiders would face all season. The thought of flinging his soft offensive line against them almost seemed cruel.

"Show your speed," Hester told his boys. "It will be the only friend you got."

The day before leaving, spider lightning streaked across the sky from an encroaching storm and drove the team indoors. The Raiders clustered inside a drab industrial arts class where Hester kept an office, since the team locker room was too small to fit them. As rain lashed against the roof and rattled the thick metal doors, Hester addressed his boys.

"We on some lists that call us the best this or that in the country," he said. "All it means is that every team we play's gonna have us circled. You're marked every time you're on that field.

"Yall got a real good football team. You could be a *great* football team. All the ingredients are there. But you're only as good as the bunch. This is the group that we coaches have been waiting on. This here is the season to win. So make your mark."

From the back row of chairs, the quarterback stood and addressed his team.

"Get my back," Mario said. "And I'll carry you."

"That's why you been given a team," Hester replied. "Now go and lead them."

• • •

PROBLEMS PLAGUED THE Raiders from the outset. The school had yet to hire a trainer, forcing players and coaches to administer wrappings that fell apart and littered the field. In a repeat of Tallahassee, a miscommunication resulted in the team having no water and coaches scrambling to Walmart to buy it in bottles.

Municipal Stadium was equipped with artificial turf, which appealed to a long-held belief in the Glades: that boys who grew up running the spongy muck were twice as fast on the hardtop. But the late-summer sun was broiling by the noon kickoff. Heat waves bounced off the black rubber in the turf, giving it the feel of hot charcoal underfoot. Then, of course, there was the Dallas line.

The boys from Skyline were indeed huge, with broad, corn-fed physiques that made a mockery of even Glades Central's biggest players. On the first play of scrimmage, they trampled over the Raider offensive line, as if leaping over a row of folding chairs, and flung Mario to the ground. The first drive ended with an interception, and afterward they gave him no rest. Each play found the quarterback scrambling to get rid of the ball as soon as it touched his hands. He would end up tossing two interceptions and getting called for as many intentional-grounding penalties. The Raiders' inexperienced OL continually jumped offsides, aborting any forward progress. By the end, Glades Central would commit fifteen penalties for a loss of 148 yards.

And when the Raiders finally fought their way into scoring position, Jeffery Philibert, one of the few seasoned big men, went and lost his mind in the heat. Immediately following a play, Philibert grabbed a Skyline defender by the jersey and hurled him to the turf. He then straddled the boy's chest, and, to the horror of his coaches, began hammering both fists into his face. ("He was grabbing my balls," Philibert would say in his defense, but the state athletics board still handed down a four-game suspension, further weakening an already porous Raider offensive line.)

But for every misery Dallas inflicted on Mario, the nimble Raider defense answered with two. They pounced on the hulking Skyline offense like a pride of cats, suddenly alive at the rumble of the drums. Behind the cheers of five hundred Raider faithful in the stands, Hester breathed easy, watching the great muscle of his squad begin to flex.

Along with Jaja, the lightning Raider defense was anchored by Dominique Gibson, who, like his teammate, evoked the old breed. They called him Boobie, just like his father, Frank Williams, who was married to KB's sister Tangela. This meant that Boobie was KB's nephew. And like his uncle, the junior linebacker had already led a complete and troubled life before wearing the maroon and gold.

As a boy, Boobie had lived in Macon, Georgia, with his mother, Cassandra. Early on, he showed a whip-smart intelligence and a love for numbers. He made the math team and wore a pair of thick, black-framed glasses, none of which brought him any peace among the neighborhood boys. Then again, neither did his older brothers, whose reputation as troublemakers often made Boobie an easy target. "Kids would try me because they thought I was soft," he said. By the fifth grade, Boobie had been kicked out of two schools for fighting.

Boobie's older brothers later got mixed up with gangs and guns, and such a life was hard nourishment for a boy looking to grow up fast. At age twelve, he was arrested for theft and vandalizing city property. In 2006, Frank pulled Boobie out of Macon to live with him and Tangela. In the few short years that followed, everything in Macon fell apart. In February 2008, Boobie's brother Derrick died in a car accident and another brother was sent to prison. During that time, Cassandra became gravely ill with kidney disease. She died in July, just months after burying her son. When Boobie heard the news of his mother, Frank said, "he fell over backward on the floor."

Trouble and sorrow had hardened Boobie by his seventeenth birthday, leaving him so old in the face that he seemed an impostor walking the halls of a high school. Girls swooned over him because of this, and boys feared him and gave him room. He still wore the black-framed glasses, usually coupled with an Oxford shirt and sweater, which worked to soften his flinty persona. The last time he'd taken the ACT, he'd scored a 23 out of 36. So comfortable with himself, one evening before a game, he sat before his teammates and recited Maya Angelou's entire poem "Still I Rise" with flawless cadence.

He'd started the Skyline game on offense, running the ball. On his very first carry, the boys from Dallas sent a message by spearing him so hard in the chest he would later spend the night in the emergency room with a bruised lung. Barely able to breathe, Boobie still pounded the Dallas line all afternoon for a game-high eighty-six yards, then played sideline-to-sideline defense as linebacker.

The tandem of Boobie and Jaja shut down the feared Skyline rushing attack, slipping into the backfield to bury the running backs the second they touched the ball. Jaja and Robert Way also sacked the Dallas quarterback three times and forced an interception. At halftime, Dallas had yet to enter Raider territory.

By the third quarter, with the score still 0–0, the heat took control. Players dropped to the turf from cramps, swatting helmets and crying in pain. On the Raiders, they were dragged off and plied with salty pickle juice, spilled cups of which littered the ground and enveloped the entire sideline in a hot vapor of vinegar.

The stout Dallas defenders soon began to wilt, enough to allow Boobie two handoffs that drove the Raiders downfield. Struggling for every breath, the powerful running back carried four Texans on his shoulders for ten yards into the end zone. The extra point attempt was a dud.

Ugly as it was, the Raiders won, 6–0.

• • •

LATER THAT NIGHT, Mario returned home and turned on the computer. The write-up in the *Post* gushed over the first-time quarterback's tenacity and echoed Hester's postgame message to the team: that against one of the toughest defenses in the country, Mario had proved himself.

But the quarterback saw only the venom that came despite the win. He spent the night reading forums and message boards that condemned him as too fat and short for the position, not the caliber of athlete to lead the mighty Raiders—a senseless coaching choice to be remedied at once. The same anonymous fans who'd showered him with encouragement that summer had not only turned on him, they were carving him up. Staring at the screen, he felt himself slowly come apart.

There was Super Mario, the No. 1 QB who crawled down Main Street in the tricked-out Lumina: candy blue with twenty-four-inch rims like disco balls in the sun, and the arcade hero himself airbrushed in a panorama across the back. There was Mario with the gold chains and high fade, the candlelight eyes, and a smile that could cut through a fog. There was the locker-room jock who bragged of older friends and easy pussy, who prepared for games with rapper Murder Man Flocka pounding in his head, singing, "GUN SOUND, luv dat luv dat GUN SOUND." There was Mario with a polished swagger that suggested ready violence if crossed.

But that young man now lay discarded like a shucked suit of armor. Exposed now in the darkness of the room, illuminated by the cruel, flickering screen, was the quiet, sensitive child. The teachers' favorite. The orphan who longed to remember the feel of his mother's embrace.

He'd been too young to know every detail, just that she'd been sick, the walls of her heart weakened by disease and made worse in the labor of six children. But Mary Rowley felt her happiest whenever swarmed with little ones. The chaos of her second-grade classroom infused her with energy, made her whole. And the madness of so much family at home kept her mind off a strained marriage.

Her husband, James, worked in the mills of U.S. Sugar. Once the cane season was finished, he followed harvests as a packinghouse foreman. He was a papa bear in the wide eyes of his children, strong arms and a round belly, a man whose talents over a kitchen stove braising oxtails and simmering stews only matched his generous appetites.

Summers he'd pile the van with kids for weekends at Walt Disney World or family reunions in Georgia. But he never stayed home long. For he was a road man at heart, raised up in the migrant fields and driven by seasons like the leaves on a tree, and its wildness had infected him. He'd disappear for days on a jag, come home stewed and raving, and empty out the house. When the road would call to him again, Mary could only pray as the sound of his truck faded toward the highway.

They'd been high school sweethearts at Glades Central and stayed together as Mary tucked into her studies at Florida Memorial University, graduating magna cum laude, later earning a master's in early childhood education. She'd always wanted a big family; her own parents had stopped at four, and Mary thought that a shame. And having children became her odd way of coping once her husband's behavior became more erratic.

After she'd had Jamal, her sixth child, she'd suffered a mild heart attack. Doctors diagnosed her with cardiomyopathy, her heart so weak the specialist came into the room asking, "Where's this old woman?" and found meek little Mary, all of thirty-three. The cardiologist suggested a heart transplant, given her age, but Mary refused, and together with her sister Gail told the doctors, "We believe in prayer, not transplants."

No more children, then, he said. The next one will kill you.

Three years later Mary was pregnant again and ashamed to tell the doctors. Gail pushed her to the cardiologist, who said a Cesarean might be the only way she'd live through the birth. Who knew what her heart could take? But the delivery went fine, thanks to answered prayers, and Mary went home with Jamarious Rowley, blessed with those same round eyes and fat cheeks as his daddy.

A month later, while standing at the chalkboard in front of her class, Mary hit the ground with a massive heart attack, her eyes dialed white.

She died twice in the course of an hour. Doctors shocked her back to life and told her children she wouldn't make it through the night. She lay in a coma for three days, a small woman sprouting tubes and wires to a machine that moved her lungs, monitored her fragile heart. James made fleeting appearances, staring through the window at the still, unresponsive form, not knowing what to say.

Gail would not leave. Every fifteen minutes when nurses opened Mary's door, she would swoop in and stand over her sister, shouting, *"Fight, Mary! Wherever you are, YOU FIGHT!"* She would sing, "God has smiled on me, he's set me free," and remind doctors as they made their rounds, "My sister is gonna walk out of here."

When Mary finally awoke, the children whom she adored surrounded her bedside, tear-streaked and jubilant. Her oldest daughter, Canisa, then fifteen, had been charged with caring for Mario, keeping him in her bed at night to feed and rock him back to sleep. Canisa stepped forward with the bundled newborn and handed it to her mother.

"Ooh, that's a pretty little baby," Mary said. "Whose baby?"

Gail said, "That's your baby!"

"Who, Jamal? 'Mal bigger than that."

"Jamarious. *Your* baby."

Mary walked out of the hospital, just as Gail had promised. Doctors later opened Mary's chest and installed a defibrillator in the event her heart ever stopped again. One afternoon, Mary told Canisa she was feeling dizzy. She flopped down on the sofa, then jumped as if a bear trap had sprung inside her. It was the defibrillator, kicking her heart back into gear.

Her disability checks couldn't cover expenses, so Mary briefly returned to teaching. But the chaos of a classroom proved too stressful for her heart, as did caring for her own beloved children at home. The responsibility now fell on Canisa, who took young Mario as her own. Living for a time with Gail on doctor's orders, Mary would tell her sister, "My baby's never gonna know what happened to his mama."

Gail was a dreamer. She'd had an awful one the night James arrived to take Mary home: someone had kidnapped one of her granddaughters, just babies at the time, and left her clothes strung along the back porch. The dream haunted her all the next day, until she realized it hadn't been her granddaughter at all, but Mary. The clothes in the dream were the ones Mary had forgotten in Gail's closet.

Two days later the phone started ringing: relatives saying something had happened when Mary was at the doctor. Her defibrillator's not working. *Gail, pray!* Then, five minutes later:

"Gail, you got somebody in the house with you?"

Oh Lord, why?

"Mary just died."

She'd been to the hospital for bloodwork, Canisa wheeling her through the halls, when her mother craned her head and said, "I'm tired, I wanna go up there," and pointed up, the strangest glow across her face. *Where*, Canisa thought, *upstairs?* Canisa took her mother to the ER, just to be safe, and the minute after leaving her with doctors she heard them shouting, *"Code Red!"*

Mario, just seven years old, was outside playing football when he heard the horrific wail of his sister Jamekia. Told his mother had just died, he ran screaming down the street. A neighbor woman found him at the filling station, lying on his back in the parking lot, a scene of bloodcurdling sadness. *"My mama! My mama!"* he cried.

James had just arrived in Georgia and rushed home. In the weeks after the funeral, he fell into a black fog, utterly consumed with shame. Wouldn't eat or rise from the sofa. Told his daughters he'd never been the husband his wife deserved, never taken the brief seconds to tell her he was sorry. Now she was dead. Five months later he collapsed one morning while shaving and never woke up. They called Canisa to release the body. Gail held Mario as he trembled and cried, as all sense of the world left him and spun out of reach.

It was Canisa who raised her brothers and sisters, forgoing her own youth to shuttle back and forth from football to band practice, to help with homework and fill out college applications. It was Canisa who froze in her tracks when Mario told her flatly one day, all of ten years old, "I don't wanna live no more."

Sometimes after dinner, she would still open Mario's door to find him fetal on the bed, that emptiness inside him having spiked like a fever. She would take her brother in her arms and hold him, assure him that it was not his fault, that God took those we loved for reasons unknown. Yet in the middle of the night, she would often wake to find her mother standing by her bed, an apparition lamenting softly, "I was supposed to be here, I was supposed to be here."

· · ·

FOR MARIO, THERE were a pair of absolute truths that had remained constant throughout his life: that his parents were never coming
back, and that one day, whatever it took, he would win a championship
with the Glades Central Raiders. These two lines of truth did not run their
separate courses, but fused to form an ironbound obligation.

His father had played baseball at Lake Shore, but threw himself into
Raider mania once the team won back-to-back titles in the early seventies.
As long as any of his boys could remember, he'd waxed enthusiastic about
one of them belonging one day to that superior order of men—a champion who could always trade upon that status in the muck and float upon
its everlasting memory.

With three other boys playing football, his odds were at least favor-
able: His oldest, Tori, was a blue-chip strong safety in 1990, but none of his
Raider teams ever made it past the semifinals. It was the same story with
Frank, the next oldest, who graduated in 1992. Five years after James died,
his son Jamal's team also made it to the semifinals, only to lose to Sarasota
Booker High by three points. After Jamal, there was only Mario.

"He was the last in line," said Jamal. "So he felt like it was up to him."

Ever since his parents died, Mario had wanted to be a quarterback. It
was the position he began choosing in the pickup games outside his family's three-bedroom home on Northwest Avenue G. His constant teammate
was Canisa's son William Likely, who was two years younger and would
later play safety and running back with Mario on the Raiders. On afternoons and weekends, the two would trade off threading passes through
oncoming cars and the farm trucks parked along the street.

And whereas many boys christened themselves a Jerry Rice or Randall
Cunningham, Mario always played himself. "He never pretended to be nobody," said Jamal. "He always said, 'I'm my own man.'"

In Belle Glade's youth league, he quarterbacked for the Eagles, who
practiced in Pioneer Park. In those immediate years after losing his mother
and father, playing quarterback gave him purchase in the bottomless
world. To him, there was no feeling like having the game in his hands,

like charging downfield with a squad of friends and managing a victory. Winning made people happy, and helping others to win made him generally less inclined to want to die.

"There is a void there," Gail would say. "He needs to fill a void."

Unfortunately for Mario, his body had not grown much by the time he arrived at Glades Central. The JV coaches saw his wrestler's physique and immediately slotted him at defense. But the desire to play quarterback still burned inside him, and by then he'd found someone who possessed that same kind of fire.

At the University of Florida, quarterback Tim Tebow had just won the Heisman Trophy. The coverage surrounding his stellar season profiled the quarterback's life as the son of Baptist missionaries and his breakout career at Allen D. Nease High School in Ponte Vedra Beach, where his state records for total career offense (13,042 yards), career passing (9,922 yards), and touchdowns scored (161) still remained.

But the story that pulled Mario off his seat involved the night Tim Tebow broke his leg. The Panthers were down 17–0 in the first half when the quarterback took a brutal sack that snapped his fibula. His coach thought it was a charley horse, telling him, "Toughen up. This is the stuff legends are made of." Not only did Tebow finish the game on one leg, but he ran for a twenty-nine-yard touchdown through traffic.

"Tebow's a dog," said Mario. "That guy never quits. He's got the fight in him. That's what I aspire to be."

But there was a story about Tebow and his mother that provided an even deeper kinship. Pam Tebow had discovered she was pregnant with Tim while she and her husband were serving as missionaries in the Philippines. The exact details of the story have changed over the years. In one version, the discovery of her pregnany came while recovering from amoebic dysentery. The heavy drugs used to treat the illness had damaged the baby, the doctors said. The fetus had separated from the uterine wall, and the baby would most likely be stillborn. The doctors advised her to terminate the pregnancy for her own safety.

"They thought I should have an abortion to save my life from the beginning all the way through the seventh month," she told the *Gainesville Sun* in 2007.

She refused, relying on prayer and faith instead. She carried the baby to term and gave birth to a "skinny, but rather long" son, who, of course, grew up to become one of the greatest college quarterbacks in history.

In a 2010 interview with the organization Focus on the Family, Pam Tebow said doctors advised an abortion after discovering not a baby, but "a mass of fetal tissue." Whichever story is true, the message remained the same: like Mario, Tim Tebow wasn't supposed to be born. Which could only mean that he had purpose; he was here for a reason.

The confluence of everything that had happened in Mario's life seemed to occur on that sorrowful night the Raiders lost to Cocoa. He'd played his guts out. Half a dozen tackles, two for a loss. Not only had he not delivered his father a ring, but he'd watched his quarterback lose his confidence after throwing a costly interception in the third quarter—a casualty at the bow that sank the entire ship.

While the rest of the team tossed their helmets and retreated to the locker room, Mario stayed on the field watching Cocoa receive their gold medals. And when that was finished, he just sat there and stared at the scoreboard. That's when Hester tapped him on the shoulder.

"Come on, let's go."

"It hurts," Mario said, crying. "It hurts bad."

"Believe me, homeboy, I know. I've been there."

"We'll be back next year," he told him. "We're comin back. And I'll bring us here."

It was that moment, looking into his linebacker's eyes, when the coach recognized something in himself, that player with a swollen heart standing alone in the end zone. In Mario, Hester saw that kid who would run into traffic, the player who would lower his shoulder and charge headlong into a house on fire.

"Some people think it's just a game," Mario once said. "But it's more than a game for me, it's about my life."

• • •

THE SECOND ROUND of the Florida-versus-Texas showcase matched the Raiders against Denison High School, a regional 4A power north of Dallas. The team would have to fly to Texas, and for many on the Glades Central squad, it would be the first time they'd take an airplane into the greater world beyond the canefields.

The morning of the flight, the team gathered in the dark school parking lot to await the bus. Night sounds still seeped into the predawn stillness. Bullfrogs moaned in the canal, and egrets flushed from the cane in search of food. Headlights sliced through the darkness, dropping off boys and bulging equipment bags.

Daylight revealed fresh haircuts—high, clean fades still with the whiff of the barber's oil. They wore starched khakis, sneakers scrubbed white, and polished loafers. Their maroon sport jackets—bought years ago for one of those fabled gladiator squads of yesteryear and recycled—drooped over shoulders and swallowed skinny wrists.

Few boys had slept the night before, their minds reeling over air travel. A group discussed:

"I hear you not supposed to fall asleep on the airplane. If you do, you crash."

"Man, that superlicious."

"*Superstitious*, fool!"

They squeezed aboard a yellow cheese wagon at 5:00 a.m., sitting atop suitcases, with arms and legs folded in the seats. The bus cut a straight line down the cane and sawgrass prairies toward Fort Lauderdale's Hollywood International Airport. Three hours later an American Airlines jet lifted off the runway as if bound for deep space. A chorus of moans and whimpers rose from the cabin.

Don'Kevious Johnson, a hardened linebacker who'd grown up amid gangs and gunfire in the trailer park near Glades Central, now covered his head in a blanket. Another carefully pulled down his window shade and announced he was going to be sick. For the businessmen on board, it was a rare and welcome bit of entertainment. Each one turned to the terror-stricken young man in the oversized coat beside him and chuckled. "First time on a plane, huh?"

• • •

AFTER THE RAIDERS freshened up at their hotel, a bus dropped them for practice at DeSoto High School's Eagle Stadium, the site of the following day's game. Standing in the parking lot, the Raiders gazed upon the $12 million brick monstrosity that sparkled under the sun, and concluded that Texas was where God had intended high school football to be played.

A local coach guided the team to the indoor field where they'd practice, along the way passing a state-of-the-art training room where a staff of student trainers waited eagerly, dressed in matching polos. The stadium had been a bond issue approved by voters, the coach explained. It was like hearing another language. Outside one building sat a row of white Chevy Tahoes, emblazoned with the school crest.

Coach Q could only shake his head. "Only time yall be riding in something like that, it be taking you to jail."

After dinner that evening, the Raiders sat in the stands to watch one of the most heavily hyped matchups of the showcase. Their archenemy Cocoa High School was playing the Abilene Tigers, who were ranked number two in the nation. The brawny west Texans and their locomotive running game were the heavy favorites and took an early 10–0 lead. But just as they'd done to the Raiders nine months before, Cocoa patiently and methodically came from behind and picked them apart. Cocoa running back Chevelle Buie, who'd run for two hundred yards and two touchdowns against the Raiders to seal the victory, found the end zone three times in the second half against Abilene. Before the Texans knew what had happened, the clock was at zero and they were no longer winning. It was a thing to behold.

Before bed that night, Hester gathered his team on the dark pool deck of the Hampton Inn. With the whine of semis on the highway in the background, he lectured them on the little things.

"You notice the way those guys played tonight," he said. "Disciplined. Not one of them walked off that field. They ran and they ran together. Aint a selfish cat on that team. Aint nobody freelancing on that team. That's how yall need to play tomorrow, like a family."

He reminded them of their assignments, to drink plenty of fluids for the blistering Texas heat, and to eat pickles for the salt, which the team had brought by the case. ("A lot of yall believe in that pickle stuff, so go get that pickle," he said.) He spoke of their duty to represent their home; so far in the showcase, he said, Florida teams had beaten Texas in every matchup except one. But most of all, Hester told them, go to bed tonight visualizing perfection.

"Nights before games," he said, "I would lie in bed and visualize every single play to the point where I couldn't make a mistake. *Why?* 'Cause I'd already seen it. I'm putting this in yalls head now.

"Lay down tonight, wake up in the mornin. You already seen it. See myself catchin that slant, pirouetting, putting my hand in the ground and going seventy-seven yards for the touchdown. *I already seen it.* Kick return. Eighty-eight yards back. *I already seen it.* Two or three interceptions. Fifteen sacks. Why? *'Cause you already seen it.* Because if you saw it, guys, what must that mean? *What does that mean?* If you saw it, *it must have happened.*"

That night on the embattled gridiron of his mind, the unlikely quarterback envisioned four touchdowns, then delivered exactly that many the following day against the Denison Yellowjackets. Despite ten starters having to sit out the first quarter for skipping practice that week, the Raiders' athleticism dominated the bigger, slower Texans from the first possession.

Halfway through the first quarter, Mario's nephew William Likely stunned the crowd by juking past what looked like every Denison defender on a seventy-five-yard punt return for the score. The quarterback took over from there. After his much-criticized debut against Skyline, this week found Mario more at ease. By the middle of the second quarter, he'd thrown two touchdown passes to Jaime and another to KB—a flying horizontal grab over two defenders into the end zone. He would also find Davonte three different times for fifty-six yards.

By halftime, the score was 39–2. The Raiders were well on their way toward a Lone Star sweep. But as players sat in the locker room cooling off and eating pickles, Hester fumed over a litany of stupid mistakes.

In terms of discipline, the Raiders seemed to have learned nothing from Cocoa the night before. Once again, the offensive line crumbled to the touch, allowing Mario to be sacked six different times. After the previous game against Skyline, coaches had become so frustrated by the OL's incompetence that they'd singled out one lineman in practice to set an example.

Brandon Rodriguez was a sweet, plump-faced kid, tall and lumbering. At six foot two and 255 pounds, he was one of the big guys who'd so unnerved Hester that summer by skipping workouts. As the OL practiced its man-on-man blocking that week, Brandon would repeatedly get toppled and let go his defender. Nothing his coaches told him seemed to stick. Having seen enough, Hester finally blew the whistle and pulled Brandon aside.

"We goin one-on-one," he said, then ordered the defensive line to circle around him. One after another, they raced into Brandon's chest and knocked him to the dirt.

"Move your feet, Brandon!" coaches yelled.

"Get mad, man!" his teammates screamed.

Delbert Clarke hit Brandon so hard that somehow his own contact lens ended up in his mouth.

"We gonna have to take Brandon to Walmart," Coach Q said. "That boy needs some gunpowder for his oatmeal."

That day against Denison, it wasn't just the offensive line that stymied the Raiders. Special teams were also a mess, and their costly miscues would haunt the team for the remainder of the season. In the first quarter they allowed a blocked field goal. Minutes later, backup quarterback Greg Davis bungled the snap on an extra point. Instead of yelling "Fire!" and tossing it to the tight end who was headed for the post, the way he'd been taught, Davis tried to run. The Denison defenders read it perfectly and planted him on his back, then plucked the football off his chest and ran it ninety-nine yards for the safety. Special teams later botched *four* separate two-point-conversion attempts. Nothing they did seemed to work.

Kicking and special teams had long been the Raiders' handicap. Whereas receivers and sprightly skill players sprang from the muck in bunches, good kickers were about as frequent as snow days.

"Only once in a blue moon do the Raiders ever have a good kicker," Hester said. "I've never understood why. It's just not something we're good at."

One would assume that a school so rich in raw athletic talent—and with an abundance of Hispanic, Haitian, and Jamaican students—would have a decent soccer program to feed the football gods each fall. But the Raider soccer team was worse than lousy, even more terrible than the baseball team, and had actually gone winless the previous season. Its sorry showing was enough to propel Marvin McKenzie, a pensive Jamaican immigrant, to abandon his lifelong dream of soccer stardom and play a game he'd always considered brutish and silly.

Marvin had grown up in the town of Anchovy, just south of Montego Bay on the northwestern coast. His family was poor, like most everyone else around them. When not in school, Marvin and his friends would spend their days on the beach roasting breadfruit over a fire, playing soccer with borrowed shoes, and always dreaming of America.

"The news of my life came today," Marvin wrote in his journal in August 2008. "I could not believe I got my visa. It was my dream and God came though for me. I still can't believe it's real. I will never forget where I'm coming from."

His father, a construction worker, had finally sorted out paperwork and sent for Marvin and his sister. Growing up, their image of America had been shaped by the two channels that came through on their television. It was of slick cars and beachfront estates, an image soon shattered when they arrived at their tiny apartment on Southwest Eighth Street, where black mold spotted the walls and nightfall was to be feared.

After the discouraging soccer season, Marvin tried his luck at football. He'd avoided football players since arriving at Glades Central, finding them to be pompous and disruptive in class, showboats. But as always, the Raiders were desperate for a kicker, and Sam King, the special-teams coach, saw promise in Marvin's leg. It had taken most of the preseason to get his approach right, and he still had a bad habit of lifting his head and throwing off his stance. But here in Texas against the Yellowjackets, that was hardly the problem. Both times Marvin was called out to kick, the whole line fell to pieces before he even had the chance to miss.

Luckily for the Raiders, the Yellowjackets could never fully capitalize on the special teams' mistakes, thanks to another powerful showing by the defense. Linebackers Boobie, Jaja, and Don'Kevious Johnson worked with sudden quickness, wrapping up the Denison running backs the second they reached the open air. They held Denison to 152 total yards and forced three late fumbles, with Boobie running one back for a fifty-six-yard score. Jaja would notch eighteen tackles on the afternoon, plus two sacks on quarterback Jordan Watson.

By the fourth quarter, the Raiders led by a score of 56–17. The game was so lopsided that for kicks, Hester allowed Benjamin to join the defense, the six-foot-six receiver prowling the Raider secondary like a lion lunging for buffalo. It was a slaughter.

The next morning as the team waited for the plane home, Benjamin—clearly proud of his performance—spotted a group of girls in the terminal and announced, "I saved three touchdowns. I'm a athlete, baby!"

CHAPTER

Kelvin's mother, Christine, had a proclivity for athletes. The one true love of her life was James Otis Benjamin, considered to be one of the greatest running backs ever to pump feet over the muck. He'd been a blockbusting god at Lake Shore High on the eve of integration, going 2,300 yards for twenty-two touchdowns his last two seasons, then to Florida A&M. But during his first year of college, Chris announced she was pregnant. After Kelvin's sister Tangela was born, Otis hung up his cleats and started driving trucks for U.S. Sugar, yet for years the memory of his electrifying power still drew college recruiters hoping to pull him out of retirement.

Otis had a second career as hero in the eyes of his daughter. Tangela's memory is occupied with fog-filled mornings when her dad would rustle her awake for predawn workouts on the dikes. Even then, Otis maintained an athlete's frame. They'd ride bikes to Okeechobee's great wall, where Otis would pound up and down the hill in shorts and striped tube socks before regimens of jump rope and sit-ups on a flat board, his pint-sized trainer giggling as she counted off, ONE-TWO-THREE.

Even after Otis slipped into drugs years later, some say because of overwhelming sorrow for what could have been, he remained present. Living on the streets, his life in shambles, he'd still slip past the house at night to give his daughter a kiss through the window screen.

At thirty-six years old, he suffered a stroke in North Carolina, where he'd gone to piece his life back together. Hearing the news, Chris drove up and found him in a coma, his brain already gone, then held his hand while doctors switched off the machine. "He was the greatest man I ever had," she would always say of him. "He loved me."

After Otis's death, Chris began dating a professional golfer who'd drive over from the coast every few months, a man who showered her with money for bills and gifts for her children. When she became pregnant again, she was certain it was the golfer's child, until nurses in the hospital handed her the baby boy with skin the color of cinnamon.

To Chris, that meant one thing: that the real father was Tony Barnett, the lanky Jamaican who owned the restaurant on Fifth Street. "Tony Dread" was a man she'd sneaked around with against her best intentions, a man she claimed to hate but couldn't resist. Tony had seen her growing belly in the subsequent months and had the audacity to claim it for his own, even predicting a boy "pretty like you, but tall and red like me." When Tony visited Chris in the hospital and saw that Kelvin was a mirror image of himself, he could only beam with pride. "I told you he was mine," he said.

As much as she hated being associated with Tony, with his Rasta locks that hung down to his backside, he was a good father to Kelvin. He'd pick him up on weekends and parade him on his shoulders through downtown, bragging to the shopkeepers about his son. He paid bills, covered day care, and even took Tan and the others for days at a time—his "little piglets," he called them.

But when Kelvin was three, Tony was arrested on marijuana charges and eventually deported back to the island, forever barred from entering the States. In the months that followed, Kelvin would cry for his father, asking Chris, "When's Daddy coming back?"

I'll let you know, Chris would say.

Tony would call every so often, but the promises of his returning slowly began to deteriorate over the watery gulf that separated them.

Chris raised her three children on her own while working a variety of jobs, which included at a day-care center and fast-food restaurants. Every so often she'd get help from a local electrician whom she'd also started dating.

Growing up, Kelvin was a big kid. His mother described him as physically awkward, a boy who was more comfortable playing video games than running for touchdowns. Nonetheless, during summers he'd still join his friends spray painting the yearly gridiron onto the asphalt for daily pickup games. He even followed them into little league, considered to be the entry level for every future Raider, but soon quit when coaches made him run in the heat. With football, his heart just wasn't in it.

"Other kids always talked about their favorite players, but I never had any," he said. "I didn't even like football. My mind was always elsewhere."

By junior high, Kelvin was already pushing six feet tall. And while football coaches were unable to utilize KB's size and strength, others enjoyed its advantages. Older boys befriended him and roped him into their schemes. When Kelvin was fourteen, he was arrested for theft after he and others went on a spree of terrorizing younger kids and stealing their iPods. His mother begged for leniency from the judge, who sentenced Kelvin to a year and a half at the Okeechobee Juvenile Offender Corrections Center, located sixty miles from Belle Glade in the swamps on the lake's north end.

The company Vision Quest ran the program, which Kelvin described as "summer camp, except you can't go home." Inmates took long, meandering walks through woods and learned to handle the extreme heats of an Indian sweat lodge.

"We did rituals and chants in those sweatboxes," he said. "A man then dumped water on the rocks. But I'd be cheatin. I'd be over there breathin by the hole in the tent."

During recreation time, many of the boys at Okeechobee would organize pickup games of football. Benjamin had nothing else to do, so he often ended up playing. Even with half his heart in the game, his unmatched size usually guaranteed his team would win. Slowly, the realization began to sink in. "This is something I can be good at," he thought. On Friday nights, a crowd of boys would gather around the radio and listen to Raider games broadcast live on the AM gospel station WSWN (whose motto was "Only sunshine reaches more homes than Sugar 900"). It was Glades Central's 2006 championship season, when receivers Deonte Thompson and Travis Benjamin were slicing up secondaries to the rumble of the hometown faithful.

"*Damn, bro,*" the kids would shout to Kelvin. "You from Belle Glade, right? That could be *you.*"

Kelvin agreed. "It was then I decided to get serious and play football," he said. "I wanted to be part of that."

Kelvin needed more male influence in his life, so it was decided that he'd live with Frank and Tan when he was released. Boobie was also living there, having moved from Georgia.

Frank Williams became the father Kelvin never had. He was a big-shouldered bear of a man who drove trucks for his dad's sod business. When he was growing up, everyone had called him Boobie, just like his son. And like Otis Benjamin, Frank had been a standout running back with a scholarship to Florida A&M. That is, until doctors discovered an abnormal heartbeat. Loyola Marymount basketball star Hank Gathers had just died of complications from the same problem. After one look at Frank's medical records, FAMU revoked its offer and no other college would look at him. Forced to retire in his early twenties, Frank came home and took a job with U.S. Sugar.

But home life had not delivered the kind of excitement he craved, or the money. In 1994, one of Frank's neighbors was dealing cocaine. Some guys from the coast approached Frank looking to buy a pound, so Frank agreed to broker the deal. In less than an hour of easy work, he pocketed $9,000.

"The most I'd ever had in the bank was five hundred," he said. "And I gave most of it to my mama to help with expenses. So the sight of that much money was exhilarating."

A month later the same deal came around. Before long, Frank was running lots of deals—so many that he didn't realize some of his contacts had been busted in a federal sting. When he was on his way to work one morning, a whole posse of sheriff's deputies surrounded his car. They carried a sealed indictment. Frank's dad put up the family house for bond. In the end, Frank ended up pleading. Just twenty-two years old, he was sentenced to serve forty-eight months in federal prison.

But that was years ago. Frank was grown up now. And he certainly didn't look like any hardened criminal. These days he worked a forty-hour week on the muck, and at night, he was a husband and father to a houseful of football players. One of them, of course, was Boobie, whose brickhouse physique and quick feet made people remember the old Boobie of 1987. Another was David Bailey, Tan's son from a previous relationship, who was a Raider defensive back. With two small boys of their own also playing football, Frank and Tan ran the house like a minicamp, which was the perfect setting for Kelvin once he cycled back into the world and took hold of the game.

Their little house on Northeast First Street was part sports bar and locker room, with football blaring year-round on the flat-screen television, thanks to the NFL Network. Each night, a stampede of boys smelling like sweat and wet grass invaded the tiny kitchen to empty the pots that Tan left on the stove.

"KB has always looked at us as his parent figures," Frank said. "He knows his sister's gonna make him do what he's gotta do. He craves that structure."

• • •

OF THE FIFTY-FOUR players on the Raiders' roster, Hester estimated that only about six had fathers living at home. Most players had little contact with their biological fathers and received little to no financial help. Many had never laid eyes on the men at all. The only exception seemed to be the Haitian players, whose parents remained together yet would still separate for extended periods of time to return home or follow harvests.

The absence of fathers was a subject little talked about on the team, but one that defined each boy and stitched his wings against the battering winds. Belle Glade was a town of children rootless from their lineage and scattered wild.

In the case of Davonte Allen, it was his grandfather Julius who stepped in to assume the role, laying in the boy a foundation of stone. Davonte had practically grown up in Julius and Nora's home in South Bay, the little community four miles south of Belle Glade. And his childhood was lived between the six rows of pews in the tiny Church of God Tabernacle (True Holiness), where both grandparents delivered the good word three times a week.

Davonte's mother, Delia, was twenty-three when she became pregnant with him. She was fresh off a two-year degree at Lincoln College of Technology in West Palm Beach and dating a handsome Jamaican named Ruel Allen. Working two jobs, Ruel did his share to provide money for diapers and bills when the baby arrived. But he also enjoyed his nightlife and friends, and Delia knew he wasn't the marrying kind. So, when Davonte was three months old, she left Ruel.

"Sometimes we sidetrack before we realize, 'This is not how I was raised,'" she said.

Working two jobs herself while caring for an infant, Delia soon realized the way she was raised was also better for her son. Julius and Nora ran a rigid household, well oiled with daily routine. Delia's younger brother was still in high school, so the family structure was very much intact. When

Davonte turned three, he moved into a small bedroom at his grandparents' home, where his mother would visit almost daily. "I wanted him to be in a normal environment, around a family that loved one another," she said.

Outside of his congregation, Julius drove a truck for a delivery company. He was a slender man with a thin face and a cast-iron voice who saw the world in stark black and white. He was the kind of man who only bought his cars in cash, explaining why with an answer more resembling a personal creed:

"I learned how to suffer, and I wait."

He'd waited until he was twenty-six to marry Nora, even though they'd been steady sweethearts since high school. "It's just the age I'd always decided," Julius said. "Ever since I was a child."

The pastor ruled his home with a firm, quick hand. But with Davonte it was rarely needed. The boy took to discipline early. One of the only times Julius remembered having to spank him was when he was five, after being told repeatedly not to run under the racks in a department store.

"I rapped him about five times on the butt," Julius said. "After that, when we'd go to any kind of store, he would shove his hands down and say, 'Granddad, keep your hands in your pockets.' He did that for years. He knew not to touch things."

Under Julius's roof, the mornings began with prayer and scripture. Nora would lead the children in a daily devotional, and before stepping out into the void, together they would recite the Twenty-Third Psalm. After school, homework had to be finished promptly, and if there was none, children were expected to read quietly at the kitchen table until supper was ready. Television and video games were closely monitored. Once, when Julius discovered Davonte playing Grand Theft Auto—walking in as Davonte's avatar robbed an old lady and knocked her to the pavement—he ripped the disc from the machine and cracked it in half. And of course there were cars to wash and the lawn to mow.

"If you don't do the yard and you need twenty dollars, I'm sorry," he'd say. "Life is not easy. It's hard, and nothing is free."

Julius's father was a Jamaican immigrant named Uriah Gordon who'd arrived in Belle Glade in the 1940s to work for U.S. Sugar. But the conditions were so oppressive in the camps that he soon quit. With only $1.65 in his pocket, he caught a bus to Hartford, Connecticut, and found work as a union painter. Uriah still lived in Hartford, and during summers, Julius and Nora would take Davonte to visit, even driving one year into New York City. There was the annual summer camp in Charlotte and another in Tennessee. One year his aunt took him to the Bahamas. And when Davonte returned home, it was to Glades Day School, where summer travel was nothing extraordinary, unlike the situation across town.

"Davonte's been to places most other kids have never been," said his mother. "And I thank God that he doesn't have an attitude that makes him think he's better. He knows that everyone is the same."

His family was also encouraged by his strong faith, which they saw as a bedrock against the prevailing winds. This close relationship with God was often evident on his Facebook page, which he used for daily affirmations in a world designed to drag him down:

"They say what goes up must come down but God please don't let me fall . . . !"

"Only one man is perfect & thats GOD and some people fail to realize that . . . real testimony by D. Allen you gotta like it! Haha!"

"Letter 2 Jesus . . . Please bless me 2 see you more clearly love u more dearly and follow u more nearly . . . amen . . . sincerely, D. Allen #6."

Ruel Allen still remained in Davonte's life. Delia would often take her son to see him at the Silver Spoon, the Jamaican restaurant he owned in Lake Park. They spoke each week by phone, and Ruel was good about putting money into Davonte's account whenever Delia asked. He also showed up for football games. That distant relationship was more than most boys on the Raiders had with their own dads, and it was something for which Davonte felt fortunate. But there was little question in his mind over who his *father* was—the man whose shadow had never left his side.

"Davonte sees me as a role model," said Julius. "I'm happy that I could be there to teach him the values of life. He listens to me because he sees that I practice what I preach. It takes a man to raise a boy into being a man."

• • •

HESTER'S OWN FATHER had disappeared before Jessie was born, and this abandonment had shaped his own values about loyalty to family and raising boys into men.

His oldest son, Jessie junior, was ten by the time Hester left the game. And although the family moved numerous times in the preceding years, with Hester frequently on the road, there were no gaps in Jessie's memory when it came to his father being around. "Growing up, he was always my best friend," Jessie said. "I wanted to be just like him. I idolized him."

Among Jessie's fondest memories were the frequent trips to Red Lobster, where his father kept a standing comedy routine. To those who knew him well, Jet was a spot-on mimic. Inside a quiet booth of the restaurant, Hester's walls would come down as he twisted his face into an assortment of characters for his son: Brer Rabbit and the Tar Baby, the Three Bears, and a crazed old neighborhood curmudgeon named Mister Ed.

"My parents thought I liked going to Red Lobster for the food," Jessie said, "but it was really to hear those stories. My dad's super quiet, but if you get to see the side that I saw, he's very funny."

Jessie had recently graduated from the University of South Florida, where he'd played his father's position and become a star on his own merit. But his chances at playing professionally had been dashed after a foot injury his senior season. He was now living in Tampa and considering a career in coaching.

Hester's two youngest boys remained at home. Jarron was a freshman at Glades Central and Jymetre was eight. There was rarely a moment when Hester did not have at least one of them by his side.

After school, Jarron would usually sit in the truck and wait for practice to end, fighting boredom with homework or video games. ("I'm just not into football," he once said. "Nobody seems to understand that.") Jymetre, however, was a born player and student of the game. He could recite the Raider route tree like it was Mother Goose, much to the pleasure of Jet's assistants. Later in the season, even when the Raiders played on the road, Jymetre would shadow his father along the sideline at most every game. With his hair done in perfect cornrows and always clutching a football like a teddy bear, he would gaze at the procession of violence, profanity, and blood with a look of wonderment. Come Saturday mornings, he would shine as quarterback, receiver, and running back on his own little league team in Wellington.

"The boy just cries whenever he loses," his father once said with a glow of pride on his face. "He takes it real, real hard."

Throughout Hester's own days as a young player, watching friends wave to their fathers sitting in the bleachers, he'd always had to settle for his grandfather, Willie, whom he loved.

Growing up, he knew his real father's name was Lorenzo. He also knew he'd been a decent player for the Lake Shore Bobcats, and that he no longer lived in Belle Glade. For most of Jessie's childhood, Lorenzo was just a myth that would take blurry form whenever strangers stopped him with the occasional *"Don't you look like yo daddy!"* or whipped him into confusion with *"Aint we cousins?"*

But after Jessie's senior season, after the All-American selection and publicized commitment to Coach Bowden and the Seminoles, Lorenzo suddenly appeared like some rare species out of the wild.

He stopped by the house one afternoon, but Jessie chose to speak with him out in the yard, rather than invite him inside. After all, the man was a stranger.

"I've been hearing about what you've become," Lorenzo said.

The first thing Jessie noticed about his father was how polite and well dressed he was, how fit and healthy. A man with a fine life somewhere else—Washington, D.C., he said. It was as if Lorenzo had been watching all that time from behind some invisible curtain, through the dark nights with Cora's fits and Anthony's seizures, the pangs of hunger and thousands of hours under the sun, just waiting for the right time to spring.

"I wanted to see him," Hester said, "to see what I came from. But there was no emotion, no thoughts in my head. At that point, there was nothing that man could do for me."

Jessie shook his father's hand and posed for a couple of pictures. He thanked Lorenzo for bringing him into the world, then asked him to forget about ever having a relationship. They would see each other only one other time, when Lorenzo appeared at RFK Stadium when the L.A. Raiders played the Redskins. When Hester's boys asked if they could ever meet their grandfather, he told them no.

"Your history starts here," he said. "This is where history begins."

To sort through his own history was a confusing and painful endeavor. Lorenzo, for what he was worth, had pulled free a telling strand and left it buzzing like a live wire. A few months before his visit, it was discovered that Jessie had a half brother named Steve Sneed, a boy his own age whom everyone called Clyde. But this was more than just a small-town coincidence. Clyde also happened to be Jessie's teammate on the Raiders—and one of his best friends since elementary school.

CHAPTER

7

The tight web of relations in Belle Glade often meant a shared ripple when tragedy struck. Several nights after the team returned home from Texas, there was a double shooting on MLK Boulevard that left a thirty-year-old barber named Adrian Brown dead. The day after the murder, it was revealed at practice that Brown was a former quarterback for the Raiders and a distant cousin to both Coach Q and a sophomore running back named Aaron Baker. The young woman who carried water for the team had sat with Brown while he died.

The shooting revealed just how closely violence touched every player. Those living downtown knew well the sound of gunfire in the night and the thumping blades of the Trauma Hawk, whipping through the dark to save someone in their golden hour. Nearly every player on the Raiders' roster had lost an immediate family member to violence, drugs, or illness. Heart disease was chronic in the Glades, as were diabetes and the organ failure that ensued.

Coach Q had recently lost a daughter to kidney disease. Baker had lost his mother to drugs. Robert Way's stepfather, Xavier Evans, had watched his mother, four uncles, and a sister slowly die of AIDS. The virus had devastated Hester's family as well. AIDS later killed his half brother, Steve Sneed, as well as his younger sister, Agnes, who passed away in 2001 after struggling for years with drug addiction. She was forty years old.

Death was ever present and real, acknowledged each morning on players' Facebook pages that read, "I thank God for lettin me see anotha day."

There were pages set up in memoriam for Willie "Gene" Thomas, the friend of Robert Way whose murder still reverberated across the school and team. So did the recent killing of a former student named Ja'Quavious Willingham, who was shot in a parking lot in West Palm Beach.

Willie Gene's death had come as the result of a long-standing beef between gangs in South Bay and the trailer park next to Glades Central. It was a feud that crackled to life every few weeks. One afternoon the entire team was evacuated from the practice field after gunshots rang out from the warren of trailer homes, which sat just across the fence. Inside, while coaches played reruns of *Hawaii Five-O*, the boys carried on as usual. "Damn," said Don'Kevious, whose neighborhood was once again under fire, "this shit always be happening, man."

The beef penetrated deep into the school, but it was one that Hester and his staff had managed to neutralize on the team. Two of the starting running backs, Baker and Tyrone Page, hailed from the trailer park and South Bay, respectively, as did several other players. Geography had never interfered on the field. But off the field, players often lived in fear.

Page's own father had been murdered when the boy was just three: Twonreon Johnson was sitting in his mobile home in Wingate, North Carolina, talking on the phone with a girlfriend when a group of men threw open the door and shot him in the chest.

Page was living in South Bay with his grandma at the time. As he got older, friends and relatives constantly commented that he was a spitting image of his dad: dark skin, the angular face, and deep-set eyes that could smolder.

But for Tyrone, his father appeared in his memory only twice. The first was when he was two or three. Twonreon handed him a couple of dollars and told him to go across the road to the little grocery. "I don't even re- member what I bought," said Page. The second memory was of seeing his father's body lying in the casket. Tyrone had tried to cry, but he couldn't. He couldn't even tell you what his dad had been doing in North Carolina in the first place. The man's whole existence, and the origins of his own, were forever wrapped in mystery.

For having been around such a short time in his son's life, Twonreon's death had cast a long shadow, one that haunted Page and clouded the image whenever he tried to picture his own future. Lately, he said, he was having problems with trailer-park kids at school. The boys were following him to class, eyeballing him in the hallways. When he'd been sitting outside the Pizza Hut recently, a few had crept past in their car and pointed at him. Page felt marked. In his heart, he feared his father's same tragic end.

He'd steered clear of this beef by attending Royal Palm Beach High School near the coast, driving thirty minutes each morning to class. But like Davonte, who also lived in South Bay, he'd transferred to Glades Central for his senior year in order to bolster his chances of recruitment.

As a running back, he'd already had eleven carries against Skyline for forty-two yards. Coach Randy had recognized his potential for both trou- ble and greatness, and latched on to him. He began calling both Page and Baker on the weekends, getting them out of Belle Glade for day trips to Orlando and West Palm, exposing them to people and culture, trying to let in a little light and positive reinforcement. He hoped, by season's end, to also get them a highlight reel.

"I'm looking to get as far away from this place as possible," Page said. "My dad lived until he was twenty-one years old. If I stick around here, I probably won't even make it that long."

• • •

BUT, SADLY, SOMETIMES it didn't matter how straight a path a player chose to walk, how careful a boy was of his ownself. The death of Pahokee's Norman "Pooh" Griffith was a shocking reminder of such vulnerability. At Glades Central, it had come in August 2000 with the murder of senior linebacker Jyron Seider.

Jyron was the son of Jay and Cathy Seider; Jay was the longtime girls' track coach and athletic director at the time, and Cathy was one of Glades Central's most beloved secretaries. Nicknamed "Big Country" because of his six-foot, 220-pound frame, Jyron was known as a go-getter. In addition to school and football, he worked as a short-order cook at Black Gold, pumped gas at Doc's filling station, and even had a car-wash business on the side.

He'd been waiting for his girlfriend to get her hair done one evening on MLK Boulevard, and joined a dice game to pass the time. As he played, a man approached the group and, for reasons unknown, shot Jyron in the forehead. Two different suspects were arrested, but charges against both were eventually dropped.

The murder took place during the first week of football practice, two weeks before the opener. After Jyron's funeral, the Raiders dedicated the season to his memory, scrawled his number, 54, on helmets and wristbands, and vowed to bring home a third straight championship in his honor. Throughout the season, they huddled around his jersey each game at halftime. Teammate Santonio Holmes also wore one of Jyron's T-shirts underneath his uniform and remembered how his friend always had a way of showing up.

"His spirit followed us each week," he said.

After winning their first four games that season, the Raiders ran into trouble one Friday night against the Cardinal Newman Crusaders. They were losing 27–18 in the third quarter, a twenty-five-game winning streak about to be snapped unless something happened, unless someone on the team stepped up.

Then, suddenly, a bank of lights went out above the Raider bench, delaying the game and crushing the Crusaders' momentum. "That's Jyron! He's trying to shake us up," the Raiders screamed, then proceeded to score twenty-three points in the final twelve minutes to pull off the upset.

In the regional playoff game against Rockledge, whose field-goal attempt with nine seconds remaining would have tied the score, they believed it was Jyron who summoned that gust of wind and blew it wide. And once they made it to the state championship game, it was Big Country whom the Raiders rallied behind as they were losing to the Titusville Astronauts. Jyron remained in their sights as they drove eighty yards in the final quarter to clinch the lead and secure the title. With the championship season delivered to their fallen friend, the team gathered round his jersey one last time, touched it, held it to their faces, and finally said good-bye.

"It's something that will never leave my memory," said Holmes. "I will hold on to that experience forever."

• • •

IN MID-SEPTEMBER, the Raiders hosted their first home game in Belle Glade, happy to have the trusted muck finally beneath their feet. As they dressed before warm-ups, the memorials and rituals for the dead and condemned were on full display. Tributes were scrawled on eye-black patches for those no longer with us: RIP GENE, for Willie "Gene" Thomas; RIP QUAY, for Ja'Quavious Willingham; RIP POOH, for Norman Griffith; RIP JUICY, for former Raider Stanfield Watson, killed in a car accident on Southern Boulevard. FREE SWIM: a tribute that was followed by a wide receiver's downward gaze and the response, "Swim my homeboy locked up. He out in November." Mario wore FREE CHRIS for his sister Canisa's longtime boyfriend, who'd recently been jailed for an alleged shooting.

Cubby said a prayer for his older sister crushed in the Haitian earthquake, her body now buried in the troubled ground of Leogane. Cornerback Crevon LeBlanc honored his father, who was struck by a heart attack on I-95 while en route to their family vacation. LeBlanc had practically run into the interstate to flag down a motorist for help, but it was too late. Now before each game, he discreetly took a handful of grass from midfield, crossed his chest, and let it scatter in the breeze.

The orphans observed their own silent ceremonies. As with Mario, Baker whispered a prayer for both his mother and father, who were long dead. Greg Davis walked alone to the end zone to address his departed parents, took a quick knee, and asked them for guidance.

For Boobie, death and mourning mixed in a pageant of seventeen tattoos spread across his naked frame. His right arm read RIP DERRICK CLARK for his brother killed in a car accident. And across the left, IN MEMORY OF CASSANDRA GIBSON. The masks for comedy and tragedy peered out from both shoulders. LAUGH NOW and CRY LATER hung like headlines over his chest.

As with death and incarceration, there were rituals involved with winning. Pickles brought good luck. So did the Wrigley's Spearmint Gum that statistics coach Dennis Knabb handed out before every game, the little green sticks carrying the same weighted juju as a service rifle. Davonte stuck a rosary down his right sock. Several coaches wore the same clothing every Friday, even down to the same socks and underwear. And for away games, the bus carrying offense always pulled out of the parking lot before the bus carrying defense.

But few team rituals carried more importance than the game-day prayer by the flagpole, administered by the team's longtime spiritual adviser, Desmond Harriott. Pastor Dez was a grandfatherly Jamaican with silver in his temples and a deep, resonant voice that appealed to heaven in Queen's English. Surrounded by scruffy teenagers with their foul street patois and sagging jeans, he always appeared like the archetypical Irish priest in the boys' home, something out of an old Cagney film. Two of his sons had also been Raiders; one had been drafted by the Chicago Bears and later played in the Canadian pro league.

"Give us strength, O Lord," Dez began, his voice cutting through the hot September wind. He asked God to place his angels around each boy to protect him from injury and harm, to make sure the quarterback's aim was true and his receivers' hands did not fail in their work. He gave thanks for the talent placed in every boy.

"And one last thing, Father God," he concluded. "We ask you for the victory."

• • •

FOR ALL THEIR attention to ritual and prayer, the Raiders' performance that evening began disastrously. All week at practice, coaches had warned that American Heritage, a private school in Delray Beach, was not to be taken lightly. Last season they'd tacked up 129 yards against the Raiders by air and another hundred on the ground and had led 14–0 before the half. Glades Central had barely escaped with the win.

Just as Hester predicted, the Stallions came out strong and bent on revenge. They rushed Mario from the first snap and rattled his cage, sending him into a panic. The Raiders were forced to punt, and once they had the ball again, Mario fumbled on the Raider twenty-yard line, allowing the Stallions to kick a field goal and take an early lead. The mood was frantic on the sideline as the great warship came under attack and began taking water.

Hester had seen it coming. Nothing had gone right that day. Everything just felt off, out of sorts. In the shop classroom where they'd retreated after the prayer to watch film and change, his coaches had lost control. Orders were ignored. Instead of watching film as they were instructed, players had spiraled off into their own orbits, blasting music, watching porn on their smart phones, wandering around campus looking for girlfriends. And once the team was suited, the coach had gone ballistic when several players turned up with black socks instead of the uniform white. Little things. Trivial when looked upon individually, but crucial to the discipline of a winning squad.

Immaturity was certainly nothing novel for a high school football team.

But moments such as these brought to light the generational divide. They underscored a common perception by former players that their proud tradition was in danger of extinction, slowly withering in the soft hands of today's spoiled youth.

It was a conversation you heard throughout the Glades, that the trouble with boys today—from crime downtown to the lack of discipline on the field—was because they no longer had to work, that because of better unemployment benefits and labor laws, kids today had never come to appreciate what they had from the perspective of a vegetable row. Since fewer people traveled for the harvests the way they once did, parents had lost that grip of control. And despite working two jobs and barely keeping the lights on, many parents still insisted on spoiling their children with flat-screen televisions, PlayStations, new phones, and designer sneakers. Lost in the process was a work ethic and a mental toughness that carried onto the gridiron, and with it an attention to the little things.

It was true that on the Raider squad there were only about five boys who'd joined their families on mule trains or in packinghouses during corn season. Aside from those few, no one had ever bent over a row of vegetables or lost a drop of sweat for a wage. In their defense, the players would tell you that summers were too busy with football practice and out-of-town seven-on-seven tournaments. The kids felt pressured to attend those tournaments in order to get playing time, which was the only way to get exposure and college scholarships, which is what everybody seemed to expect from them anyway.

That generational divide was a constant source of vitriol for old-timers such as Preston Vickers, a former Raider linebacker and U.S. Marine who often volunteered at practice. That week, as the team ran through two-minute drills in preparation for American Heritage, Vickers observed a group of second-string players goofing on the sideline and launched into a tirade.

"You guys don't take it seriously," he shouted at them. "Yall don't realize where you playin. This here is bigger than you all. This here is tradition. What yall need is discipline, 'stead of all this horseplayin and cussing. That's when accountability will set in—"

He was suddenly interrupted when the boys, ignoring him, broke into freestyle rapping.

"See there! Aint got *nothin* to do with football. You boys aint *focused*, man. You all spoiled. Everything been handed to you, even the tradition itself."

He told of the 1998 state championship game against the Madison County Cowboys, when the Raiders were playing like dirt. The quarterback, Jerry Campbell, had thrown two interceptions that had both led to Cowboy touchdowns. Come halftime, with the Raiders losing 14–7, Vickers happened to be in one of the bathroom stalls when some teammates shoved Campbell against a wall and threatened to beat him if he blew the game.

"Rest is history," said Vickers. "Second half that boy threw for three touchdowns and over two hundred yards. He knew those boys was for real. Those boys came to work. They knew, they *knew*, what they had to do."

He then looked out at the current crop, rapping, sitting on helmets, loafing at the water cooler while the rest of the team practiced.

"These cats, they nothing but *babies*. The wake-up call has to come from a player, not a coach. What this team is missing is a *leader*."

However, among the die-hard fans in the community, some of the same criticism was being lobbed at Hester's coaching staff. Fans already took issue with the fact that several assistant coaches had never played football for the Raiders—or played at all, for that matter. Around town, people were also starting to complain about the staff's behavior and how they represented the team. Some hated the way Jet wore his hat backward like a teenager, hated Coach Q's flashiness, how he "dressed like a pimp," and how at practice "Jet's boys" appeared just as disorganized and disengaged as the players themselves.

The criticism had stepped up the previous week after it was discovered that Coach Q had landed himself in trouble with the administration.

While in Dallas, Coach Q and another assistant had left the hotel after the team was in bed to go visit a local club. Afterward, Glades Central principal Anthony Anderson suspended them from participating in the home opener.

Although some of Hester's assistants may have lacked hands-on experience when it came to teaching Xs and Os, their presence and reach on the team were undeniable. There wasn't a kid on the Raiders who didn't love Coach Q, or hesitated for a second to take the piss out of Sherm or Coach JD. A bond existed beyond the game. Aside from Vickers's occasional rants, Jet and his coaches did not rule with fear.

• • •

BEFORE THE HOMETOWN crowd against the Stallions, the Raiders remained a rudderless ship. Tackles were missed. Receivers refused to block and improvised routes, running ten yards instead of five, hopelessly tangling the offense. Standing on the sidelines with his son Jymetre, Hester identified the problem, and it wasn't his coaching staff.

"You got all these people telling these kids what to do, how great they are, how the coaches don't know nothin," Hester said, gesturing to the crowd, which had started to groan. "Well, now they're seeing what happens."

Benjamin did manage a beautiful, one-handed catch for thirty yards to move the team into scoring position, but the momentum was quickly squashed as the Raiders lost it on downs.

The offensive line had yet to improve. Even if they'd held, it was no use. Play after play, Mario would dash out of the pocket, "running from ghosts," as Hester would say, and immediately get hammered to the ground. In the second quarter, after driving to the Stallion ten, Mario was sacked in the backfield for a loss of twenty-five yards. Third down and thirty, sacked again. Fourth down and thirty, Hester threw up his hands and went for it. Mario was sacked again.

An interception by the Raider secondary moved Glades Central once again into scoring position, but a wild snap sent Mario chasing the ball across midfield, only to be buried under a pile of enemy jerseys. The whistle blew for halftime, leaving him crumpled on the grass.

As the team trotted off the field toward the locker room, their path took them underneath the home bleachers, where a group of local men rained curses down like stones.

"Hey Jet, yall messin up our team, man!"

"Mario, you sorry piece of shit!"

"Hey Mario, you suck, bro!"

"Hey Jet, take yo' ass back to West Palm!"

Frantic and demoralized, the squad gathered beneath an oak tree outside the locker room and Hester tried to calm them. He felt out of his body. A migraine twisted his brow, forcing him to squint in the dark. Perhaps he'd been wrong about this team after all.

"There's something about this bunch that's killing me. Flat-out killing me," he said, then exhaled in resignation. "But I'll be here till you kill me."

The Raiders returned to the field with renewed vigor, which was quickly crushed when KB was hit on a reverse and flipped upside down, landing on his back and writhing in pain. The doctor would later diagnose a deep-thigh contusion. He limped toward the bench to the hushed silence of the crowd.

Mario rallied them back with a thirty-yard pass to receiver Robert Burgess in the end zone, only to have the Stallions answer with a ninety-yard return for a touchdown to make the score 10–7 in their favor. With seven minutes remaining, Mario punched through the line for another score, giving the Raiders a slim lead. On their next possession, on fourth and short, the Raiders looked likely to lose the ball when KB hobbled back under the lights.

It was a welcome show of initiative by the Raider captain. Benjamin had asked Hester to return, he'd even called the play. He caught a short slant between two defenders, then leaped toward the first-down marker with his long arms outstretched. The effort was just enough to set up another score by Page to give the Raiders a ten-point lead.

The Stallions quickly answered with a touchdown and two-point conversion to make the score 20–18, but their rally was too late. Once again, the Raiders managed to survive.

Despite the win, reaction to the team's lackluster home performance was immediate. Hester's phone rang all weekend with fans calling to complain about everything from the fat quarterback to the jelly-wristed O-line. He did not answer, nor did he bother wading through the flak on Internet message boards, as he was certain his players were doing. At Monday practice, he reminded everyone that anger and insults were part of playing in the Glades, that it was nothing new. Players who shut down from a little criticism could not become better, could not lead their team. And the Raiders' problem, he knew, was that a true leader had yet to emerge.

"Every one of yall is like that lonely ant, spinning around trying to find the others to lead him back to the mound," he said.

• • •

THE PERSON HESTER was waiting for was Mario, but the quarterback was too lost in his head. He'd gone home after the game in a funk. He could not find his rhythm. Was not playing like he knew he could. First of all, he was too manic. He was playing quarterback like a linebacker: full-on beast mode with the brakes ripped off. He was jittery, easily spooked, and just plain nervous. It was no wonder the fans were circling like buzzards over the cane rows. He had to learn to calm down, to internalize the criticism and use it as fuel. *That* was the stuff that legends were made of. But living it was another thing. Living it was hard.

Lying on his bed that night, he could still hear the town rising up against him.

"Pay them no mind," his girlfriend said, rubbing his neck.

He'd been dating Les'Unique Hessing since last summer. She was a Raider cheerleader, older than her years, with long legs and a diamond tattoo on her stomach. After games, she would sit with Mario in front of the television and rub Tiger Balm into the muscles of his arms and back, which had seized up like a dry engine.

Around his boys, Mario was quick to dismiss the seriousness of their relationship, saying, "I don't trust no females. Everybody fuckin everybody in Belle Glade." But the truth was that he'd let Hessing inside where few people had been. It was Hessing whom Mario had once called in the middle of the night, half asleep and distraught, saying his parents had just visited him in a dream. Someone had said, *Who's knocking at the door?* And when Mario opened it, there stood Mary and James as vivid as yesterday.

He'd even taken his girlfriend to visit their graves on Mary's birthday, leading her to the mausoleum at Foreverglades Cemetery, where his parents lay buried side by side in the walls. Afterward, he'd paid her no mind as he sat there talking to their photos, telling them about his day.

Mario shared everything with her, even the secret he now harbored— one that threatened to destroy his whole pursuit.

The secret was that Mario was playing with a torn ligament in his throwing shoulder, the kind of injury that ended seasons for good. The injury had happened during the summer seven-on-seven in Tallahassee while he and Benjamin were connecting for touchdowns to the great thrill of the crowd.

An out-of-town doctor had taken the X-ray, then given him pills for the pain that now raced through his arm every time he passed, every time he went down in a smothering heap. He told no one, so horrified of being benched and watching it all slip away. For he was meant to play quarterback and lead the Raiders, and there was no turning back now.

Other fears crept in with the pain. He was scared that by pursuing his conviction, he was also gambling a potential college career as middle linebacker, a position for which he'd been recruited as a junior. The weight of his decision grew heavier each afternoon he walked into the shop class to dress for practice. Colleges had once again begun their seasonal courting. In a basket by the door sat dozens of faxes from football programs far and wide, a fresh stack arriving each week before game day.

"Dear Kelvin," a letter from University of Alabama's head coach Nick Saban read. "People will be talking about someone's great performance tomorrow . . . make them talk about you!"

"Dear Jaime," the coach from Western Kentucky wrote. "The WKU football coaching staff wishes you *good luck* as you lead your team to victory . . ."

At the bottom were the inspiring words from Jim Rohn, the rags-to-riches motivational speaker cum locker-room swami: *Leadership is the challenge to be something more than average.*

The stacks of correspondence were mostly addressed to KB, Jaime, Jaja, and Boobie. But picking through the basket, there were no good words for the quarterback. He would have to make them notice, broken body and all.

CHAPTER

8

For the rest of the students at Glades Central, college could be an elusive if not fantastical quest. But it was one Jonteria Williams had been on for so long, it was hard for her to remember an afternoon or weekend with an open, unscheduled hour.

She is entering the seventh year of her journey when we see her cheering on the sidelines of the Raider home opener, a journey that began the year her mother explained that her father was in prison and not coming home. It was then that Jonteria declared, rather unceremoniously, the end of her childhood.

That same year Jonteria told Theresa, her mother, that she wanted to become a doctor, and together they'd embarked on this mission. Every step beyond that point was calculated with the one goal of getting a scholarship into medical school. The pom-poms, the college boyfriend, and her bedroom at home, solid pink and bedazzled with Hello Kitty, remained her few sanctuaries of normal teenage life. But even cheerleading looked favorable on a college application. After all, she was the captain.

Theresa watched her daughter from the third row of the bleachers, where she sat with other moms. Her presence was constant, for her daughter's life was her own. In fact, even during years when she worked two jobs, Theresa had not missed a single practice, game, banquet, or award ceremony since her journey with Jonteria had begun. If her daughter could make such a commitment, then so could she. It was the least she could do after what had happened with John, the man who'd set both their paths in motion.

It was 1990. Theresa was at the car wash, drying her burgundy Pontiac, when John Williams appeared out of nowhere like Billy D. He wore a muscle shirt and kept his hair permed in loose Jheri curls. The aqua convertible with the top down *had* to be his.

"You need some help with that?" he said. "I'll help you."

Before Theresa could refuse, he'd grabbed the chamois from her hand and was wiping down the car, smiling like he'd just found his best friend.

"I was like, *oh no*," she remembered.

Theresa had just ended a long-term relationship and was not looking to get involved. She'd dated a man named Jerome for over four years, and together they'd had a daughter, Jawantae, who was then two years old. Jerome was a good guy, she said, but he'd always floundered when she brought up marriage and making a life together, just the three of them. So finally she broke it off.

The very last thing Theresa was looking to do now was hook up with some guy she met at a car wash. *Who does that?*

"But he wouldn't give up," she said. "He pursued me."

Theresa mentioned something about working at FHP, not thinking John would figure out that it stood for Florida Highway Patrol. She was a dispatcher there, and two days later when she answered one of the lines, it was John.

"You didn't think I'd find you here, huh?" he said, laughing.

He started calling her every day. Sometimes twice.

"Finally," she said, "I broke."

She wasn't attracted to John at all, not at first. But after they'd dated awhile, she eased into him. He was steady and owned a business. He wasn't spooked by kids, and even seemed to enjoy spending time with Jawantae. Plus, he had that way of making her feel like the last woman alive.

The two were married three years later. By that time, Theresa also had Jonteria. The four of them made a nice life together. John bought them a three-bedroom house in the Lake Breeze Mobile Home Park outside Pahokee, just across the street from Theresa's mother. John and his father owned a fleet of trucks they used to haul corn, so as long as it rained and shined in Georgia, business was good. John would leave the first of every June and be home by the Fourth of July picnic at Pioneer Park. The rest of the year, they worked the corn and pepper seasons in the Glades.

Then, one day in July 1999, her husband never came home. Theresa called his phone, then started getting worried. She called his brother. *Have you heard from John?* But he had not. The next day she got a collect call from Georgia. It was him.

"I'm up here in jail," he told her.

"*Jail?* What happened?"

"Flip and some other guy robbed a jewelry store and they say I was the getaway driver."

"Were you?"

"No, no."

"Should I come up there?"

"No, I'll be home soon." But he never came back.

"He had no reason to be with those guys robbing a jewelry store," Theresa said. "He had a successful business. No reason. It totally surprised everybody."

A judge sentenced John to ten years. Meanwhile, back in Belle Glade, Theresa was alone with two kids, a car payment, and a mortgage. And every day she woke up with the weight of those obligations she brimmed with resentment.

"I never even went to see him, I was so mad," she said. "He called at first, then I realized I was getting these humongous telephone bills. I told him to stop calling and just write. He was remorseful. But it was too late. My mind was made up."

That next year, Theresa filed for divorce.

It was a case of cruel coincidence, for nearly the same thing had happened to Theresa's mother, Bernice. At age thirteen, with her parents' reluctant approval, Bernice had boarded a Blue Bird bus in Selma with a boy named Jessie and set off for an adventure into the north country. Jessie was older, a family friend, and he'd heard there was good money in the apple orchards of upstate New York, right outside of Albany. Theresa's older sister, Ethel, also went, and once the season was over, the three of them fell in with the gypsy caravans and eased their way down to Georgia for corn.

By age sixteen, Jessie had given Bernice two babies. One morning in Albany, with Bernice pregnant with their third child, Jessie left for work and never came home. No phone call. No letter. The man simply vanished. Alone with three children, Bernice came to Pahokee, where the beans and corn brought better pay. For a year they stayed with a woman named Eva Hill, known affectionately as Big Mama. Her home was a way station for the rootless, its many rooms filled with families of migrants seeking their footing.

"Big Mama's house was huge," Theresa remembered, "with lots of babies crawling around, and she'd take care of them all. By the time my mom came home from the fields, she'd have us bathed, fed, and ready for bed."

Bernice worked the cornfields on the slow-moving backs of mule trains, which were like miniature packinghouses on wheels. She then took a job cooking for the Jamaicans who cut the cane. After moving into their own place, Theresa remembered, her mother would wake at three o'clock each morning to fry chicken for their lunches, then leave for work by four. All day she'd prepare giant vats of rice and beans, stewed oxtails, or mustard greens, then roll them into the steaming cane rows on trucks to serve the men. Once the cane harvest was over, Bernice would go back to packing corn and peppers.

"Her hands were so rough and callused," Theresa remembered. "At night they'd crack."

Hard as life was for Bernice as a single mother, Theresa still carried fond memories of her childhood in Pahokee. But it certainly wasn't how she'd envisioned her own children growing up. At least Jonteria and her sister Jawantae knew their fathers, she thought. Theresa had no memories of Jessie, not even a photograph.

While John was at home, Theresa had given up her dispatch job to be with the kids. Now that he was gone, she had to scramble to keep a roof over their heads. Soon she was working two part-time jobs, one at the Boys and Girls Club from six until eight in the morning, then at a day-care from eight until four in the afternoon. She did this for six years, rushing out to get her daughters from school, then bringing them back to work. They spent so much time in the car that Theresa used the miles for reading. Anything Jonteria had in her school bag, her mother would make her read aloud.

All these years, Theresa told the girls their father was just "away." It wasn't until Jonteria was in seventh grade that she sat them down at the city park in Pahokee and told them what had really happened.

Not long after, Jonteria started talking about wanting to be a nurse. Not in the same way kids dream of becoming astronauts and race-car drivers, but really asking specific questions.

"I just saw my mom struggling and I knew that doctors and nurses made good money," Jonteria said. "It just became that thing I focused on and nothing else."

Right out of the gate, her confidence cut a path. We see her at age thirteen, short, beaming behind large, buggy glasses, the pride of a kid having won an award. The prize for the local newspaper's character contest was getting to read a PSA on the airwaves of WSWN Sugar 900.

"She is certainly outgoing enough, articulate and uses great sentence structure by which I was impressed," the station manager, Harvey Poole, told a reporter who captured the moment. "Fear factor is not a part of her makeup."

"It comes naturally," the eighth-grader replied. "I am happy I can speak and smile at the same time."

The story described Jonteria's eagerness to help tutor her fellow students and assist teachers. But it made no mention of the social downsides of ambition, the jealousy that brains and confidence can incite, or the daily serving of abuse she had received every day since getting to junior high.

Popular girls lacerated her with name-calling, pelted her with wads of paper in the hallways, and made fun of her glasses. Most painful were the girls in her same gifted-student program who teased her to fit in themselves, leaving her no shelter. The problem became so bad that Theresa had to routinely visit the school and demand better protection. Finally one day Jonteria, fed up, smashed one of the girls in the face with a water bottle.

High school offered asylum. In order to curb dropout rates, Florida law requires incoming freshmen to declare a major area of study and slots them into appropriate career academies. Glades Central, historically one of the worst-performing schools in Palm Beach County, had recently opened academies in engineering and criminal justice, but its toughest was medical science, which required a solid understanding of algebra and a 3.0 GPA all four years. Jonteria threw herself into it.

The academy gave students Licensed Practical Nurse Certification by the time of graduation. Part of the requirement was an internship at the local hospital, Lakeside Medical Center, where it didn't take long for Jonteria to trade up on her dream. She would be a doctor—not one chained to her pager twenty-four/seven, but an anesthesiologist. "You still make good money," she reasoned, "but you also get to go home."

Her goal before leaving high school was to be valedictorian, a title that would sparkle on any college application and guarantee free money. To bolster her chances at the top scholastic honor, she dual-enrolled at the nearby community college, taking courses like statistics and anatomy in the evenings after school. "I felt it was something I had to do," she said. "Or else someone else was gonna jump over me."

• • •

AND TO PROVE she wasn't just brains, Jonteria set out to become popular. She began running to get into shape, circling her neighborhood in the morning near the sugar-mill smokestack that defined the city's skyline. That summer before her sophomore year, Jonteria tried out for the Dazzling Diamond Dancers, the saucy drill team that performed alongside the Marching Maroon Machine Band. She made the cuts. She got contact lenses. Before long, she was grinding her hips in a pair of skimpy shorts across the halftime field.

But the Dazzling Diamond Dancers weren't enough. Jonteria wanted more—she wanted to be a cheerleader. The next summer, after spending all day on her feet at the grocery store, she stayed up four hours each night practicing toe touches and herkies and learning how to throw her tiny voice when reciting from a list of chants.

"Let's get phy-si-cal, get down, get dirty, get mean. WHAT?! Let's get phy-si-cal, gon' stomp right over your team."

She was one of seventeen Raider cheerleaders her junior year, holding her own among girls who'd never lifted a finger to be popular and beautiful. And it was *fun*, like living two separate lives.

But Jonteria was competitive by nature, maybe when the other girls were not. She was just wired to go above the minimum. Perhaps it was because she'd choreographed some cheers that won the Raiders a cheerleading award, or because she never talked back and took instruction. Whatever the reason, just before the start of senior year, head coach Connie Vereen made Jonteria the captain. And with that honor came a fresh set of enemies.

"Even though I had the better skills, I didn't think she would pick me,"

Jonteria said. "These girls had been there since they were freshmen and I made captain my second year. Some of them were jealous, and not very friendly about it."

As captain, her directions were ignored. Girls sniped and yelled at her, turned their noses, and refused to get in set. Jonteria didn't want a fight. She bit her lip and carried on.

Suddenly, being at the top wasn't so much fun.

· · ·

EVEN BEFORE JONTERIA became a dancer, she started dating a football player. Theresa hadn't let her date until she was fifteen, at which point Jonteria brought home Vincent Harper. He was a junior and two years older, played offensive line for the Raiders, and was built for the position, at six foot one and 250 pounds; Jonteria barely came up to his chest.

They met in algebra class. For a big guy, Vincent had a booming voice and he liked to joke. "Who is this guy who's so loud?" Jonteria blurted out in annoyance one day. She was just a freshman, but did not tolerate fools. Vincent just looked at her and got louder. One day on the band field, he asked her out.

When Jonteria brought Vincent to meet Theresa, she also made him bring his mother. The four of them sat in Theresa's living room.

"I told him my expectations and requirements, and his mom did the same," Theresa said. The first rule Theresa laid down was *NO SEX*.

"I want her to live her high school years without being tied down," she told Vincent. "I want you all to go back to the old-fashioned tradition of dating. You don't have to go out just to have sex. There are other things you can do to enjoy each other."

Remarkably, it seemed to work. One day, Theresa got a call from one of the school administrators. "Ms. Williams, oh my god," she said. "I have never seen a couple behave like this. They actually *act like a couple*. They hold hands. He holds her books. He opens the car door and takes her to games."

Theresa told Jonteria, "The most important person to protect is you. No one is gonna protect you. And if sex ever crosses your mind, please tell me. Please let me know."

Later one weekend night, Vincent picked Jonteria up to see a movie in West Palm. But half an hour later, Theresa heard the car door slam and the engine race away. A minute later, Jonteria came inside, visibly upset.

"Are you okay? I thought yall were going to the movies."

"Oh, Mom, I'm fine. I just remembered what you told me. Guys are something else."

"Wanna talk?"

"No. Just know that I remembered what you told me."

Theresa let it rest. A few days later, she asked Jonteria again. *What happened?*

"Nothing, Mom. And that's what I mean. Nothing happened."

When Theresa saw Vincent again, she waited until they were alone and confronted him.

"Did you forget the rule?" she asked. "You just put my daughter out and didn't even wait for her to get inside? Were you that upset that she didn't have sex with you?"

"Ms. Williams—"

"'Cause if she had, I know you'd have walked her to the door."

Jonteria never came home upset like that again. But Theresa still worried about Vincent pressuring her. She knew how easy it was to fold when a man wouldn't give up on what he wanted. After a while you could persuade yourself to accept anything. It wasn't until Vincent graduated and moved off to college that Theresa's mind was put at ease.

She'd taken Jonteria for her first gynecological exam. When it was over, the doctor came out and said that Jonteria was still a virgin.

"I was smiling from ear to ear," Theresa said. "I'm thinking, *all right!*"

As they walked to the car, Jonteria looked at her. "Mom, why are you smiling like that?"

"I'm just happy."

"You don't have anything to worry about."

The memory still brought a smile to Theresa's face. "She is dedicated. She is determined," she said.

"Jonteria is a moral force in an immoral world."

· · ·

VINCENT WAS NOW at Hampton University on a football scholarship. The two of them texted every day and tried to speak as much as possible. She'd adapted to long-distance love easier than she'd imagined.

"My friends don't agree with our relationship," she said. "They have trust issues that keep them from having a long-distance relationship where you can be apart and still trust the person. Vincent's in college, but we have trust in one other."

At the same time, she would acknowledge with a sigh, "Whatever happens, happens. Both of us are young."

For Jonteria, there was little time to pine. Now, as a senior, her schedule was dizzying, starting each morning at six and ending near midnight. There was school, cheerleading practice, work at Winn-Dixie, her internship hours at Lakeside Medical Center, emptying catheters and giving sponge baths, in addition to finishing her final courses at college. By graduation, Jonteria would be only six credit hours from an associate's degree and two years closer to medical school.

She was also vice-president of the Twenty Pearls sorority, secretary of the National Honor Society, treasurer of the Health Occupations Students of America, a member of the Elite Club, and the salutatorian of the senior class. Jessica Benette, the only other girl in the medical sciences academy to dual-enroll in college with Jonteria, had been given the coveted valedictorian slot. Jonteria was graceful in her concession. After all, Jessica's mother had passed away.

"Jessica deserves to go to whatever college offers her a scholarship," she said. "So good luck to both of us."

The admissions applications from the universities of her choice filled a giant folder in her room: University of Florida, Florida State, University of Miami, and Florida Atlantic University. The applications to UF, FSU, and FAU had been sent weeks before to meet each school's early-decision deadline. But she was still laboring over the details of the application for Miami—her top choice ever since she'd dedicated herself those seven years ago.

"Miami has the number-one medical school in the state," she said. "The smartest kids in Florida go there and it's private, which is also a draw. I want to go somewhere private, to be accepted there. It's always been the dream."

Florida Atlantic was Jonteria's second choice, mainly because of price. It was located in nearby Boca Raton, offered a decent medical school, and cost only $18,000 per year—the price of just one semester at Miami.

Since 2004, Theresa had been working as a dispatcher at the hospital. But her salary paid only $25,000 a year. Even with Jonteria's contribution from Winn-Dixie, there was nothing left over at the end of each month. The family had no savings. Having grown up so poor, Jonteria felt that taking out student loans would be like digging herself into a deeper hole. She would try to pay for college on her own, and to do that, she would need a full scholarship. So, at the end of each night, her mind numb from exhaustion, Jonteria would sit at her computer and distill the subtle tragedies of her life in hopes of getting free money.

"My father was sentenced to ten years of incarceration in Georgia," she wrote to the Ron Brown Scholar Program, for ten grand.

"The first thing that comes to mind when a person says Belle Glade is football," she wrote to the Albert Lee Wright Jr. Memorial Migrant Scholarship, for $3,000. "Glade Central Community High School does in fact have one of the best football teams in the nation, but I'm living proof that we are much more than that."

She wrote letters and essays to Coca-Cola, KFC, Walmart, McDonalds, and Bill Gates—each one tailored to meet the award's specific requirement. The Coca-Cola Scholars Foundation Award, for instance, worth $20,000, usually went to a student who could prove significant hours devoted to community service. This made her worry. She would need more of those.

"You can't just be a good student," Jonteria said. "You have to prove you're an all-around good person."

· · ·

"COMMITTED TO WINNING in Academics and Athletics."

That was the motto that appeared everywhere at Glades Central, in the cafeteria, on the walls of the gymnasium, even as a reminder along the bottom of the Raiders' season schedule. While a commitment to winning football games thrived independently of the school administration, Glades Central's academic record had long been an embarrassment.

Perhaps Glades Central's greatest curse was its geography, and wrapped within that curse was its defining irony. Stranded in the western outback of one of the nation's wealthiest counties, engulfed in the sea of cane and vegetables that drove the region's economy, Glades Central remained the poorest high school in the state of Florida. Every student qualified for free or reduced-cost lunches. Its minority rate was 99 percent, with first- and second-generation Haitians and Hispanics making up over a third of the student population. When these students did arrive, all had varying levels of education and knowledge of English.

The school's remoteness made Glades Central a singular challenge to the district, said Dr. Camille Coleman, a former principal. The town's isolation and poverty narrowed students' frame of reference and knowledge of the larger world. Coleman remembered helping students prepare for the Florida Comprehensive Assessment Test (FCAT) one year when they became stumped by a sample passage describing a cottage.

"Even reading the sentence, they could not figure out what they meant by a *cottage*," Coleman said. "Finally I told them, 'Remember *Little House on the Prairie*?' and they were like, 'Oh yeah, I know!' When you're not as traveled and your bubble is small, your language and vocabulary is going to be limited."

Since 1998, Florida had used the FCAT to measure student learning from grades three through ten. The state required kids to pass the FCAT to advance and to graduate. And for schools, the state passed down grades according to their FCAT scores and how they improved the lowest 25 percent year to year. Schools with high grades received more state and federal funding, while low performers were subject to state intervention.

The high-stakes nature of the test was incredibly controversial, with critics complaining that it unfairly awarded schools in wealthy neighborhoods while suffocating poor schools that needed the extra funding to improve. In the dozen years of FCAT, Glades Central had never received anything above a D grade. Four of those years had brought Fs, including two in a row starting in 2007, prompting the state to issue vouchers to students who wished to transfer to private schools. Auditors appeared randomly in classrooms, checking for state-mandated curriculum. The state had also threatened Glades Central with takeover or closure.

The scarlet letter associated with the FCAT and twelve years on the state's list had also caused a revolving door of principals at Glades Central. Since 2000, four had been hired and dismissed. The chaos and inconsistency at the high school angered many parents and older residents, who fondly remembered an easier, less stressful time. For a quarter of a century, Glades Central had known only one principal, Dr. Effie C. Grear, a woman considered the grand matriarch of Belle Glade and an inspiring and iconic figure to the region's African Americans.

Grear had been raised poor in Huntington, West Virginia. Her father, a minister, had suffered an accident and died when Effie was in high school, leaving her mother to raise the children on a meager salary as a maid. In the mid-1950s, after putting herself through West Virginia State College and Ohio State University, where she earned a master's in music, Grear had taken a job teaching in a migrant camp school outside of Belle Glade. She'd served as band director at Lake Shore High, then as assistant principal through the turbulent integration of schools. In 1975 she took over Glades Central, and for the next twenty-five years she oversaw the education of Belle Glade residents, most of whom she still remembered by name.

The memory of Dr. Grear's tenure still carried a golden hue, symbolic of a simpler era, before joblessness, crime, and technology began complicating an already complicated life. To listen to anyone over forty years old, it was an era when teachers still lived in the community and kept close watch on their students, telephoning parents at the sight of children in the bars or misbehaving on the corner. It was a time when adults commanded both respect and fear, and fights on Fifth Street were settled with fists and a blade, rarely a gun.

And until the FCAT, it was also a time when poor academic performance came with little consequence to schools. For most of Grear's tenure, students at Glades Central struggled on just about every standardized test placed before them. The alphabet soup of tests given each year caused panic in the classrooms and made a public mockery of the Glades in the morning papers. Students who failed the High School Competency Test (HSCT) could retake it in order to graduate, though Glades Central still had one of the highest dropout rates in the state. Often frustrated, Grear would hold contests for A and B students, most of whom she saw off to college. But in a poor migrant community, she explained, the isolation worked like a desert island.

"Back then, they felt they couldn't see anything beyond Belle Glade," said Grear, who passed away in May 2012 at the age of eighty-four. "And for having never been out of Belle Glade, they were dispirited in trying to see anything to help them out, unless they were an athlete. If you've never been to the outside to know there's something brighter, you never have any hope of leaving."

By the time Grear retired in 2000, two years after the advent of FCAT, Glades Central had a firm reputation as a chronic academic underperformer. She'd managed to raise the school grade to a D, along with students' writing scores, but still only 44 percent of seniors were graduating. The school offered only one Advanced Placement course, and reading scores were still the worst in Palm Beach County.

The years of stigma had also weathered the staff. Teachers complained about colleagues who'd given up on teaching, instead showing movies and allowing students to run wild through the halls. There were also numerous reports of faculty having sex with students, a practice many said had persisted unchecked for years.

It was certainly one of the lowest points in the school's academic record. When it came to athletics, however, Glades Central had reached an apex. The year Grear retired, the Raiders had just won three back-to-back state football championships and were on their way to a record forty-seven straight wins. The team was ranked top ten in the nation. Football fever was at its peak, with thousands of fans packing the bleachers on Friday night and players headed to college by the dozen.

And that was exactly the problem, thought Mary Evans, who took over Glades Central in 2002 and practically flipped the world upside down. Born and raised in Belle Glade, Evans had performed a miraculous turnaround while principal of nearby Gove Elementary, the only school in the Glades ever to earn an A grade.

A month before taking over at Glades Central, she'd vowed to then governor Jeb Bush at a hearing in Tallahassee that within the year the school would be more famous for its Brain Bowl victories than for football. The governor had been so fired up by her moxie that he'd slapped his dais and volunteered to help in any way, even visit the school and paint his hair purple.

"Well, get ready," she told him.

Evans's first act of business was to "zero-base" the entire teaching staff, making every teacher reapply for his or her job, regardless of tenure. Days after the interviews concluded, a quarter of the faculty received letters that said, "I'm sorry to inform you, but . . ."

Included was Willie Bueno, the head football coach who'd taught physical education for nearly a decade. Also on the list was the wildly popular wrestling coach, Frank Lasagna, who'd been at Glades Central for nineteen years and produced a string of district titles and twenty-five state place winners.

Going even further, Evans transferred Jay Seider, the athletic director and girls' track coach who'd been hired in 1971 by Al Werneke. Not only had Seider brought home ten state track titles, but the murder of his son Jyron two years earlier had become something ingrained in Raider football history. The 2000 championship trophy that Jyron's teammates had won was removed from the main office, replaced with academic awards (the trophies were relocated to other parts of the campus). And for good measure, Evans then disbanded the Raider booster club.

"Glades Central was a failing school and that bothered me," she told the *Sun Sentinel* at the time. "I want the school to be recognized for its athletes and scholars. Academics and athletics. I say that in alphabetical order."

The dismantling of the athletic program sparked an uproar. Parents and fans argued that for most of these kids, sports was the only avenue into college, and that athletics had educated hundreds in the Glades over the decades. One columnist pointed out that if sports was such a distraction for young minds, how did Evans explain Tim Sims, the Raider track star and football player who'd been given a scholarship to Stanford?

But in the end, the sky did not collapse. The Raiders, under the new leadership of coach Larry Coffey, still barreled through the season undefeated and lost in the playoffs. In the classroom, Evans backed up her promise. Students received more-rigorous tutoring, and football players were required to sit through study hall before practice. Reading and math scores improved, some dramatically. Evans sent a dozen teachers to get AP certification and made it harder for kids to drop classes they deemed too difficult. Governor Bush even paid a visit and accepted a football signed with players' SAT and ACT scores. (Bush had apparently forgotten about his promise to dye his hair purple, though he still drew laughs after sitting down on a wad of bubble gum.)

In addition to academic reforms, Evans began working to change students' expectations of themselves. She arranged for the band to play its first-ever concert on the coast and secured sponsorship money for Glades Central girls to enter the town's annual Harvest Queen pageant, which for decades had never featured a black contestant.

"That really lifts your spirits as a young girl," said Evans, who now worked as the city spokesperson. "There were lots of things to be done here, but adults had to get off their lazy behinds and do them. We've always been recognized for football, but what about the other 96 percent? What are you going to do for them?"

But for all the incremental improvements and changes, even down to the way the staff answered the phones ("Glades Central. Expect more."), Evans's reign at Glades Central was short. In 2004, citing health issues, she transferred to another elementary school and was gone.

• • •

IN THE YEARS following Evans's gutting of Glades Central, the school weathered two more F grades, another zero-basing of staff, three more principals, and a near takeover by the state. The Raider athletic program, meanwhile, clinched state championships in both football and track.

The job of principal in the Glades had never been easy, and if anything, after Evans, it only became more difficult. In 2001, President George W. Bush signed into law No Child Left Behind (NCLB), a set of national standards designed to narrow the achievement gap between low-performing minority schools and high-performing wealthier ones, which tended to be predominantly white. The law dictated what states taught, how they tested, and how teachers were trained. It also established rules and consequences for schools failing to make yearly progress, such as allowing each student an opportunity to transfer. The law also tied federal funding to scores.

In Florida the measuring stick for NCLB was, of course, the FCAT. And it seemed that every day since Anthony Anderson had taken over as Glades Central's latest principal, he and his staff had had one goal in their sights: getting off the list, gaining freedom.

After the state intervened in a low-performing school, it controlled many parts of a teacher's day and what was seen in classrooms. There were whiteboard configurations with lesson plans categorized under the headings: I Can, I Do, We Do, You Do It Together, and You Do It Alone; a lesson plan on the door outside for the state-mandated monitors; teachers using "differentiated instruction" with individual students to identify strengths and weaknesses; classrooms plastered with students' current work; and "data walls" displaying students' progress on each test.

And because of NCLB (pronounced by faculty as "Nicolby," in a tone that evoked an overlord listening from above), the school had lost dozens of high-performing students to transfers. But under Anderson's leadership, the school managed to raise its graduation rate to 82 percent.* It brought up reading and math scores, just before the federal standard jumped again out of reach. The same had happened to principals before him, and when those administrators had failed to improve after two years, they were transferred.

"That target is always going up," said Dr. Janis Andrews, the county's chief academic officer who once presided over the Glades. "It's like the principals are in a circus and they're all spinning plates. You have to keep them all going, because if one of them goes, they all come crashing down. It gets to be exhausting."

She felt that her former boss, superintendent Arthur Johnson—who resigned in February 2011 in the midst of a scandal involving his chief

---

* The significant percentage increase since Dr. Grear's tenure is the result of substantial changes in the way graduation rates are calculated.

academic officer accused of moonlighting—had given principals too little time to make improvements. "Research shows that it takes longer to turn around something as big as a high school," she said.

Especially one where its children live within entire city blocks lacking adequate plumbing and where ninth-graders become guardians of young siblings after parents die, leave town to work, or simply vanish altogether. These were the spinning plates a principal and his staff were forced to balance on every finger and toe, and only one of them had anything to do with the school's failing grade.

Although Anderson was seen as an outsider when he arrived in 2009, he'd overcome some of the same obstacles facing his students in the Glades. He'd grown up poor in a tough section of Boca Raton. His mother died in childbirth when he was five and his father was incarcerated for drugs not long afterward, leaving a grandmother to care for him and his siblings. In September 2006, his twenty-two-year-old son, Christopher, who'd been in and out of trouble for several years, was shot and killed at a house party in Delray Beach.

"Adversity and poverty are not monopolized here," he told a gathering of faculty, parents, and students shortly after arriving. "I wasn't just dropped on this earth with this shirt and tie on. I understand pain. I've had struggles, too."

For Anderson and his staff, the daily problem-solving was from another era, one dark and cruel and hell on children. How to help the young lady who for weeks couldn't use the communal shower in her apartment for fear of the red-eyed men who lurked like wolves at the door; where to put Zeke, the shy and gifted artist they'd discovered living in a boarded-up house with a mentally ill brother, surviving on sardines and cold cereal; how to persuade the father of a senior honor-roll student to allow his daughter to leave the cornfields and finish school because she'd just been accepted to Florida International University?

What to do when dedicated students couldn't afford their caps and gowns, school uniforms, or tickets to the Senior Grad Bash? In those cases, teachers pooled their own meager pay and bought the things themselves. And what to do when, after prepping all year for the FCAT, many of your lowest twenty-five-percenters (whose scores enormously affected your school grade) didn't show up for school? Assistant principals have jumped into the yellow cheese wagon and driven through the narrow streets, yanking kids out of bed, out of the fields, anything to get them into a testing room. One AP, Angela Moore, even ironed kids' clothes while she waited.

"We eat, sleep, and dream this stuff," said Moore, who'd been at Glades Central for seventeen years. "Here you give two hundred percent."

The double shifts expected of teachers in the Glades, plus the isolation and lingering stigma as a district rubber room, made it extremely difficult to recruit quality staff. This despite one year when the county offered a $10,000 bonus for leaving a better-reputation school. Most teachers lived along the coast, so the commute was long and the travel stipend offered by the district hardly covered the rising price of gas. And what if you had to work past dark? Visiting teachers have described the mortal fear that gripped them while caught in the Glades after sunset, the curtain of blackness on either side of the highway and the canals wild with chatter. What was the incentive when there were ten other schools within twenty minutes of your house? Especially if they were wealthier magnet schools like Suncoast, where test scores and achievement were always high and teachers received bonuses every year? Schools like Glades Central only got endlessly scrutinized.

"It's a backward performance system because you're benefiting schools that are already prepared and taking away from communities that are hurting and dealing against the odds," said Dr. Andrews, referring to the current structure. "The rich get richer."

Many now felt, however, that as controversial as they were at the time, the two rounds of faculty purges had achieved their aim of a stronger, leaner, more dedicated staff. The teachers chosen to stay at Glades Central, and those who sought out the post, tended to be dogged and intrepid types with high energy and unspoiled idealism. Some were also locals who'd returned out of duty, bent on cleaning the tarnished image of their home. And after years of oversight and mandatory curriculum, said Dr. Andrews, they'd also become some of the most creative and innovative instructors in the district.

"I will put them up against any teacher along the coast," she said. "I will put the actual practice of teaching against some of our best teachers. They're just better prepared."

• • •

ONE OF GLADES Central's most highly regarded teachers and champions was a woman named Sherry Canty, an eight-year veteran who chaired the school's career academy. She'd graduated from Glades Central in 1981, the same year as Hester, then had spent nearly two decades as an emergency-room nurse before being called to teach. Canty found her passion creating the school's medical sciences academy, guiding bright students such as Jonteria into the demanding field of medicine.

While the academy only offered students the LPN certification, most, like Jonteria, had greater aspirations. They were certainly the most dedicated. The required 3.0 GPA, advanced math and science courses, dual enrollment in community college, and off-campus clinical work usually guaranteed that Canty's students dominated the top scholastic positions in the school. For the other 96 percent, the counterpart to the football dream machine was here. In eight years, every one of Canty's students had gone to college and most had been awarded full scholarships.

Canty was quick to point out that Glades Central students were also perennial winners of academic decathlons, and that in 2009 twenty-four graduates received academic scholarships to the University of Florida. Just the previous year, two had been named Bill Gates Millennium Scholars, one of the most prestigious awards given to aspiring college students today.

"The school grade doesn't tell you what's happening here at Glades Central," she said. "And neither does the football team."

CHAPTER

For the Glades Central Raiders, the middle chunk of the season schedule was expected to be light fare—"stat games," as KB and others described them, much to the annoyance of the coaches. But a few easy games were certainly welcomed and exactly what Hester needed to iron out kinks and review fundamentals with his line. Much of the week was spent in the classroom, drilling plays and formations, hours steeped in the coded lexicon of football.

"Guys, this is Sally."

"Coach, is Sally quick?"

"Yeah, Sally is quick."

"So we can chop?"

"Yeah, chop."

But as weak as the opponents appeared, the Raiders still struggled in their game against Royal Palm Beach at Effie C. Grear Field. The Wildcats' offense had gone all season without scoring a single touchdown, a truth that caused the bleachers to groan when, minutes into the first quarter, they connected for a fifty-yard bomb into the end zone against the Raider secondary.

"Come on, Jet!"

"Where the defense at?"

Penalties and turnovers plagued the Raiders throughout the game. Benjamin's kickoff return for seventy yards—his giant legs churning slowly at the start like an engine getting loose, then pure velocity, the kind of run that fed the dreams of his recruiters—was instantly erased the next play by a Raider fumble. The Wildcats then managed no more acts of greatness, which meant that for four painful quarters, the Raiders played mostly against themselves.

Little things, like the center's ballooning weight, stymied them:

"Coach," Mario screamed toward the sideline, "the ball keeps getting stuck between Cubby's legs."

"You gotta get up under there!"

After the Raiders won 24–7, even Pastor Dez channeled his frustrations to heaven when the team gathered for prayer:

"Father, it could have been prettier, but nonetheless, we thank you for the victory."

A sloppy victory in any other town in America was a victory nonetheless. Despite playing with a torn ligament in his shoulder, Mario passed for nearly three hundred yards and two touchdowns. It was his best game so far, but one that also included three interceptions. Once again, the insults had rained down from the stands, then later flooded the message boards:

"everybody knows that [Rowley] can not handle the qb position but hester keep using him. that same qb gonna have you lookin for a job next year."

"DAM JET YOU GON LET US GET TO THE PLAYOFFS OR STATE AND LOSE BECAUSE OF THE LACK OF DEVELOPMENT AT QUARTER BACK AGAIN THIS YEAR!!"

On Saturday the quarterback's Facebook status read, "ME AGAINST

THA WHOLE BELLE GLADE." For all of Hester's encouragement, for all the times he'd stood before the team saying, "I don't care what *nobody* says. He's *my* quarterback," the ever-private coach withheld arguably his best line of motivation—his own personal struggles with insecurity and the battle a city had once waged against him.

• • •

"IT FEELS WONDERFUL," Jessie Hester told the *Los Angeles Times* in May 1985, shortly after the L.A. Raiders selected him in the first round. "I'm just overwhelmed. I just can't believe I'm part of this organization."

The Los Angeles squad that Hester joined in 1985 was older, more hobbled than the Super Bowl champions of the 1983 season. Injuries had riddled the entire offense, in particular the thirty-seven-year-old body of warhorse quarterback Jim Plunkett. The Raiders had finished the previous season 11–5 and suffered a crushing loss to the Seattle Seahawks in the AFC playoffs.

By choosing Hester in the first round, Raiders owner Al Davis was hoping to fill a crucial gap in the receiver corps that had once sliced up secondaries and helped the Silver and Black to three Lombardi trophies. And it was a gap of legendary proportions. Jessie the Jet, with his 4.23 speed and thirty-eight-inch vertical leap, was being unveiled as the next Cliff Branch.

Branch was the three-time Super Bowl champion and the league's leading postseason receiver, a man of heart-stopping ninety-nine-yard-pass plays, who, in his thirteenth year in the same jersey, was still being described by his coach as "a feather . . . he just kind of flies over the ground." He was also turning thirty-seven in August and breaking down. The legendary wideout had been injured most of the previous season and had caught no touchdowns, leaving the Raiders with just Dokie Williams and Malcolm Barnwell.

Going into the draft, the Raiders had rated Hester higher than both Al Toon and Jerry Rice, who'd gone tenth and sixteenth to the Jets and 49ers, respectively. Head coach Tom Flores had said publicly that he expected the Florida burner to be more than the acrobatic highlight maker he'd been with the Seminoles.

For the shy, twenty-two-year-old Jessie, the sudden pressure was incredible and, in his own mind, seemed to magnify his every move: from the first touches in training camp before an audience of All-Pro teammates Howie Long, Marcus Allen, and Lyle Alzado, to renting the ritzy Foxhill apartment for himself and Lena, who'd just learned she was pregnant with Jesse junior, to the party invitations from Dionne Warwick and Hollywood events where Magic Johnson and Janet Jackson knew him on sight.

Look, there was Jessie Hester, the million-dollar man. The next Cliff Branch.

• • •

"I GOT THE Bonus Baby," shouted Lester Hayes, the five-time Pro Bowl cornerback, as he lined up against Jessie the first week of camp.

"Let's see what you got, Bonus Baby. Let's see if that money was worth it."

Hayes was six-two and 225 pounds, one of the greatest defensive backs to play the game, a man whose nickname was "the Judge." Hester was accustomed to beating bigger guys off the ball with his quickness, but the orders from the sidelines were to go straight through Hayes. Employing his signature bump-and-run, Hayes made the rookie pay for every step, clawing at his eyes and nose and grabbing his throat, everything but throwing a blanket over his head and beating him.

"Oh no!" shouted Hayes. "They done gave that money away!"

Hester was humiliated.

"I was never so frustrated," he said. It wasn't until he appealed directly to Davis, who appeared on the sidelines ("Let me get off the ball the way I know how"), that he was finally able to get open.

Jessie had little time to let the hazing get to his head. Before the season opener, the Raiders had already sent Branch to injured reserve and traded Barnwell to Washington, leaving the young rookie to start opposite Williams in the number-two slot.

For any rookie receiver thrust into such a fire, it was a fine season: thirty-two catches, 655 yards, and four touchdowns, some of them thrilling—like the impossible grab over the helmet of Kansas City corner-back Kevin Ross, or the catch-and-vanish between two Chargers that left them clanking skulls like Keystone Kops.

Hester's season performance set a franchise record for a first-year player, but it came with an asterisk. Hester had developed a tendency to drop passes. While the team listed only six official drops for the season, the rookie's hands soon became the subject of weekly scrutiny in the sporting press.

There were two drops in the exhibition loss to Miami, one in the end zone. The bobble against San Francisco. The potential game-winner in Cleveland that flew out of his hands at the goal line, and the one in Atlanta worth another six. The drop in Cleveland earned Hester a public lashing on the sideline from receivers coach Tom Walsh, his trusted corner man.

"When the Los Angeles Raiders had the ball and the game safely in hand, rookie wide receiver Jessie Hester had no problem catching any num-ber of elegant, exciting passes," wrote the *Miami Herald* after the Raiders were eliminated by New England in the first round of the playoffs. "But when the game was on the line and passing yardage crucial, Hester's supple hands quickly turned to stone."

Hester had "hyper nerves," the story said. The receiver could not ex-plain the drops, even to himself. They were like a curse, a virus ripping through his methodical, orderly nature.

"Mentally, I was gone," he remembered. "Marcus and these guys would try to talk to me, 'Man, just play ball. Don't listen to that. Play ball.' But they didn't know how deep it was."

After sitting out the first quarter of the '86 season with a sore Achilles tendon, Hester returned off the bench in a game against San Diego, roping in a forty-yard shot from backup Marc Wilson to win the game. The next week against Kansas City, back in the starting lineup, Plunkett hit him for eighteen yards and another game winner.

"The Jet is back," wrote Mark Heisler of the *Los Angeles Times*.

Heisler, the sharp-witted, now-venerated sportswriter, had given the first-rounder from Belle Glade a celebrity welcome upon his Hollywood arrival, then quickly shown him the ways of the wild kingdom. Hester's unraveling, like Al Davis's endless court struggles and team controversies, became the sweet pulp of Heisler's L.A. stories. When Hester's bad luck found him again, dropping three big-potential catches over three consecutive weeks, Heisler quipped, "Jessie Hester is once more putting the ball on the floor as often as Magic Johnson."

The next game, a demoralizing loss to the shoddy 3–9 Eagles, Heisler struck again: "The young Raider receivers dropped passes all over the lot, including one by Jessie Hester in the end zone. He caught two others for touchdowns, but in this league, .667 doesn't get it."

"At this point, I thought it was personal," Hester said. "I wanted to hurt the guy."

Hester spent the majority of the '87 season on the bench, still haunted by the occasional drop and never safe from Heisler's lens. Afraid to get open, he hid in the secondary and managed only one catch for thirty yards.

"I didn't want the ball thrown to me," he said. "I did whatever I could not to be open. I didn't want it thrown and have things said about me."

The next season the Raiders drafted first-round receiver Tim Brown from Notre Dame and traded to get wideout Willie Gault from Chicago. Brown had won the Heisman Trophy; Gault was a former Olympic qualifier in the 4x100 relay (unfortunately for him, the United States boycotted the 1980 games) and was considered one of the fastest receivers ever to have played in the league.

The message was clear. In August, under new head coach Mike Shanahan, the Raiders finally traded Jet to Atlanta for a fifth-round pick. As

Hester left Los Angeles, crushed and dejected, his nemesis, Heisler, didn't miss the chance to chalk the outline of another fallen star.

"Jessie Hester, the soft-spoken burner from Florida State," Heisler wrote, "leaves with a 23.7 career yards-per-catch average, but only 56 receptions in three seasons. His teammates marveled at the way he could run routes, and the opposition never could cover him, but what did they have to worry about? He dropped too many passes to live up to his billing."

In Atlanta, playing for the lowly Falcons, Hester was hoping for a clean bill in a smaller, more forgiving southern market, to sort out his problems and prove the past no longer mattered. For a while the curse disappeared; then it found him in the worst possible places, like in the end zone of the L.A. Coliseum in a midseason game against the Raiders. The crowd broiled him from above.

Hester finished the season with only twelve catches for 176 yards. When a *Palm Beach Post* reporter found him at the Falcons' training camp the following summer, he appeared a lonely and desperate man.

"I have to do something this year for myself, regardless of what anybody else thinks," he said. "If I don't do anything this year, I will be destroyed mentally."

Three weeks later, after he dislocated his toe in an exhibition game in Philly, the Falcons released him. With his career in pieces, his mind and body a mess, Hester left Lena and Jessie junior in Atlanta and retreated to the only safe place he knew. He went home to Belle Glade.

• • •

FORMER DOLPHINS DEFENSIVE back Louis Oliver liked to tell the story of the day Jet first came home after the Raiders drafted him, a quintessential hero's parade that left a vapor of stardust and wonder in its wake.

"He's driving that two-door red Mercedes down Avenue E and the town is going bananas," said Oliver, who was fourteen at the time. "He sees me and blows the horn. I immediately go home, put on my workout clothes, and head to the field. Then I run till I can't run anymore. Seeing that took my work ethic to a whole other level."

When Hester returned to Belle Glade four years later, it was nothing inspiring, and the lesson it provided was old. The world chewed up men and their dreams. And when that happened, they came home to hide.

"I was sulking and feeling sorry for myself," Hester said. "I came and stayed with my mom. I didn't want to deal with football again. I was here trying to figure out my life. I wasn't even working out. I was just in the dumps."

Depressed and restless, Hester spent the '89 season drifting. He would stay in Atlanta with his family as long as he could, but the atmosphere of football season was impossible to stand.

It was no better in Belle Glade. People talked, the way they do:

"The boy done lost his hands."

"He scared of the ball."

"I knew he'd be back."

Down at the Alabama-Georgia Grocery Store, they might slap him on the shoulder and smile, but behind his back, he knew what they were saying.

"Let's just say they was *glad* to see me back in town."

The only solace he found was at his mother's house, or sitting with Willie watching television. He visited friends, helped Zara with work. He even filed for unemployment.

That spring, Cletus Jones, his old roommate at FSU, got married in Miami and Jessie went to the wedding. Also in attendance was Hassan Jones, another of Jessie's teammates at FSU, who was now with the Minnesota Vikings. Sitting around after the ceremony, Cletus and Hassan pulled an intervention.

"Jessie, you're making a big mistake to not go back and play," Hassan told him. "You're too good a player, man. You just lost your confidence, that's all. Besides, you don't wanna go out a loser."

When he returned to Belle Glade, his older brother, Roger, staged an intervention of his own.

"I'd been hearing it all," Roger said. "People sayin how he couldn't make the pros, wasn't good enough, this and that. Jessie felt like a failure in our community. He was my brother, and it hurt me to see him like that."

Over the years, whenever possible, Roger had recorded every one of his brother's games. Now, seeing him in such a state, he went back and compiled every electrifying catch to remind Jessie of the athlete that lived inside, the one now lost out in the void.

"I've seen you catch some remarkable balls," he said. "Just take these tapes and go look at 'em. This is something you been doin all your life. Go look at the proof yourself."

Hester took the tapes back home to Atlanta, but instead of watching the highlights as his brother had intended, he focused on the rest. Sitting in a dark room by himself, Hester went back and watched every dropped pass, every missed block, every glaring contradiction to the athlete he thought he had been. After he could stomach seeing them a first time, he watched them over again.

"The good times were easy to relive," he said. "Mentally, I had to deal with the bad and accept those things that had happened. I had to ask myself, 'Could I have really made that play?' and then answer with the truth. That was the only way I was gonna move on. I had to accept myself as a person who made mistakes and learn how to be better."

But it wasn't until a few weeks later, back in Belle Glade, that he finally came around. Jessie was at his grandparents' house with some cousins, who were trying to perk him up, when Willie, who was sitting in his recliner watching *Gunsmoke*, had finally heard enough. Willie told everyone in the room to shut up, then turned and looked at Jessie.

"Son, nobody forgets how to catch a football," he said.

"This man never said nothin," said Hester. "I mean *nothin*. And just like that. All that noise and talk was gone. The way he said it—he was right. It was then I knew I had to go back and play."

• • •

HESTER RETURNED TO Atlanta and spent the next six weeks in heavy training. He hadn't worked out in almost a year since his toe injury, so he started slow: first jogging around his sprawling apartment complex, then speed work. Pretty soon he was clocking forties and picking up time. It felt good, like being in his old skin. His agent placed him back on the market, and soon he was getting calls to try out for the Patriots, Eagles, and Colts.

The quarterbacks coach from the Raiders, Larry Kennan, was now offensive coordinator with Indianapolis, which Jessie saw as a plus. And other than Andre Rison, who was the Colts' number-one receiver, the roster was mostly guys Hester didn't recognize. The smaller midwestern market looked to be a genial and welcoming place for a man aiming to start again.

"I thought I could prove myself easier on that team," he said.

It didn't take long. Just before the season opener, the Colts traded Rison to Atlanta, while number-two wideout Clarence Verdin sat out with an injury. After five games, Hester became rookie quarterback Jeff George's go-to utility receiver, having caught fifteen passes, including a career-high eight receptions in a loss against Denver.

"It's like I've been reborn," he told the *Sporting News*.

• • •

THE TRANSFORMATION WAS nothing miraculous. Rather, it came about as the result of two small changes. Little things. For one, Hester simply became a better student of the game. In his short time in Atlanta, he'd worked with a receivers coach named Jimmy Raye, who'd introduced a more fundamental approach to seeing the position. It was a revelation.

"Jimmy Raye taught me to pay closer attention," he said. "He was real hands-on. Before, it was guys telling me to look for the ball at ninety degrees, and meet the ball at forty-five degrees. Jimmy's putting it on the board and showing me on the field. He's showing me that one subtle move that otherwise I might have missed or forgotten. I put those in my notes. I started watching for that move in other guys and taking notes on them. My career took off after that."

Hester's note taking would become so meticulous and ritualistic that later in his career his teammates would dub him "the Professor."

Also, while he was still in Los Angeles, Hester discovered that he had trouble with his vision. He had requested to see an optometrist and confirmed one of his fears. It turned out he had amblyopia, or "lazy eye." In his case, his right eye was weaker than the left.

"I started remembering old basketball games, football games, seeing the ball coming, then suddenly turning back and it was gone," he said. "I guess I somehow compensated for it in high school and college, but in the pros, the competition was just too much that it didn't work anymore."

He'd told few people aside from the team trainer, fearing it would be seen as an excuse. Instead, he'd sit in his apartment—a more modest affair in Inglewood that he'd traded down for after his struggles began—and perform eye exercises: looking left to right, focusing on two objects and making them one. He began doing this daily. By the time he reached Indianapolis, his vision had greatly improved.

"The combination of me maturing mentally and being able to see the ball more clearly gave me more confidence. For once, I was able to be me."

Unfortunately, the early nineties were lean years for the Colts, who won a total of five games in Hester's first two seasons. But Indy proved to be the ideal for redemption. At the end of his first season, his numbers nearly equaled those of his entire career so far.

By Hester's third year with the Colts the dreaded curse had not only lifted but reversed its cruel order. Hester could not *stop* catching the ball.

By the time he left the Colts in 1994, he'd caught passes in sixty-two consecutive games, a franchise record that dated back to the days of Johnny
Unitas. Acquired by the Rams, Hester returned to the West Coast not as a
disgraced superstar but as a man on a streak—one the reporters were calling one of the longest in the NFL.

The Jet was back.

CHAPTER

10

The fairy-tale comeback of Jessie the Jet was a story known by few, if any, players on the Glades Central squad. The coach was such a guarded man that he did not provide the story to KB as a cautionary tale of hubris and human fallibility, and not to the quarterback struggling with his own "hyper nerves" and a doubt about his own potential. Just like Jet, they would be forced to learn these lessons the hard way, to gut them out alone.

For Mario, the next test was a game against rival Clewiston, the home of U.S. Sugar, located fifteen miles up the west side of the lake. It was the forty-fourth meeting between the two towns, this time at Cane Field, where the stands and sidelines were mostly white, and the first place all season where country music blasted from the press-box speakers during warm-ups. A narrow canal ran behind the field, which was framed by high sugar-cane, sending up billions of gnats and mosquitoes.

As Benjamin had predicted, Clewiston provided the stat game for the ages. The Raiders won 55–0 and scored on nearly every possession, including a ninety-yard punt return by KB that even the Tiger crowd had to applaud for its beauty. Benjamin, Jaime, and Davonte would end the night with two touchdowns apiece.

Clewiston's offense never showed any sign of life against the Raider defense. Robert Way, after recording two sacks the previous week, rolled off the weak Tiger line all night like a slippery fish and dropped the quarterback three times. Even Joshua Knabb, a kicker for the Raiders and the only white player on the team, managed a vicious tackle on the offensive line.

"Joshie got him a pancake," Boobie shouted, slapping his helmet.

Clewiston provided the Raiders with a much-needed statement game, another year of bragging rights around the lake, and for the time being it silenced the critics. But the game had been wrapped in turmoil like most games before it, caused mostly by the general lack of seriousness so often mentioned. After three years it was finally chipping away at the usually understated head coach, whose moods were swinging wildly.

He'd exploded earlier that afternoon as the team suited up, leaving those in the room stunned by the rare display of emotion. The boys had misbehaved during the team dinner, he said, wearing headphones, ignoring instruction, straight disrespecting. As he lectured the players once again on their poor attitudes, he noticed one of his wide receivers, Jaqavein Oliver, lying down, apparently asleep.

Oliver was a smiley, droopy-eyed kid who was content spending his Saturdays perched on the canal banks, fishing for bass. He'd been cut from the squad the previous season, then returned that summer in better shape and quickly showed skills. He'd completed a pair of clutch first-down catches against Skyline and American Heritage, and was now competing with Davonte for the number-three slot. But today the boy certainly wasn't helping himself.

"Get up," Hester screamed. "Get up, get up, get up!"

Oliver flung himself against the wall, eyes wide, nowhere to escape.

"You got a problem with authority, bwah?"

"Man, you can't be doing that," Oliver tried, but Hester was already in his face, his breath hot on the boy's cheek.

"I can do that because I'm your coach, bwah. I'm your coach and from now on you WILL LISTEN TO YOUR COACH."

Hester jerked back, as if released by a spirit. He took a breath, rubbed his brow, then scanned the room.

"Don't yall ever make me get out of my character again," he said, then calmly walked out the door, leaving only the sound of the track lights humming overhead.

It was an extreme leap of emotion for a man who, just two weeks before, had displayed such extraordinary tenderness. During the tense game against American Heritage, a junior cornerback called Slick had nearly come to blows with defensive coordinator Tony Smith, who'd groused over a missed block. The fight had caused a wild scene along the sidelines, with players screaming, *"Take his helmet, Coach!"* while fans watched from above and shook their heads.

Tempers had flared once again as the team gathered after the game, until Hester physically pulled Slick from the pack and took him aside. Down on both knees, he whispered softly to him, caressing his flak vest and shoulder pads, as a mother would a child. The second Hester's hands made contact, the boy went slack and began to cry.

"You gotta remember they're just children," he said, walking away. "And you gotta pour on that love. Just keep pouring on that love."

So, the following Thursday at practice, as the Raiders prepared for one of their most important home games of the regular season, nobody knew what to expect when Hester stood before them with that same furrowed brow which preceded each of his "I'm disappointed in you" speeches. And sure enough, the speech came.

"On a serious note, guys," he said, looking down, shaking his head. "There's always somethin, aint it? *Always somethin.* Well, this somethin is this: we got a cat who can't play tomorrow. A serious leader, too. So serious that yall might not even win without this cat. This here's a cat who done disappointed his team, his family."

He paused for an entire minute, letting the silence sink in.

"Don't yall wanna know who I'm talkin about?"

"Who is it, Coach?" someone whispered.

"Huh? I can't hear you."

"We wanna know who it is."

"You what?"

"Who's the person?"

"Say it again."

"*Who it is, Coach?*"

Hester's face broke into a smile as he grabbed his crotch.

"*DESE NUTS!*"

The boys roared with laughter, and all the tension from the past weeks seemed to drift away. Tomorrow was homecoming.

• • •

HOMECOMING IN BELLE Glade was like Easter Sunday and Fourth of July wrapped into one glimmering extravaganza. It was a day when parents dressed their children in lavish costumes to peacock down the boulevard, a time to eat well, drink heartily, then gather around the lights for the evening beat-down on the muck.

It was a day when everything must shine, and preparations began early. The trucks and flatbed trailers for the morning parade gathered along the canal at eight, waiting to be dressed, while, nearby, Haitian women stood over sleepy-eyed little girls, speaking rapid Creole while braiding hair and mending dresses.

The store and social club across from Glades Central was abuzz all morning with men sprucing up for the big day and placing bets on the victory against the Boca Raton Bobcats. Behind the counter, an old woman holding a fistful of cash barked into a cell phone, *"Raiders 24, Boca 10,"* while down the hill along the ditch, Ray King ran a makeshift barbershop under a blue tarp. A cluster of men sat waiting in folding chairs for five-dollar shaves and ten-dollar cuts, reading magazines, staring into phones, and swatting mosquitoes that poured from the stagnant creek nearby. Over near the street at Joe Whitey's car wash, rag men crouched on their knees polishing a gleaming row of twenty-four-inch rims with studied detail.

By noon hundreds gathered along MLK Boulevard, which ran through the tumbledown heart of town, feasting from sidewalk stands selling lemonade and pulled pork, boiled crab with eggs and potatoes, and buttery pound cake. And nobody batted an eye when suddenly the streets filled with muscled white police wearing weapons and tactical gear.

The floats were both spectacular and confounding, each bedecked with elaborate Asian and Egyptian scenes that rolled in high relief against the pillbox boardinghouses and Dixie Fried Chicken. There were floats of schoolkids dressed as pharaohs and queens, heads topped with shiny paper crowns and gold ribbons woven into braids as if done surgically. Floats of young black boys masquerading as Chinese emperors in silk pajamas; tuxedoed chauffeurs driving horse-drawn carriages with tiny girls smiling under pink paper umbrellas.

And once the floats had passed—the pageant queens! There was a chosen queen for every class in every school, from Miss Rosenwald Elementary to Walkeria Carter, Miss Glades Central. The girls sat perched atop the hoods of slow-creeping Mercedes and tricked-out ghetto chargers, their long, flowing gowns spilling over the sides like melted wax.

Leading the procession was Jonteria, representing the Raider cheerleaders. She wore a brown strapless dress that she and Theresa had picked out at a Fort Lauderdale boutique, Theresa reminding herself of the importance of the event as she'd laid down $200. But it *was* gorgeous and complemented Jonteria's golden hair extensions her cousin had spent seven hours weaving. The flaxen curls now draped over her shoulders as she rode atop the covered bed of a pickup, her hand raised at her side, waving like Lady Di.

* * *

IN SHOP CLASS before the game, the boys were bug-eyed with excitement. Waka Flocka Flame thumped from their headphones as the team decked themselves in pink: do-rags, wristbands, and socks, all in recognition of National Breast Cancer Awareness Month. Mario paced the room in silence, his eye black reading simply, I'M BACK.

So was Jaime, who walked through the door looking fragile and listless; he'd come straight from the emergency room. "I had a fever today and went to the hospital," he said. "I was so weak. But the nurses told me to get up on outta there 'cause I had a team and fans who needed me too much."

And in lieu of speeches, Hester stayed in his office and let his boys be boys.

"This is gonna be a night you never forget," he said before cutting them loose. "Homecoming night. It's all about having fun and putting on a show."

The Raiders ran out into the night air and down the sidewalk, through the fragrant clouds of pit smoke and the cheering throng of fans. They formed a howling pack near the goalpost, banging helmet against helmet, body against body, anxious for that first touch of click-clack.

And once the whistle blew, they indeed put on a show. On the Raiders' second possession, the Bobcats blitzed with all their linebackers, and running back Neville Brown read it perfectly, taking the handoff from Mario and darting through the gap for seventy-five yards and the score. Another touchdown by the fevered Jaime Wilson had the hometown crowd up on their feet; then, two possessions later, KB slammed on the overdrive for a forty-three-yard burst up the sideline to send them reeling. By halftime, the score was 34–0.

. . .

A DOUBLE-DIGIT LEAD at halftime was expected fare for the home-coming crowd. But this year also brought something special. The Raiders were retiring the numbers of three of their biggest stars, who gathered now at midfield. Standing next to Hester were Jimmy Spencer and Fred Taylor.

Spencer, Class of 1987, was part of the early crop of studs to leave Belle Glade after Hester and play in the pros. Like Jet, Spencer had been recruited by just about every major football program in the nation. He ended up choosing Galen Hall's Florida Gators, then later was drafted by Washington. Over the course of a dozen years, Spencer had been part of five NFL teams, ending his career with the Denver Broncos, where he later became an assistant coach. He still lived in Denver and worked as a minister.

Taylor had flown in from Boston, where his New England Patriots were taking their bye week. The Pro Bowl running back had spent his first eleven years in the league with the Jacksonville Jaguars. Alongside his cousin Santonio Holmes, Taylor was Belle Glade's biggest active celebrity. His youth and Sunday-ready physique stood in contrast to the older men at his side. When he'd moved through the crowd, there was a noticeable wake of both admiration and some upturned noses, a reaction that spoke to the complicated relationship between the poverty-stricken town and its rich and famous men.

. . .

"I CRIED MY eyes out the first time I left Belle Glade," Taylor said.

He was fifteen, on his way to basketball camp in Johnson City, Tennessee, and seeing the world outside of Palm Beach County for the first time. Leaving home was a common, dominating memory for most every player who'd ever competed on the next level. For Hester, it was a recruiting trip to Ohio State in the dead of a midwestern winter. And for most, the fear was quickly overwhelmed by a sense of awe at the great unfolding world. Staring out the windows of buses and planes, many experienced a jarring new understanding of home and history.

"Belle Glade will get a grasp on you and won't let you go," Taylor said. "But those people who can get away and experience life elsewhere, that's often all it takes to motivate them."

Guys soon realized the power their hometown held, both to destroy and to evoke a sense of wonder. For young men striking out in search of identities, the muck defined who they were and branded them on the outside, especially in football.

"We had a chippiness about us, the way we played, our bravado," said Hester. "Muck players have edge. They're raw."

Louis Oliver had once stood before the starting Gator secondary and announced, "I'm a safety from Belle Glade. And as long as I'm here, aint none of you muthafuckers gonna play." It was edgy all right, given that Oliver was just a skinny freshman who'd walked onto the team with an academic scholarship.

Whenever Santonio Holmes caught a touchdown on national television, such as the one to win Super Bowl XLIII, he'd often find the nearest camera and strike a flexing pose, the emphasis on the "561" area code tattooed across his right bicep.

But outside football, the stigma of Belle Glade followed its own like an offensive odor. "In college, people from Belle Glade would say, 'I'm from the Palm Beach area,'" said Taylor. "There came a point where I just embraced it, but that took a while."

The muck instilled a sense of place, but for many, the place itself remained too hot to touch, save for one or two fleeting visits a year for family or charity events.

"I'll never forget where I'm from," said Holmes, who came back each year to host a kids' football camp with his cousin Fred. "But I certainly don't miss it. Just hearing about the shit that happens here daily—kids getting shot, the gangs. That's not what I remember. I hardly recognize this place."

That same new reality had hit another former player, Santonio Thomas, particularly hard. Thomas, whose local nickname was Fat Man, had helped anchor the defense of the 1998 and 1999 championship teams, a defense so feared it was known across the state as the Legion of Doom. He'd signed with the Miami Hurricanes, and after graduating with a degree in sociology and secondary education, he'd spent three seasons in the league with New England and Cleveland.

The Browns waived him in September 2009, after which he retreated to a quiet, two-acre spread in the Georgia pines. His wife later accepted a job in Fort Lauderdale, and once Fat was back, Hester invited him to coach the offensive line. At the start of the Raider season, fresh after arriving, he'd brimmed with excitement about the new adventure.

"I'm just happy to come back and prepare these players for the realities of college," he said, then mentioned a desire to maybe get his teaching certificate and stay at Glades Central.

Two months later, however, the optimism and glee were nowhere to be found. Shortly after the Clewiston game, Coach Fat sat in the shop classroom as the team dressed, and tried to diagnose the newfound depression that filled him.

"You know when you come from a place and there's nothing but positive energy, then you go to a place where there's a lot of negativity?" he said. "I'm just feeling a lot of negativity in my life right now. I'm feeling like I can't escape it here. Like it surrounds me from every direction."

Much of the negativity that pros experienced was rooted in jealousy. Because for every young man who made it to the next level, there were forty who did not, guys who didn't have the discipline or skills or support structure at home, or who'd made it part of the way, only to get spit back to earth by the big machine.

The earth and its days are evil, the scriptures say, and many cannot walk circumspectly once they're free upon the land. In 2001, former Pahokee star receiver Keo Green, twenty-five years old, shot and killed his girlfriend and then himself after a police chase down Highway 80. And there was Roosevelt Johnson, twenty-four, the Raider defensive tackle who'd cycled out of Southwest Mississippi State and returned home, only to empty his pistol one night at some men who'd insulted him on a homemade rap tape. Johnson had missed the men and killed Lanetra Brown, a mother of three. And like Coach Vickers, everyone liked to use Jerry Campbell's rousing comeback victory in the 1998 championship game against Madison County as an example of toughness and character. Yet they left out the part where Campbell, back home for several years, got picked up for robbery.

A crowd of older boys usually gathered on Saturday afternoons in Pioneer Park to play pickup ball with current Raiders. Several years out of high school, with no college and few job opportunities, some of them were already caught in the swirl of gang life and had spent some time in jail. ("Some a them boys be carrying guns right now," said one Raider, watching from the bleachers.) They relished occasionally burning rising talents such as Jaime or Boobie, but few Raider players even bothered exposing themselves.

"People try to bring us down," said KB. "I don't even get involved."

The more ambitious ones gathered on the community center field, where the Muck City Starrs, the regional semipro team, met on crisp February nights for practice. The Starrs belonged to the sixteen-team Florida Football Alliance, its roster filled with former Raiders and Pahokee Blue Devils whose dreams had been upended for myriad reasons. Most were now in their mid-twenties; the oldest player was forty-one. And many were still hoping to get noticed, either by a small college or the lower-level pros, such as the Arena League. Over the years, several Starrs had gotten second looks in Canada.

There was Jarrell Moore, the defensive back who'd been forced to quit Miles College before his freshman season when his brother was murdered on Avenue D. He'd come home in 2007 and gone to work in the fields, chasing the mule train. Now twenty-three, he led the FFA in interceptions and was hoping to be in shape for the Canadian league's next tryout in Orlando.

"I'll feel like it's the last shot I have," he said.

For the Muck City Starrs, the quest for a second chance was certainly not as easy as the first time around. With no sponsorship, the team had little money for equipment or travel. Many players still wore their old pads from high school; their silver helmets were gashed, reconstituted relics. Injuries to aging bodies were rife and dream-crushing. With no bus, players drove themselves to games, some as far away as Tallahassee, a six-hour journey.

"We make our money from car washes," said Jarrel Ford, the team's owner. "There are no NFL players giving back to us."

While the Starrs were not expecting any handouts, there were plenty in town who were. And perhaps this, above all else, was what kept many pros from coming home. Some had been burned early in their careers after donating to what they thought were local charities, only to discover the money had simply disappeared. But most just felt judged and harassed by people they hardly knew.

"You have people in that town who had the same opportunities as you, some even more," said Louis Oliver. "You make it, and they don't make it, and suddenly they think you owe them something. It's like, how did *you* help me to get where I am?"

After Hester's first season in Los Angeles, he was standing outside his mother's new house when a car full of men rolled up. They were high school acquaintances who heard he was back in town. One of them asked Jet for gas money to drive down to Miami, then flashed a gun.

"They were off to rob someplace and wanted me to go," he said.

When he refused, one of the men said, "We know where you live."

He told them to hit the block. When they circled back around, he'd left ten dollars by the gate.

Mindful of such stories, many of the pros who came home for brief periods made it a point to lie low, never pulling out rolls of cash or wearing heavy jewelry. Flashiness had never been part of Hester's nature, and the fame and money he garnered while in the league did little to change that. Aside from owning a few sports cars during his playing days, Hester had never been comfortable with extravagance.

For her book *Battle's End,* Caroline Alexander tracked down her former student athletes from the 1981 Seminole football team to follow up on their lives. In 1994, she found Hester at his family's modest ranch home in Wellington that he'd bought several years earlier. Entering his ninth year in the league, he was the same Jessie whom Alexander remembered: polite, thoughtful, and downplayed.

"He was dressed very simply in jean shorts and a T-shirt," she wrote. "Shining with mesmerizing brightness from his wrist, however, was a gleaming diamond-studded Rolex."

Throughout their interview, Hester kept fingering the watch "with something approaching disdain," until finally he addressed it. "This is a flashy watch," he said. "But I didn't buy this—my *money* bought it." Lena had purchased the Rolex as a gift, he explained. At first, Hester had carried it in his pocket until coins started scratching the face. Terrified of leaving it lying around, he had no choice but to wear it. "She thought that I would like it," he said. "I told her, you know . . . don't do it again."

Now, more than a decade into retirement, Hester drew a pension from the NFL and earned money on his properties, although most months he wound up floating many tenants who couldn't pay their rent. Lena worked full time and the family still lived in the same house. "With the same old bathrooms that were here when we bought it," Lena once said, annoyed. "He'll use something till it can't be used no more."

Aside from the gold nameplate that Jet wore around his neck, his only outward indulgence seemed to be a few gadgets: an iPad and video camera, and in place of the diamond-studded Rolex, a bulky watch phone that he often labored over with a stylus.

These toys, along with Hester's pension (the amount of which was often debated in town), were enough to inflate his mystique and incite wonder and misconception. "You know Jet," his assistants would sometimes say to punctuate a conversation. "He don't gotta work."

"The man's a millionaire," another once said. "Yet he still chooses to come home and help these kids."

But the real reason Jessie returned to the Glades after retiring was not "to give back to the youth of his hometown," as Coach Knabb told the Friday-night crowd on homecoming. Not yet, anyway. All of that would come later. What brought him home was the fear of losing his family.

In the early nineties, while he was still playing for the Colts, his mother had been shot. One of her boyfriends had pulled a gun on another man. The gun went off and the bullet struck Zara's leg, putting her in the hospital. There were other issues with Zara that Hester kept private. And long before these incidents, Jessie's sister Agnes began struggling with the addiction that would eventually lead to her death.

A thousand miles away in Indy, Jessie felt powerless. In addition to his mother and Agnes, both Anthony and Cora still required assistance. It was becoming too much for Roger and their grandmother to handle. The two were calling more and more, asking Jessie to come home.

"I thought I'd best get a little closer in case something happened," he said. "I felt like I carried weight with the family and I was in a better position to hold things down."

So he came back and bought the house in Wellington, far enough away from Belle Glade where Lena wouldn't feel so "countrified." And for years it was where Jessie would return each evening after days back home, deflecting the same dark forces that would later come against him as a coach.

CHAPTER

11

Leaving home was on KB's mind. Not just leaving, but the whole buildup to the great exit, when he would stand on Glades Central's auditorium stage on Signing Day and bestow on the university of his choice the gift of his talents.

Whereas Hester had gone into hiding during his recruitment, Benjamin relished the courting, devouring the bait of praise and promise that the recruiters left in trails toward their locker rooms.

After KB's junior season, there had been a rush to secure an early commitment. Alabama head coach Nick Saban had personally visited Benjamin at Glades Central just months after the Crimson Tide had won the national championship. The coach had seen KB's highlights and told him he had the build and style of Julio Jones, the Tide's standout receiver.

"He was down-to-earth," Benjamin said of Saban, whom *Forbes* once called "The Most Powerful Coach in Sports." "I didn't really know who he was."

But by senior year, Benjamin had narrowed his choice down to the University of Florida and Florida State. Both programs had already hosted him at summer camps and tournaments and each felt it had a shot. Following September 1, the date by which NCAA rules allowed coaches to begin personally contacting players by phone (one call per week until season's end) and visiting practice (only to watch, never to speak), both programs assigned their receivers coach the daily task of winning his favor.

For the Seminoles it was Lawrence Dawsey, the former FSU wide receiver who'd played seven years in the league, mainly with Tampa Bay. During the Raiders' homecoming victory over Boca Raton, in which Benjamin had three catches for over seventy yards and a touchdown, Dawsey stood tall by the Glades Central end zone in a pair of pressed jeans and cowboy boots.

"This place, they got speed like nowhere else," he said. "Every year you can find a receiver, DB, or running back. It's just unreal. These boys can run."

Dawsey had extra help on the ground from Mike Morris, another former Seminole. Back in 1990, Morris was one of the top ten offensive guards in the nation until a broken foot ended his playing career. He'd grown up in the Liberty City neighborhood of Miami, site of devastating race riots in the late sixties and early eighties that left it one of the poorest and most violent sections of town. So tough, Morris would brag, "it makes Belle Glade look like Candyland."

And like Belle Glade, Liberty City produced phenomenal athletes, so many that the Miami Hurricanes built their championship football program in the 1980s from players recruited primarily from that area.

Morris went into law enforcement after college and was now a lieutenant with the Palm Beach County Sheriff's Office. His turf was Belle Glade, and all over town the mucksteppers knew him as Big Mike. He'd put on weight from his playing days, and even then he'd struggled to keep himself under three hundred pounds. In a town where many felt under constant siege by the law, Big Mike could be trusted. If you wanted to report something in confidence, you called Mike. If your boyfriend was locked up and you needed information, you called Mike.

His pickup was a constant fixture in the quarter, where he'd crawl with the windows open so people could approach and present their case. Often he'd stop outside the boardinghouses and ask if there were any kids inside, then pull out backpacks filled with school supplies. At the Popeye's Chicken on Main Street, not even the mayor was given such a rousing welcome.

Still wistful about his college days, Mike remained a fervent booster for Florida State. He and his wife, Melanie Bolden, one of the vice-principals at Glades Central, took handfuls of students each year to FSU and other colleges for motivational tours, helped them fill out admissions and scholarship applications, and volunteered as mentors. Kelvin Benjamin had been one of the kids they'd adopted, and now Mike was determined to use his leverage to deliver him to the Seminoles.

For the University of Florida, it was Zach Azzanni, a young and tenacious receivers coach who channeled the polished intensity of his boss, Urban Meyer. The Florida head coach had first hired Azzanni as a graduate assistant a decade earlier at Bowling Green. Now back with Meyer after three seasons at Central Michigan, "Coach Z," as he was known to players, already carried an aura of Gator dynasty.

The first time Azzanni actually saw KB up close was at basketball practice during Benjamin's sophomore year. Azzanni was visiting on behalf of CMU when one of the football coaches steered him toward the gym and said, "You gotta watch this kid run around." Benjamin didn't need pointing out, with his long arms, loose hips, and powerful legs. He was the biggest guy on the court, playing like a slippery point guard.

It took Azzanni all of two minutes to imagine what kind of damage KB could do to a secondary. He also realized Benjamin could be the biggest recruit of his career. By the next season Azzanni was recruiting for the Gators and held the power to make it happen. He started e-mailing and called when he was allowed to call. Over time, he got to know Chris, Frank, and Tan and started building a relationship.

"With a kid like that, you have to be on top of it daily," Azzanni said. "There were so many people in his ear. His mind could be swayed every single day. I never took a break recruiting him."

During the summer after his junior year, KB attended a football camp in Gainesville, where he outshone some of the best recruits in the nation. For being so raw, Azzanni said, "he had a savvy for the game. He had a knack for getting himself open. Our guys were just in awe of what he could do. I don't think even KB knew how much he could do."

That kind of raw naïveté helped explain why KB, whenever discussing his own recruitment, did so without the slightest trace of vanity. On the field, he rarely boasted. Rather, one got a sense that Benjamin was as genuinely astonished by his newfound gifts as were the coaches pursuing him.

"Coach Z called me last night," KB said one day at practice. "Said I'd be a threat on their team and get them to the national championship. Said I'm not like a regular receiver with the height and speed I got. It's not all hype. I know it's true."

• • •

DAWSEY'S BOSS, JIMBO FISHER, had been calling Benjamin since the Raiders' game in Dallas, joking that KB should swing up to Norman, Oklahoma, where the Seminoles were playing the Sooners, to score a couple of touchdowns.

"Coach Jimbo tells me I got Randy Moss syndrome. That's how he describes my style," he said.

It wasn't just Fisher and his assistants who made the comparison, but Randy Moss himself. At the annual Heath Evans Foundation 7 on 7 Championship held that summer in West Palm Beach, Moss appeared on the sideline in a golf cart and followed the team through several matches.

After the competition was finished, KB described how the All-Pro wide receiver approached him.

"You look good out there," Moss told him. "In fact, I look at you and see myself when I was younger."

"That's crazy," answered Benjamin, of all things to say.

"I don't get nervous around celebrities," he added. "Randy Moss is my size. In fact, I'm probably a little bigger." (Which was true: KB had Moss beat by two inches and twenty pounds.)

On the Saturday after the Raiders' homecoming victory, Benjamin traveled to Gainesville for the Gators' game against LSU. The school had invited dozens of potential prospects from around the state to mingle with players on the sidelines, talk with coaches, and see the facilities. But after the game, which the Gators lost, it was KB whom Coach Z tapped on the shoulder and ushered into the locker room to meet the head coach. On Monday, Benjamin could hardly contain his excitement as he recounted the exchange.

"Coach Meyer seen me and said, 'What's up, freak?' He always calls me that. He calls me that because the way I'm built, you see. He aint never seen no one my size who can run so fast. And because I got a long wing-span and stuff like that. And because I'm crazy on the field and be catching balls like crazy and stuff like that. He says they don't have that big target, *that first-round NFL draft pick*, on the team right now. That's why they been losing."

A few days earlier he'd expressed concern that the UF offense, now without Tebow, was having trouble executing in the red zone. On his list of pros and cons, it was one of the biggest strikes against the Gators.

"But I been thinking about that lately," he said, reconsidering. "And you know, they don't have me yet. I'm not on that team."

He paused to tie his cleats, then added, "Anywhere I go I'm gonna get play."

Didn't it depend on the program? he was asked.

"Not really," he said. "Anywhere."

• • •

ANYWHERE WAS EXACTLY where Mario hoped to end up. His great exit had not revealed itself. When he was a junior, Hampton University had pursued Mario as a linebacker. Coach Stephen Field, the team's recruiting coordinator, had recently called Mario again and reaffirmed their interest.

Among the coaches in the Glades, the small historically black college in Hampton, Virginia, had a reputation as a kind of bottom feeder—albeit a worthy one—that snatched up muck players who'd been kicked out of bigger programs for either bad grades or trouble.

It was where Pahokee's Nu'Keese Richardson had landed the previous year after getting booted from Tennessee. The wide receiver had caused so such commotion when he'd spurned the Gators and 'Canes and signed with Lane Kiffin's Volunteers that photographers used to follow him around the Walmart in Knoxville. But a week after scoring his first touchdown as a freshman, he was arrested for armed robbery outside a Pilot convenience store. Kiffin banished him from the team, and after getting three years' probation, Richardson was seen at Hampton's spring practice.

And just months earlier, former Raider running back Antwon Chisholm was about to begin his freshman season at Marshall University when he was arrested for first-degree robbery in Huntington, West Virginia. According to police, he and several teammates allegedly robbed a pizza deliveryman outside their dorm. Marshall immediately revoked his football scholarship. Days after posting bail, Chisholm was also on Hampton's rotation. "And without learning a damn thing," Hester said.

Two former Glades Central coaches were now at Hampton, including Willie Snead, the head coach who'd won the 2006 title, ensuring that the pipeline from the Glades to Virginia would remain steady. After Coach Field's phone call, Mario was ebullient and relieved, even adding HAMPTON PLAYMAKER #1 as his text-message signature. But after six weeks he'd received only one other phone call. Still, it was enough to keep his hopes alive. "They know I got a positive mind-set," he said. His signature now read: I'M THA MAN IN MY CITY.

Marshall University was another school that had established a recent presence in the Glades, hoping to tap its talents for years to come—and, if at all possible, to lure KB to the program that had produced his NFL idol, Randy Moss. Marshall's weapon in that campaign was JaJuan Seider, the son of Glades Central's former athletic director and older brother of Jyron, the slain Raider linebacker.

JaJuan was the handsome, easygoing quarterback for the storied 1994 Raider team that went on to produce many NFL players, including Fred Taylor and Reidel Anthony, both first-round draft picks. Along with Ocala's Daunte Culpepper and Shaun King in St. Petersburg, Seider was part of a rising group of young black quarterbacks in Florida that were being heavily recruited by colleges nationwide.

With offers from Miami, Tulane, Clemson, and Notre Dame, he eventually chose West Virginia. But after playing under the shadow of Marc Bulger for three long years, Seider transferred to Florida A&M, where he made up for his college career in one season, passing for 2,512 yards and twenty-seven touchdowns and earning an All-American honor.

The San Diego Chargers selected him in the sixth round in the 2000 draft. One night after training camp, while having a late dinner with fellow quarterback Jim Harbaugh, Seider received word that his little brother had just been murdered in Belle Glade. With his family devastated and mourning at home, JaJuan spent the season in a fog of grief and depression. The Chargers released him the following year.

"I could never get back into it," he said. "It was just too much to deal with. I just had to be with my family."

JaJuan was now the running backs coach for the Marshall Thundering Herd, and one of his official duties was recruiting in the muck. To him it was clear that signing KB was a long shot, especially with the Gators and Seminoles fighting for his attention. So JaJuan had turned his focus on other players, particularly Robert Way and Davonte, the latter of whom also happened to be his cousin. The Herd had made offers to both players, and JaJuan was setting up their official campus visit for later that season.

When JaJuan was in town, he was usually joined on the sidelines by his old friend and teammate Roosevelt Blackmon, who now worked as Glades Central's assistant athletic director. Watching the adulation and attention heaped on young recruits must have left a grin on Blackmon's face. For if there was ever a story to inspire a fat, struggling quarterback or a half-pint lineman, it was the story of Roosevelt Blackmon.

Blackmon's nickname growing up was Tadpole, and his size was true to label. When he'd tried out for the mighty Raiders as a freshman, the coach had looked down at the scrawny, ninety-five-pound weakling and shaken his head. The best they could do for him was water boy. He'd hauled water his sophomore year, too, the only role he could manage on a team stacked with talent.

By senior year he'd added sixty pounds and made starting receiver, but he was no glimmer in any recruiter's eye. Roosevelt Blackmon was not among the names in the basket of faxes and correspondence. So he made it happen himself.

One of his class assignments that fall was to write to a college and request an admissions application. Blackmon sent letters to Florida and Miami, listing his home address as the Raider football office. The next week, the letters started appearing in the basket, never mind what was inside.

"Tadpole, the Gators want *you?*" someone asked.

"Mmm-hmm."

Blackmon graduated without a single offer, yet still determined to play football. An attempt at being a student at Bethune-Cookman University in Daytona Beach failed, so he returned to Belle Glade and found work where he could, scrubbing tires at A&D Used Cars. And whenever someone died, he dug their grave at the cemetery.

But his dreams were very much alive.

"A setback is a setup for a comeback," he would tell himself, hoisting his shovel.

One of his teammates had made the squad at Morris Brown, a Division II black college in Atlanta, and he felt Blackmon might also have a shot. But when Blackmon arrived and enrolled at school, he was informed the football team had been placed on probation and was not giving scholarships. Feeling sorry for him, the coaches did what they could. They put him on the meal plan and made him the water boy. Without financial assistance, Blackmon had to take a job working night shifts at Winn-Dixie, stocking shelves. During holidays, he'd drive home in a beat-up Chevy Spectrum that barely pushed sixty.

At Morris Brown, while Blackmon was washing uniforms and lugging water bottles, he was also working out with the team—tossing footballs, learning plays, talking smack. His chance to prove himself finally came the following year. Off probation, the Wolverines extended to Blackmon a scholarship as a defensive back.

In his first game against Clark Atlanta, he had four tackles and two interceptions. For the rest of the season, Tadpole was like a caged man set free. By his junior year, he was a two-time All-American. His next season, he was playing in the Senior Bowl and was roommates with Fred Taylor, by then a stud Gator running back whom he'd once kept hydrated.

Taylor was a shoo-in for the NFL, and his other former teammate Reidel Anthony had gone the previous year. Blackmon never mentioned that as a water boy at Morris Brown, he would stare into the glass trophy case and ruminate over the small handful of players who'd made it to the league. Standing there, he would address the reflection staring back, the gravedigger and shine boy muckstepper without a scholarship or a hundred dollars in the bank: "I'll be the next man," he'd say.

An invitation to Pro Day at Georgia Tech—where a scout for Detroit had gushed over his 4.38 forty—had reinforced this conviction. Blackmon was so confident he'd be picked in the first three rounds, he'd driven home to Belle Glade in April for the draft, bought a trunkload of food and champagne, and invited all his friends and family to celebrate his ascent into glory. But after two days of watching the television, after everyone had eaten his food and gone home, his phone still had not rung.

He was in church that Sunday, having just given his offering, when his uncle rushed in and said the Green Bay Packers just called.

"Yall hear that?" the preacher announced. "Tadpole pays his tithes and gets called by the NFL."

He played three years in the league, with Brett Favre's Packers and then the Cincinnati Bengals, who eventually released him. In 2000, he returned home to Belle Glade and pursued another dream of working in the school.

"People say, 'Oh, you didn't make it,'" said Blackmon. "But I *did* make it. And I was happy to come back and say it doesn't matter where you go to college. No matter where you're at, if you want it bad enough, they will find you."

CHAPTER

12

After coming off two easy victories, the Raiders entered week seven feeling giddy. It was mid-October. The stifling muck air was beginning to thin and give way to the cool winds of autumn. And the suspense over *where* KB would mark his place in history was the talk of Raider nation, from under the tarp at Ray King's barbershop to the booths of Dixie Fried Chicken.

With the Raiders having pummeled two mediocre teams and the playoffs just weeks away, it seemed the last thing people were discussing anymore was whether KB and the Raiders were actually any good. Could the cocky, undefeated Raiders learn to embrace the little things and play to their potential, or had the near beating they'd taken in week three not taught them anything at all?

Week seven took the Raiders to Fort Lauderdale to face the Dillard Panthers. The team carried a lackluster 3–3 record, but battled in a tough division, a wild-card squad capable of giving the Raiders another painless stat game, or sneaking up as American Heritage had done and putting them on their backs.

The Panthers' number-one weapon, Wayne Lyons, a six-foot safety who had offers from Notre Dame, Nebraska, and UCLA, had recently torn a ligament in his knee and was out for the regular season. His absence in the secondary would help the Raider passing game, but Hester expected Dillard to take it right back on the ground. The Panthers did quick counts and almost always ran the ball. Their running back, Otis Wright, had legs like an ox and was capable of hanging a hundred yards rushing on you before you could blink.

After practice on Thursday, Hester gathered his team in the twilight and attempted to light their fire.

"Guys, we got a scenario where we goin into somebody's house tryin to take their baby. That's the scenario this time. We tryin to take *their* baby. They see us comin. They know we out there."

"We the dingo," someone said.

"That's right, we the dingo. And because they know we out there, guess what we need to be prepared for? Traps. Be prepared for the ambush."

He instructed each boy again to go home and visualize the field in his sleep, to see every snap, correct each mistake, and rise having already played the game. But in his reading of the oracle, perhaps Hester saw something else.

"This is the chapter of the book where it gets interesting," he told them. "Now you gonna see what all the main characters fixin to do. Chapter seven tomorrow, guys. This is where it all unfolds."

• • •

ON GAME DAY, the ensemble cast of "Chapter Seven: Dillard" played mostly to type. Half the team were late for walk-throughs and film, causing

Hester to get so angry he locked dozens of them outside to languish in the sun. Once again, there was horseplay when coaches asked for focus and rolled eyes over the boring parade of "tradition."

Before the game, Coach Fat, the two-time champion, attempted to rally the boys by pointing out that Dillard had scheduled the mighty Raiders as their homecoming game—a bitch-slap back in his day.

"Everybody knows you schedule homecoming against a team you can beat," he said, trying to boil their blood. "We would have *never* stood for that kind of shit when I was playing. That's a fuckin disrespect to this program. Yall should be insulted."

But Coach Fat was turned to the wrong page; this was no Legion of Doom. A voice rose from the back of the room: *"Maaan,"* it said, "we aint into that stuff."

The voice was KB's. By now, the rah-rah speeches of old high-school heroes bored him to tears. The old slights and burden of tradition sparked no fire within his guts. He'd even said one time, "These old guys take this stuff way too seriously. I'm just tryin to have fun." And when KB spoke, the team listened.

Benjamin led the ensemble cast onto the field of Dillard's Otis Gray Jr. Memorial Stadium, strutting through their warm-ups. And when the Dillard Panthers appeared, KB stood at midfield and let them know the dingo was at their door, shouting, *"We comin for you, baby! We comin!"*

The dingo came out snapping and drew first blood. Benjamin took the kickoff sixty-seven yards, stiff-arming defenders into the dirt. Mario then found KB on a twenty-yard corner route over two Panthers and put the Raiders on the one-yard line. Page punched it into the end zone.

"That's right, bwah! Raiders comin!"

But the boys had not played the game in their dreams the night before. For if they had, they would have seen the traps laid everywhere. The ambushes at every snap. Confusing, because in that dream, the Dillard Panthers were nowhere in sight. The big bad dingo kept hanging himself, twisting the chains tighter and tighter.

(Below) Raider head coach Jessie Hester, "Jet."

Senior wide receiver Kelvin Benjamin, "KB."

Senior quarterback Jamarious Rowley, "Mario."

(Below) Senior wide receiver Davonte Allen.

Jonteria Williams with her parents, Theresa and John.

Jonteria Williams in her bedroom.

(*Below*) Junior linebacker Jatavis Brown, "Jaja."

(*Below*) Junior linebacker and running back Dominique Gibson, "Boobie."

Coach Hester and the Raiders.

(Below) Sophomore running back Aaron Baker.

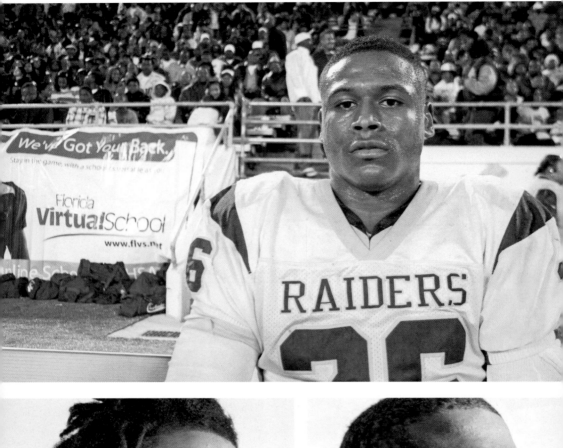

Senior defensive end Robert Way.   Junior offensive lineman Tavious Bridges, "Gator."

(Below) Assistant coach Randy Williams.

(Below) Defensive line coach Sherman Adams.

(Below) Greg Moreland, "Coach Q."

Assistant head coach Sam King.

Frank Williams (Gibson's father) among the fans at Effie C. Grear Field.

(Below) Sugarcane fires near Glades Central's Effie C. Grear Field. The thick smoke from the annual harvest is an integral part of football season in the Glades.

One of the boardinghouses in Belle Glade's notorious migrant quarter, home to the town's poorest residents. Many of the buildings are condemned and feature shared toilets and showers.

The greeting wall at Effie C. Grear Field lists past championships and players who have gone pro.

After the Raiders stopped the Panther offense and forced them to punt, Benjamin stood in the backfield for the return. But instead of another thrilling run, the ball bounced off his fingers and wobbled beneath his legs. A Dillard lineman pushed him aside and smothered it on the ten. Two plays later, Otis Wright broke loose into the end zone for the score. The extra point attempt was no good.

Raiders 7, Dillard 6.

The Raiders ended up turning the ball over again on a botched fourth-down attempt, placing it right back into the hands of the unstoppable Wright. For if anyone had played the game in his mind the previous night, it was him. Wright exploited every block, every missed tackle. The only thing the Raiders didn't give him was a welcome mat. Wright would have thirty carries by the end of the night. Here he led the Panthers on a forty-yard drive to set up the first of two touchdown passes from quarterback Ernest Merritt to William Dukes. The Panthers easily executed the two-point conversion.

Raiders 7, Dillard 14.

The next drive, Mario came storming back, but on unsteady legs. He'd suffered a deep-thigh bruise in the Raiders' homecoming victory over Boca Raton that had left him unable to run. The doctor had given him more pain pills and told him to rest. But Davis, the Raider second-string quarterback, had been suspended that week, leaving only Jems Richemond, who had little experience. Before the game, Mario had lied and said he felt fine. After all, he thought, the leg couldn't hurt any worse than a torn shoulder.

As if sniffing his wounds, the Dillard line kept him running all night. On the second play of the Raiders' next drive, the offensive line disintegrated and left Mario exposed. He scrambled out of the pocket, but couldn't find speed. He dashed toward the sideline in a mad hobble and saw Davonte standing alone on the twenty. The throw was perfect. Davonte juked a defender, made him miss, and trotted into the end zone.

But the snap on the extra point attempt was too high, forcing Mario to throw it away. The Raiders would not convert on another extra point for the rest of the evening.

Raiders 13, Dillard 14.

Glades Central quickly got the ball back, but went nowhere. Once again, the Dillard defenders pushed aside linemen Travis Salter and Corey Graham as if they were sidewalk traffic, chasing Mario ten yards into the backfield and pile-driving him into the grass.

On fourth down and fifteen, Hester called a time-out and implored the quarterback to look across the middle. "Check down," he told him. The underneath receivers running "hot routes" across the middle had consistently been open, he said.

Most of Hester's route sequences had a built-in hot route. Two outside receivers would run the straight post, usually deep, while the others would stay shallow for the underneath option—usually a dig route to the outside or a crossing route over the middle. The hot routes were designed for emergencies, to dump the ball quickly in danger and pick up yardage. But because of Mario's height, he'd always feared the middle.

"I can't see it," the quarterback would say.

"Just look for the defender," Hester would tell him. "If you can see the defender, the middle is yours. The receiver will be there. Just trust in yourself."

But Mario couldn't find the confidence. He consistently favored the outside, often leaving receivers wide open.

"*Check down,*" the coach told him again.

Oliver and Jaime were the hot reads across the middle, and just as Hester had said, both ran completely open. But Mario panicked and rushed the pass. He overthrew Oliver and the Raiders lost the ball again. Capitalizing on yet another turnover, Wright chipped his way downfield and set up another Merritt and Duke touchdown pass.

Everyone on the Raiders was having a bad game. It was as if a sickness had ridden in on the moist ocean air and seized even the strongest, most competent players. Boobie was next to fumble, on the Raider thirty-eight.

As if to make amends, Boobie and Jaja buttoned up the Panthers' next drive and forced the punt. But on the Raiders' first play, Page bobbled the ball on the handoff and fumbled. The Panthers took over on the ten. Within seconds, the score was 28–13.

As the defense skulked toward the sidelines, Mario paced up and down the bench. *"We straight! We straight!"* he assured his teammates, who stared ahead in disbelief, looking gray.

The quarterback rallied late in the second quarter, launching a perfect eighty-yard pass to Davonte, who was waiting in the end zone as if he were born there. But the touchdown was called back for an ineligible man downfield, one of the many Raider penalties on the night. Three plays later, Mario launched it again, this time finding KB on the twenty. The entire sideline shrieked as the Big Ticket bobbled the ball once again but managed to hold on for the score. The attempt at a two-point conversion was a dud. The Bad News Bears were finally saved when the whistle blew for the half.

As the Panthers commenced their homecoming ceremony, leading undefeated Glades Central 28–19, the Raider coaches huddled for a plan:

"They leavin the middle open and blitzing that middle linebacker late," said Coach Andrew Mann.

"On the outside, they playing five to seven yards off," said Coach Bruce Hytower. "If you go with a two- to three-receiver set and run your bubble screen, you'll kill 'em all day long."

"I know you don't wanna do it," said Coach Fat. "But you gotta change the snap count. No huddle and speed the tempo."

"If Mario just takes his time," said Coach Hall, "them receivers are all open."

The coaches then turned to Hester, whose mind had settled on a simpler approach. They'll just have to scrap it out, he said. He gathered the team at the far end of the field.

"As you guys can well see," he said, "we gave these people twenty-eight dang points. Fumbles, fumbles, fumbles. And you guys understand this started early today with you cats coming in late. All the cats I locked outside, those are the cats messing up. When we gonna get it right, guys? When we gonna be responsible? Is it so hard to be on time? Good thing is we have two more quarters to play. You cats settle down. All this moping is ugly, man. We playin completely *stupid*. It's an easy fix, guys. O-line, I better not see my quarterback running around. I don't care if they bring twenty people. Stop being lazy. Move your feet. Make it your job. This half, aint *nobody* gone touch your quarterback. It's simple, guys: they don't score no more. *No more.*"

"It's time to talk about identity," said Fat. "Now's the time to find out who yall really are. Yall can put your head down like last year in the state game, or yall can rise up like Raiders. What yall gonna do?"

"No more!" someone shouted.

"Yeah, no more!"

But the Raiders could not dig themselves out. On their first possession of the second half, the Panthers tipped Mario's pass for an interception. The Raider fans in the crowd booed and hissed, except for a lone voice of support—Aunt Gail, who screamed over the rancorous din until the veins bulged in her neck.

"Mario, honey, don't you get frustrated!"

As if things couldn't get any worse, KB fumbled the ball again. On another punt return, he caught the ball on the Raider forty-three and quickly found himself in traffic. As he spun out of a tackle, he left the ball unprotected at his side, waving it around like a loaf of bread. Then he lost it. The ball flew out of his fingers and onto the snarled clay field and was immediately recovered by a blue Panther jersey.

Dillard kept the ball another eleven plays, with Wright hammering the Raider line and driving them across the plain. Perched at the five-yard line, Merritt once again handed off to Wright, who slipped into the end zone.

The coaches lost their minds on the sideline. *"Hit that motherfucker in the face mask!"* Randy shouted at the line. *"Buckle that bitch's knees!"*

The Glades Central fans fell silent along with the Raider bench, who stared down at their feet, unwilling to look. The sight caused Mario to well with fury. He marched up and down with his fists clenched, screaming into their downcast faces, *"Get up! Get your ass up!"*

Then, once again, he came back. In the fourth quarter, Mario hit Oliver for two quick strikes up the left side. When his OL dissolved around him, the quarterback took off running on his bad legs for twenty yards and the first down. The next play, he found Oliver in the end zone. But the pass to Oliver again for the two-point conversion was too high, leaving the score 35–25.

With Glades Central now within striking distance, the quarterback went into the crowd. He climbed the chain-link fence separating the track and waved the fans to their feet and into a thunderous chant of *DEFENSE!*

On the field, the Panthers mercilessly chewed the clock, going for the kill. With five minutes left, Robert Way managed to bat the ball away and recover the fumble on the Panther forty-five.

On their last chance at victory, the Raiders mounted a drive.

"We goin Rocket Right, 989," Hester yelled.

But the Panthers blitzed with everything and plastered Mario to the clay. They knocked him down the following play, but not before he turned it loose, a high floater to Davonte at the ten. On the next snap, he found Oliver, who trotted in for the touchdown.

But this time for the Raiders, it was too late. The two-point conversion attempt was batted down and the clock hit zero.

Dillard won, 35–31.

"Lose with grace!" Hester yelled. "Do not throw your helmets."

It was Hester's first regular-season loss in a three-year career as a head coach, an occasion he let slip past without ceremony. Instead, he addressed his weary team at the end zone.

"Guys, nothing needs to be said. When you get home, look yourself in the mirror. Ask yourself, 'Did I do what my coach asked me to do?' This is a football game that you lost. The sun's gonna rise tomorrow. But you lost. So what are you gonna do about that?" He looked at Salter, his offensive lineman.

"Salt, can we beat Cocoa? Today?"

Salt shook his head. "Nah."

"Then what are you gonna do to make yourselves better? The question is, guys, what is our ultimate goal?"

"To win state," said Mario.

"Huh?"

"*TO WIN STATE!*" the Raiders shouted.

"Don't forget that," the coach said. "This is where we start being a team. Today."

CHAPTER

Dear Kelvin,

Play hard this weekend at Dillard. Keep
in mind, talent wins games but teamwork
and intelligence win championships.

—fax from University of Arkansas head coach
Bobby Petrino

I f the Glades Central Raiders needed one thing to correct their path
to meet Cocoa, it was to lose to a 3–3 team like Dillard. As Hester
saw it, losing was a release. Gone was the boyish bravado and the
weight of a national ranking that had hung around their necks. Only humility remained, the greatest teaching aid of all.

If ever a player should be humbled, it was Benjamin. Despite eighty-
eight yards and a touchdown, he'd fumbled twice and given up fourteen
points. When the coaching staff met afterward to review film, they grew

even more exasperated watching the rest of his game: not blocking, not running hard to meet plays, not lining up correctly. The little things.

"He say anything about those fumbles?" Coach Randy asked.

Hester shook his head. "That boy don't own up to nothin."

As Hester knew too well, everyone had bad games. But with KB, the performance against Dillard seemed to say everything about his season, his attitude toward work and discipline, and the great disappointment they all feared he would become. The only positive thing to come from it, said Randy, was knowing that KB would soon be gone.

Because Benjamin had repeated two grades in school, he'd reached the maximum age allowed for high school athletics. The Florida High School Athletic Association rules forbade students older than nineteen years and nine months to compete in organized sports, a limit KB would reach in two weeks. Which meant Glades Central's next game against Boynton Beach would be Benjamin's last as a Raider. His teammates would have to carry on without him.

Publicly, coaches reacted as expected when losing a superstar.

"No question about it, that's a big loss, the kind of talent he brings to the team," Hester told a reporter after the Dillard game.

On paper, that was true. Benjamin remained the second-highest scorer on the team behind Jaime. His mannish physique and natural athleticism were enough to guarantee at least one highlight each Friday night. And those moments could be rapturous to witness. But in the locker room and on the practice field, coaches were now seeing KB as little more than dead-weight, a poison in the well.

As team captain, his open refusals to run hard and do push-ups, his sleeping during film, his blasé indifference, were what coaches saw as a key contributor to the team's internal problems. The behavior had already in-fected Jaime. Watching the Dillard film, Jaime would pop off the line, then start walking once the ball went elsewhere, refusing to block. When Mario passed him over again, he appeared to pitch a full-on tantrum.

"KB's just a distraction at this point," said Coach Randy. "We already got too many prima donnas on this team. But we gonna show everybody that we don't need them to win.

"Listen, Randy Moss is the best damn receiver in the game of football, and the Vikings just told Randy Moss to go fuck himself. You're never indispensable."

"KB's certainly not a game changer this year," said Coach JD. "Defenses aren't even changing their game plans because of him. I think we'll do better without him."

No one was more disappointed by KB's performance than Hester, who, like any head coach, had allowed himself to dream about the juggernaut they could've built with such a phenomenal talent. There were even times during the season when Hester considered kicking Benjamin off the team but changed his mind.

"You have to give a guy a choice to want it or not," Hester said. "If you tell him to leave and go, he'll say that people didn't care. Whatever happens, the only thing KB can ever say is that he let his team down. He can never say we gave up on him.

"Some kids can't handle success. The more success he had, the less he wanted to work. You start believing what you read. He knew that physically in high school he didn't have to work. And he didn't."

But the reality was that KB had never asked for the captain's role, something that tended to get overlooked in the mania of a title-seeking season. Benjamin was nearly twenty years old and playing on a team of mostly sixteen- and seventeen-year-old boys. He was in a steady relationship with an older woman—Mika Lemene, a former Raider cheerleader who was twenty-two and worked a full-time job at the Boys and Girls Club. KB had spent more than a year in jail and grown up without a father, and his mother had lived on the fringes of poverty and trouble for so long that each day she woke up in her apartment on the edge of the canefield and rang his phone was a small miracle.

Benjamin respected Hester and loved being a Raider. ("I didn't know anything when I first came here," he once said. "He taught me everything.") But unlike Mario, he had nothing to prove with the maroon and gold. For KB, the Raiders were merely a means to an end. His future was locked, and his mind was miles ahead.

• • •

IF ANYTHING, HESTER was hoping that Benjamin's exit would make room for a true leader to fill the vacuum, and for other kids to find their confidence to shine.

"A lot of these guys have been too intimidated to step up with KB around," he said. "After he's gone, we'll see who the true players are."

The morning after the defeat, the coach had gone out for an early look. Each Saturday following a game, the team was urged to attend a nine thirty prayer breakfast at the Baptist church, hosted by Pastor Dez, one that also drew many players from the Glades Day squad. Before leaving Dillard on Friday, Hester had made attendance mandatory, using it as a gauge to see "who had the guts to face themselves and their teammates" after such an embarrassment. When Hester arrived at the church that morning, he saw Mario, Davonte, Oliver, and about twelve others. He did not see KB or Jaime.

As the players sat down to plates of scrambled eggs, bacon, and cheese grits, Pastor Dez preached on the deception of beauty. He told of being a boy in Jamaica and loving the flavor of mangoes. One year he found a tree near his home and devoured the low-hanging fruit. Thinking he'd stripped the tree clean, he noticed another one. It was red-ripe and succulent to the eye, the most delicious-looking mango he'd ever seen. But it hung on the highest branch, making it irresistible. So Dez started climbing, battling ants and slippery limbs, until he finally reached the mango and held it in his grasp. But when he bit into its flesh, he found that it was full of worms.

The same message could be gleaned, he said, from one of the parables Jesus told about the sowers of wheat. In the parable, which appears in the book of Matthew, enemies have entered a field of good stout grain and sown it with seeds of darnel, a weed resembling wheat.

"Looking at this field from afar," Dez explained, "some stalks are broad and upright, looking tall and mighty, while others are leaning toward the ground. But walk into that field and you'll discover the tall plants are only barren weeds, while the smaller, more humble stalks are full and heavy with fruit."

If anyone in the room fit that description, it was Davonte.

His transition across town from the small private Glades Day School to Glades Central had been much greater than the single mile it covered. The schools were different in almost every way. Glades Day was mostly white and more affluent, with yearly tuition for the upper school at $7,975. Many of the teachers were Glades natives whose families had lived there for generations. With an enrollment of 328 students across the twenty-two-acre campus, classes were smaller and academic performance was higher.

But when it came to football, the only difference was the alternate universe that seemed to separate the two. Just like the Raiders, the Glades Day Gators had won six state championships, along with seventeen regional titles. Their Friday-night home games also drew hundreds, including many who still attended decades after sons and brothers had graduated. But unlike Glades Central, Glades Day had a spirited "touchdown club" that hosted rib-eye dinners each Tuesday night during the season and spread Gator pride by flag and farm truck, casting a visible shadow across the Raider nation.

Glades Day played in the tiny, single-A classification and had never met the crosstown Raiders on the field. There existed no fever-pitched rivalry as there did between Glades Central and Pahokee, who also played in a different division. It was as if the Belle Glade Rams and Lake Shore Bobcats had simply regrouped after the onus of history had passed.

Despite the differences, fans of both teams enjoyed each other's full support, especially during the postseason. In 2006, when the Raiders, Gators, *and* Blue Devils all won state championships—a phenomenon known as the "Muck City Sweep"—many joked that the confluence of power was just enough to usher Christ himself back to Earth.

"What fans of both schools have in common is they both roll," said Mike Diagostine, who calls the play-by-play for all three schools on WSWN Sugar 900. "Wherever Glades Day goes, the Gator faithful go, and wherever Glades Central goes, the Raider faithful go. And when they're both in the championships, both sides will come together and try to fill that Citrus Bowl. They're staying all weekend."

Glades Day started offering scholarships to local black students and athletes decades ago. And for years, that Muck City speed had given the Gators the edge over its prep-school competitors. The previous year, Davonte and his cousin Johntavis Brown were both starting receivers who could unzip the defense of a Jupiter Christian or a Zion Lutheran with relative ease. But the problem was that Glades Day rarely threw the ball, mainly on account of a steamrolling running back named Kelvin Taylor.

Kelvin was Fred Taylor's son. At age sixteen, he already bore a striking resemblance to his father, complete with heavy ink up and down both arms and a neck like a Sunday ham. Blessed with furious speed and power, Taylor was certainly the most phenomenal athlete ever to play at Glades Day, and arguably one of the best ever to spring from the muck. When the Gators took the field, few teams could stop him. During his freshman season, Taylor had averaged 185 yards per game and broken the state's single-season touchdown record with forty-nine. Now a sophomore, he was rapidly closing in on the state's all-time high-school rushing record of 8,804 yards, held by NFL Hall of Famer Emmitt Smith during his years at Escambia High.

Taylor regularly attended the Saturday-morning breakfasts. He was reserved and respectful around adults, and quietly answered questions with *sir* and *ma'am*. For instance:

So how was your game last night?

Three fifty.

Three hundred and fifty *yards*?

Yes sir.

With Taylor as their bull-necked Trojan horse, the Gators won the title in 2009, defeating Warner Christian in the Citrus Bowl the day before Glades Central dropped its game against Cocoa.

In that game, Davonte had two catches for fifty-eight yards. When the clock hit zero and the Gators had won, he ran onto the field and embraced his teammates, jumping up and down in a rare moment of public exuberance. Afterward, a runaway smile was spread across his face as he leaned down to accept the gold medal.

The Gators had ordered championship rings: a golden football with a crown of diamonds around a green emerald and the numeral 1 posted like a flag in the center of the stone. He'd worn the ring every day, loved the way it looked from different angles while he sat in church or in class. Its heaviness made him think of two-a-days in the August sun.

At night, he would place the ring beside the black King James Bible on the shelf in his room. It was his first real Bible, the one his grandmother Nora had given him when he was eight. Its pages were now marked with ink and its cover soft and weathered from a decade of service.

The ring and the memories of that day were keepsakes of a family that would always be bonded in time. But the smashmouth running Gators were no place for an aspiring receiver with dreams of college and beyond. So with a championship now under his wing, Davonte left Glades Day and the shadow of Taylor to go fly with the Raiders.

As Davonte discovered, the culture at Glades Central more closely mirrored the town: It was loud and brash and everything he was not. It was a place so insular that everyone seemed to share the same thousand Facebook friends—kids with wild and colorful monikers such as Bootz Lynch, Rivermonster Humphrey, LemonadeGame Tharpe, Badlegs Brown, and Interstate Frank. The first week Davonte arrived, his new teammates made fun of his khaki pants, which he wore in a normal fashion, around his waist. "Church boy got no swag," they teased. And when he returned several weeks later with his jeans sagging off his butt, his coaches sighed in defeat.

"They finally corrupted him," said one.

• • •

A PECKING ORDER was firmly in place on the Raider team that Davonte joined. The squad was already loaded with topflight receivers in KB and Jaime, and others who'd come up in the program. But among this corps of players whose egos tended to spiral into the heavens, Hester noticed that Davonte was one of the few to follow advice.

"He's the most teachable," said the coach. "And guys like that succeed. Davonte gets it."

A sore hip flexor had slowed him during the summer, and afterward he'd spent much of the season as a decoy for Benjamin and Jaime. There were three catches in Texas for fifty-six yards in the Raiders' rout against Denison. But the first time the game was on the line, such as it was against American Heritage—at home with a chance to score—he was wound too tight and choked.

Mario's first pass had sailed right through his fingers while he was running for the end zone. The second time, he simply ran the wrong route and missed the ball completely. "The pressure was on me, and I cracked," he said.

Hester gave the mistakes a pass. "Look, it happens to everybody," he said. Nothing was even mentioned during film the following Monday. But privately, Davonte's performance hounded him, so much that he folded inside himself. He spent the next week in deep prayer, seeking focus. He went into the Word, taking solace in a verse from Jeremiah assuring that those who trusted in the Lord would be like a tree planted by the river, whose leaves would flourish during drought and whose branches would remain full with fruit.

Two weeks later, in Clewiston, Davonte scored two touchdowns, and then another against Dillard—one of two catches for almost a hundred yards that kept the Raiders in the game until the end. His coming-out had encouraged his coaches. With KB's imminent departure, and Jaime's tendency to quit when he couldn't shine, they now began to see Davonte as the budding X factor in their quest to meet Cocoa.

"The rough edges are wearing away," said Hester, watching him one afternoon at practice. "The edge is appearing."

"But he aint *mean* yet," said Q.

"Yeah, but it'll come."

. . .

IN THE FIRST game after losing to Dillard, Davonte took the backseat to let KB go out in style. The farewell tribute to the Raider captain began on Thursday. To commemorate his last day of practice, the coaches treated the boys to a game of Bull in the Ring. Benjamin stood inside a circle of his teammates while the strongest of the squad charged him like a procession of rams. After a dozen tried their luck, the receiver was still on his feet.

On game day, the team wore eye blacks that read KB#3, and chanted his name like a war cry in the huddle. Then, beneath the primal light of a full, pregnant moon, the Raiders commenced their cathartic slaughtering of the Boynton Beach Tigers.

Every mistake of the previous week was purged as the Raiders racked up fifty-three easy points while holding the Tigers to just twenty-six total yards of offense. Benjamin had five catches for eighty yards. His final touchdown as a Glades Central Raider was a near-cinematic twenty-five-yard floater into the corner of the end zone that he brought down under double coverage.

Coach Z stood several feet away on the sideline. He applauded, shook his head, and hoped to God the next time the Big Ticket roped in another six, it would be with a green gator on his helmet.

"Dominance from beginning to end. That's what you wanna see," Hester told his boys after the beating. "Hat's off. That's a hell of a way to play."

But the win did not come without some pain. Just before halftime, running back Neville Brown and Mario were injured on the same play. First Neville went down screaming with a dislocated shoulder, which the Tiger trainer reset on the field with a sickening pop.

Mario went down as well, but before he could get to his feet, a Tiger linebacker speared him in the helmet just above the face mask, rattling his brain. Dazed and disoriented, the quarterback said nothing and remained in the game for six plays, even managing three completions. Finally he broke from the huddle and stumbled toward the sideline, weaving across the field like the town drunk. He braced himself against Hester, then staggered to the fenceline and stared into the crowd with blank, childish wonder. By the time the trainer reached him, Mario was slack-jawed and gazing up at the moon.

CHAPTER

14

On Monday after the game, a doctor took scans of Mario's brain and diagnosed him with a concussion. The quarterback was ordered to sit out for at least a week to recover. The second half of the game still remained blurry in his mind; he didn't remember wandering off after it was over and having to be guided back to the bus, or how he'd swayed like a bowling pin through an entire interview with a clearly alarmed *Post* reporter. For days after the hit, the sun burned his eyes and gave him headaches.

Monday's practice also found Neville Brown with a busted shoulder; Boobie's shoulder was sore and wrapped with a sling; Page had a quad contusion; and Kelvin Benjamin was gone. Luckily for Mario and the Raiders, the next Friday was off, allowing two full weeks to heal and come together as a team minus the figurehead star.

The game in two weeks against Suncoast would be the last of the regular season at Effie C. Grear Field. It was also Senior Night, when seniors from the entire maroon-and-gold machine—football, band, and cheerleading—got to honor their families before the fans and announce their future plans.

Jonteria Williams imagined the evening with both giddiness and trepidation. She felt excited to be recognized as head cheerleader, to be front and center under the lights instead of second fiddle to the football boys. Plus, she had good news to share: Florida Atlantic University had accepted her for admission in the fall. It was the only school to respond so far, and just in time. Jonteria was getting worried that Senior Night would come and find her empty-handed, with nothing to share but empty hopes: "Jonteria Williams . . . hopes to attend the college of her choice."

That's how Coach Dennis Knabb would say it on the PA system. It was the stock line they used for graduating cheerleaders who were too preoccupied with boys and looking pretty to bother with college. Out of the entire squad, only three ever made the honor roll. That included her best friend, Walkeria Carter, who was also in Ms. Canty's medical science academy and had been accepted to FAU. Walkeria was president of Twenty Pearls, while Jonteria was vice-president. Walkeria had also won Miss Glades Central.

"Walkeria's very outspoken," Jonteria said. "And everything she competes in, she wins. She's been winning ever since we've been in elementary school."

Theresa had been ecstatic when Jonteria got the news about FAU. It was the school she privately hoped Jonteria would choose in the end, just because it was so close to home. But there was still the University of Miami.

The application deadline for UM was January 1, still over a month away, and Jonteria refused to rush. When she hit Send, the formal request of Jonteria Williams to attend the school of her dreams would be nothing short of perfect.

So, in terms of Senior Night coming and not looking like a fool: check. But there was something else about the evening that left a queasiness in her stomach. Jonteria had asked her father, John Williams, to walk the field with her and Theresa. It would be the first time in her memory the three of them had stood together in Belle Glade in public since his release from prison—a five-minute game of pretend unhindered by the pangs of betrayal and bitterness.

"I'm just so happy he said yes," she said, sitting in her dark living room one Saturday after an eight-hour shift at Winn-Dixie. "Football has never been his thing. I think he's nervous."

Since Jonteria was only five when her father decided to involve himself in a robbery, the details of his going to prison were foggy in her mind. She just remembered him being gone. And her memory of him before that moment was merely a stark composite, constructed from her own limited recollections and the stories her mother told.

"I remember the gifts he would bring because he was always up in Georgia working," she said. "A gift you could remember. A balloon and a bike on my birthday, even though he just left the money for my mom. But we would take family trips. Once we went to Disney World in Orlando. And Boomers in Boca. That's an arcade.

"How did I see him? He was this person who could give me anything in the world. But after a while you start to notice it's not all about gifts and stuff. After a while he just wasn't there."

Jonteria had seen her father once in prison, right around the time her mother broke the news. John's old girlfriend Shirley, who also had a daughter with him, had taken the kids to the facility near Atlanta. The guards took them to a large empty room, as big as a gymnasium, where her father sat wearing a white jumpsuit. They formed a circle around his chair and John informed them that he'd been saved and wanted to become a preacher. He talked about Jesus the entire time, she remembered, then insisted they all pray. It was disorienting and confusing, and it wasn't until they were driving home to Florida that Jonteria realized she'd forgotten to ask her father what he'd even done and when he was coming home.

Seven years later, at a Christmas party at her house in Belle Glade, John walked through the door a free man. He'd recently been released from a halfway house in Georgia and had settled in with a new wife, whom he'd married while in prison. The seven years had turned Jonteria into a young woman; her father hardly recognized her.

"When I saw him, I thought, 'I look just like this man,'" she said. "We had this blank moment where we didn't know what to say to each other. Finally I just hugged him."

After being gone a decade, the reacquaintance period with his two daughters had been slow and awkward. As the oldest child, Jawantae still harbored unresolved feelings and remained reluctant. Theresa had simply been there and done that.

But Jonteria hoped for a relationship and worked tirelessly to make it work. It wasn't that her father didn't want one, she said, it was that he couldn't remember how. He was a man who'd been gone too long. When he and Jonteria spoke by phone, he mostly wanted to talk about church and Jesus, as if using her to practice a sermon. But it was a start.

"He's getting better at conversations," she said. "It's just different from what I *thought* a father would be like. I wish he were more like my mom. She's more *enjoyable*. You can enjoy her. You can hang out."

They'd had a series of breakthroughs. The first came on Jonteria's seventeenth birthday, when John had taken her to Red Lobster in West Palm. Theresa had driven Jonteria, then joined them for dinner, which was awkward, but something Theresa needed to do.

"It was a chapter in my life that I never closed, and I finally closed it when I saw him," she said. "It gave me a sense of release to know it was really over."

Their relationship never came up. The two just talked about their daughter and all she'd accomplished, one of Theresa's favorite subjects anyway.

Then one night John came over to the house. He brought steamed crabs, and he and Jonteria spread out a blanket in front of the television and had a picnic.

"It was just like I remembered as a little girl," she said.

She knew that her father probably felt ashamed about the past and worried that people in town still judged him for what he'd done. So when Jonteria called and asked if he'd escort her and Theresa down the field on Senior Night, before the eyes of Belle Glade, she was nervous he'd say no. And even though he'd agreed, seemed flattered even, she still wouldn't feel totally at ease until she saw him at school, in the flesh. "That's when I'll relax," she said.

• • •

FOR THE RAIDERS, the game against Suncoast held far more importance than just the Senior Night ceremony. A win over the Chargers would give Glades Central the 7-2A district crown and home-field advantage in the first round of the playoffs, just three weeks away. Suncoast was a magnet school and, in terms of academics, was ranked one of the ten best high schools in America. The Chargers were a perennial "A" performer and certainly a powerhouse at statewide Brain Bowl competitions. But when it came to football:

"They garbage," said Coach Randy, watching film of the team.

But what about Davison Colimon, the six-foot-two free safety and wide receiver?

"Garbage."

And the Granger brothers, Abiade and Timotheus, a power duo on both ends of the defensive line, who'd combined for a dozen tackles a game and also played offense?

"Garbage, too."

After the week off, the players also seemed little worried about Suncoast. But instead of their usual cocky ambivalence preceding such a "stat game," the Raiders entered the week like a team starting to find its groove.

On Monday the two-minute drills, while usually high tempo, grew tense and violent. The Raider defenders, led by Boobie, Jaja, and Don'Kevious, were feeling well rested and took the field snapping on the leash, ready to hit. They quickly grew agitated by the usual sluggishness of the offensive line, the inability of Brandon, Corey, Salt, and the rest to block and remember play calls, and began punishing them with force. Hester approved and began ordering blitz after blitz. Each one was carried out with maximum strength, leaving linemen flat on their backs. The usual soft touch of practice was temporarily forgotten.

Between plays, Don'Kevious bounced behind the line, barking like a dog. He and his boys wanted more. At 6:00 p.m., they begged the coach for an extended practice. The next day was a teacher work holiday, they said. Let them punish these boys a little longer. The coach agreed. The OL's suffering would not end soon. "No school tomorrow," Don'Kevious shouted. He was only getting warm. "So we gonna play till yall get it right."

As the sun began to set, the hits became so raw and painful that two fights broke out that cleared the sidelines and took every coach to stop them. Then it began to rain, the drops falling like rocks from the darkening sky and bringing a cold wind. The boys loved to play in the wet. The click-clack chewed up the field, leaving them sliding in the black muck until the light finally vanished.

"Great practice," Hester told the team afterward, standing in a downpour. "That's the kind of intensity I like to see."

Coach King added that in 2006, the last time the Raiders won the championship, there were fights like that every day—fights for all the right reasons.

• • •

THE SENIOR NIGHT ceremony took place before a small pregame crowd as the sun sank behind the cane. Junior players lined up to form a tunnel through which the seniors walked to meet their families at the other end. Each carried a carnation tied with ribbon for the proud parent or grandparent waiting with open arms. Coach Knabb read prepared notes over the PA regarding each boy's plans after high school, and which college programs had extended offers.

For those who did not know which college they'd be attending, yet who still wished to play the game, Knabb provided the stock line: ". . . who hopes to attend the college of his choice and to play the game he loves, football. And if God blesses him so, a career in the NFL."

Hoping that God would bless him so, Mario ran out of the tunnel and presented his carnation to his sister, Canisa. Davonte, with his offers from Marshall, West Virginia, and others, embraced his mother, Delia. For all the other players, the ambitions varied: Dion Blackmon was headed to the Air Force; Rashad Darisaw wished to become a sports agent; Robert Burgess had dreams of the Federal Bureau of Investigation; Courtney Porter had the humble hopes of returning home after college to teach math at Glades Central.

The last player to be called was Benjamin, who sauntered down the tunnel to the wild applause of the crowd. He would attend the college of his choice and major in criminal justice, said Knabb. But Belle Glade would have to wait until the first week of February to find out where God would bestow his blessing.

Benjamin was out of uniform, wearing a white T-shirt and a Phillies cap turned backward. He'd appeared only once that week at practice, just to say hello, and stayed less than an hour. For the rest of the week, he'd gone home straight after school, not answering calls or returning messages.

The Saturday after his last game, he'd turned up at a picnic in Pioneer Park hosted by Pastor Dez. He was moody and withdrawn and admitted that his season had been a letdown. For this, he blamed Hester.

"It felt like he didn't like me," he said. "When I first started, he would stay late after practice and coach me one-on-one. But then when I got so good, and blowed up and stuff, it's like he stopped trying to coach me. So by my last game, I was ready to stop playing. It wasn't as exciting as I thought my senior season was gonna be.

"I was promised a bunch of touchdowns," he added. "And when I didn't get the touchdowns, I didn't say nothin. Life goes on. I was just going through the motions."

He'd positioned himself near the ticket booth before the Senior Night ceremony began, chatting with teachers and greeting fans as they walked through the gate. Showing that he was still there, that he'd not disappeared. As his Raiders wrapped up the first quarter already up by two touchdowns, KB stood alone on the sidelines, staring into his phone, as if trying not to seem invested. When he sensed someone watching him, he turned around and gave a goofy grin. By halftime, with the Raiders coasting to an easy victory, he was long gone.

Up in the stands, Frank Williams was sipping gin and juice with the other Raider fathers. He'd also been watching KB down on the sidelines and acknowledged that he was feeling down. All week KB had come home and played video games with his little nephew, Willie. "Not being part of the team, it's hurting him on the inside," said Frank. "He didn't even come out of the house."

Frank planned to get a family friend, James Jackson, to start conditioning KB for summer training camp, wherever he decided to go. Jackson himself had played for the Miami Hurricanes and Cleveland Browns and now ran a fast-track program in Wellington. "I told KB he's gotta start running and lifting or his body's gonna go to waste," he added.

KB had just nodded.

• • •

ALSO SEATED IN the stands during the first half was John Williams, there to escort his daughter. He wore a four-button pin-striped suit and a blue tie. His hair remained styled in the classic Jheri curl with enough sheen to make it sparkle under the lights. He sat with Theresa while Jonteria led the cheerleaders through their routines on the track below, wincing after she fell down from an awkward jump. "Shake it off, baby," he muttered under his breath. Then, to Theresa, "I think she's jumping too high."

The Senior Night ceremony for cheerleaders took place at halftime at midfield. There was a chill in the air, so John held his daughter close to keep her warm. Theresa, dressed in a brown pantsuit, stood with them smiling, waving to friends in the stands. When Coach Knabb announced their daughter's future plans, Theresa and John walked proudly on either side, as if the past had never happened. And for a moment, as the three of them posed for photos under the lights, Jonteria let herself imagine that it had never changed, and that it would stay this way tomorrow and forever.

CHAPTER

fter beating the Suncoast Chargers 39–0 and capturing the district title, the Raiders arrived at Monday practice to a changed reality. Hester gathered the team under a crisp, blue November sky and told them to forget about the past nine games. The time for hand-holding was over. Moving forward, only the best eleven guys would take the field.

"Right now, we in the playoffs," Hester said. "Aint no more regular season for us."

Technically, there *was* still one more game remaining on the schedule. But it was no ordinary game, nothing to take lightly. In fact, many would argue that nothing beyond this game even really mattered. The Raiders could win state and send twenty kids to Division I, but history would regard the season as a failure if Glades Central lost to Pahokee.

"It's Muck Bowl time," Hester reminded them. "Nothing more needs sayin."

• • •

IN ADDITION TO sending an extraordinary number of players to college and the NFL, Pahokee and Glades Central were known for one other thing, and that was their annual shoot-out against each other. Touted as one of the greatest high school rivalries in America, the Muck Bowl drew thousands of fans and practically emptied both towns. In addition, there were those in the Muck City diaspora who treated the game as an annual pilgrimage and traveled from as far away as Alaska. The tailgating began early Friday morning and didn't end until Sunday night, leaving lower Okeechobee hidden from space under a hazy cloud of pit smoke.

Reporters from the major papers, magazines, and networks also arrived looking for good color; over half the stories ever written about Glades football in the national press were written during Muck Bowl. Even ESPN had once televised the game. More important, the matchup between the Raiders and the Blue Devils also drew a throng of college coaches and scouts looking to maximize their time. In past years, both schools reserved entire sections of bleachers just to accommodate them.

The rivalry dated back to 1943, the year Belle Glade High first opened its doors and invited the inevitable pissing match with its bean-picking neighbors to the north. For decades, the annual meeting was called the "Bean Bowl" or "Everglades Bowl" and was played on Thanksgiving Day. It was the premier social event of the season, as described in an editorial in the *Belle Glade Herald* on November 22, 1957:

"The feeling has existed for years that the two-city battle was a must on every sportsman's calendar and both schools treat the situation with all the pomp and ceremony of a Roman emperor returning from the wars."

The term "Muck Bowl" was coined in 1984 as a way to market the game as a showcase for the talent being exported from the region. But out of all the meetings, Belle Glade maintained the edge. Since '84, the Raiders had won 18 out of 26 games over the Blue Devils.

"This is our reputation in the community," said Mario.

Or, as Page put it, "This is the only team we bigger than, so we like to punish those boys."

. . .

LOCATED EIGHT MILES across the canefields, Pahokee had a history very similar to that of its sister city to the south. In the 1920s, the sleepy fishing camps along Okeechobee's East Beach were swallowed by the rush to farm the black, fertile muck. By the Second World War, Pahokee shared the title as the "Winter Vegetable Capital of the World" and, like Belle Glade, was a major food supplier to Allied soldiers. Vegetables opened banks and restaurants along Main Street, as well as hotels and a theater, and kept the lights on at the Rotary Club dinners. Before football, Pahokee was most notable as the home of country music singer Mel Tillis, who himself had played for the Blue Devils.

Don Thompson was a living relic of those early days. In 1949, when Don was nine years old, his family left their sharecroppers' farm in Harrisburg, Arkansas, forty miles west of Memphis, for the promise of abundant wages in the beanfields of the Glades.

The family settled in Pahokee, yet still rode the migrant circuit during summers up to Michigan for strawberries and cherries, Arkansas for cotton, then back home for beans. By the eighth grade, Don had arms like a pipe fitter and weighed over two hundred pounds. When Blue Devils coach Webb Pell spotted Don walking home along a dirt road one day, he slammed on his brakes.

"You're playing football for Pahokee," he told him. "Get in."

Don played middle linebacker and offensive tackle, eventually earning a scholarship to The Citadel, the military college in South Carolina; later he played at Arkansas A&M.

After he graduated, Coach Pell gave him a job as defensive coordinator. In his first year with the team, the mostly young and inexperienced

Blue Devils did not win a single game. But hope arrived the following year, when Pahokee leaped ahead of most schools in Palm Beach County and began integrating its schools. While panic gripped the rest of the town, the football coaches were beside themselves. Get down to East Lake High, Pell told Don. Invite those boys to come and play.

Black students at East Lake had the choice of attending all-white PHS or transferring to Lake Shore High in Belle Glade, which would not integrate for another five years. Don needed volunteers, and the way he sold the players on the Blue Devils was his weight program. While in college, Don had become a self-described weightlifting fanatic. He was already strong; he'd been the only cadet at The Citadel whose shirts had to be specially tailored, because his neck was twenty-two inches around, earning him the nickname "Bear." But it was at Arkansas A&M where he'd first seen a proper strength-training program, something most colleges and high schools were slow to embrace.

Boys in the Glades, both black and white, got strong by lifting crates of cabbage and throwing corn. But Don knew they could become bigger, and besides, "weightlifting is the ultimate team builder," he believed. He scoured the Glades looking for dumbbells and barbells and had little luck. Finally, a serendipitous event:

"There was a train wreck in Canal Point," he said. "I went down there when the crew was cutting those rails up and got them to cut them in certain lengths. I weighed them, then added more weight with cement-filled buckets."

Many of the black players lived in migrant camps outside of town and had to walk to school, so Don began picking them up each morning for training. He'd pull up before dawn, blowing the horn of an old '59 van that had floorboards so eaten with rust you could see the pavement. Back at the weight room, Don began fattening them up.

"I had the milk truck stop in each morning," he said. "I'd get these boys to drink a quart of this heavy cream, high-protein stuff. They'd be pumping steel and drinking milk at six in the morning. They'd get sick half the time. But I tell you something—those linemen put on fifty pounds a man. We came back that next year loaded for bear and we kicked butt."

Mixing black and white students did not happen without problems. At school, there were fights and black students staged walkouts to protest. But on the football field, coaches Webb Pell and Don Thompson saw a mostly seamless transition. Because the school was so small, the coaches were able to field a team of fifteen whites and fifteen blacks, with most everyone getting time. "The white boys were not threatened by their positions. They could all play football," he said.

As Belle Glade would experience five years later, joining the two teams had the effect of powder and fuse. The integrated Blue Devil team of 1965 included Leopold Sterling, a running back whose raw power was as intimidating as his name. "He had eyes on the sides and back of his head," said Don, "and legs like tree stumps. He could break arm tackles like wading through water."

There was middle guard Walter Boldin, aka "Baby Huey," who, at six foot eight and three hundred pounds, had to wear uniforms patched together with other uniforms. Boldin would play for the Houston Oilers, while tailback Willie McKelton was picked up by the Minnesota Vikings. Defensive back John Osborne went to the Browns.

Back then, before recruiters began their annual pilgrimage to the Glades, a player's recruitment was only as strong as his coaches' connections. Pell had ties to West Virginia and FSU and sent many players there. Don knew Red Parker at The Citadel. In 1968 he sent Parker a grainy black-and-white reel of a graduating senior named Norman Seabrooks, who became the first African American ever to play football at the military college.

As racial turmoil still gripped the South, Seabrooks staged a brave and lonesome protest against the traditions of intolerance around him. As team captain of the Citadel Bulldogs, he refused to run onto the field with his fellow teammates while the school band played "Dixie." Instead, he would run ahead, standing alone and defiant as the all-white crowd belted out the Rebel anthem in a thunderous chorus.

Whereas Jessie Hester cast a permanent light on Belle Glade, in Pahokee it was Rickey Jackson. Drafted by New Orleans in the second round in 1981, Jackson spent thirteen of his fifteen years in the league with the Saints. A six-time Pro Bowler, he was finally inducted into the Hall of Fame in February 2010, twenty-four hours before New Orleans won its first-ever Super Bowl.

Known as "City Champ" in high school, Jackson is still regarded as the best linebacker and defensive end to ever play for Pahokee. Jackson and fellow end Walter "Brickhead" Johnson made the Blue Devils murderous on offenses.

"They didn't need down linemen," an opposing coach once told a reporter. "[Jackson and Johnson] covered sideline to sideline. And if you threw, it had to be a three-step drop. You had to get the ball the hell out of there."

As Jackson's coach Antoine Russell once put it, "That joker could bust some headlights."

Both Jackson and Johnson ended up playing at Pitt. But it was little-known Cheyney University where Jackson's teammate Andre "Spanky" Waters eventually wound up. The Philadelphia Eagles signed Waters as a free agent in 1984, and for the next decade, he starred in one of the hardest-hitting defenses in the league. The hits Waters delivered were meant to maim and cripple or, at the very least, chill the marrow of an opposing quarterback. He once speared Vikings quarterback Rich Gannon in the knees twice on *Monday Night Football*. He'd done the same to Rams QB Jim Everett, resulting in a rule named after him that forbade defenders from hitting quarterbacks below the waist while still in the pocket. Dan Dierdorf called him a "cheap-shot artist" and nicknamed him "Dirty Waters."

That battering-ram style not only took a fatal toll on Waters's health, but changed the game forever. Waters committed suicide in 2006 after years of crippling depression. It was tissue from his brain that Dr. Bennet Omalu, a neuropathologist at the University of Pittsburgh, used to finally confirm the connection between concussions suffered in football and early-onset Alzheimer's, dementia, and depression. In 2010, after a flood of supporting data and lawsuits from former players, the league began ejecting and fining players for helmet-to-helmet hits, sparking debate among erstwhile gladiators over whether their profession was going soft.

• • •

ANDRE WATERS'S NAME appeared alongside those of hundreds of other Pahokee legends on the walls lining the Blue Devil locker room, names that included nine All-Americans; more than thirty NFL players; two Super Bowl champions; and one member of the Hall of Fame; along with forty-four other Blue Devils who were currently playing college ball.

The "Wall of Fame" was actually a row of Dry Erase boards with names carefully scrawled, a project Don originally started in 1985 after he returned to Pahokee as head coach, a position now occupied by his son, Blaze.

From the time his two sons were born, Don had prepped them to become Blue Devils (he'd even named his oldest boy Pell, in honor of his former boss and mentor), though it may not have always seemed that way. Don had left coaching in 1970 to pursue his growing passion for weightlifting. He bought a franchise of a company that sold universal weight machines. For the next fourteen years, the family traveled the country while Don sold weight programs to high school coaches, often demonstrating the equipment by benching the entire four-hundred-pound stack of plates.

"I'd tell coaches to give me a ten-by-twelve-foot room and I'd give them a weight program," said Don. "I sold them like crazy. I'd go state to state and stay in the swankiest hotels and live like a king. Often I'd forget what town I was in."

So did his family. During this period, Don, Alice, and the boys moved thirty-six times, switching schools and homes so often that childhood had become a blur to Blaze.

"Remember that farmhouse we lived in?" Don asked his son one afternoon. "North of Atlanta, with the chicken barn?"

Blaze shook his head.

But through it all, Don not only made sure his boys played football, he even held them back a grade to ensure they'd be more physically mature as seniors. In 1981, Don said, the program *60 Minutes* even featured Blaze and Pell in a segment about these "football holdbacks."

"What can I say?" he said, laughing. "I'm a coach at heart."

Don had always hoped and prayed that his family could one day return to Pahokee. And in 1984 his stars aligned. Pahokee called and wanted Don to build them a universal weight program. When he was finished, they said, they wanted him to deliver a state championship—something the Blue Devils had never won.

•   •   •

AT THE TIME, both Blaze and Pell were "playing good football," and just in time to become Blue Devils. Don took the job and delivered on his promise, giving Pahokee its first championship in 1989, beating Port St. Joe by a score of 24–7. By the time Don quit in 1992 because of health concerns, he'd sent twenty-two boys to DI and five to the NFL, including running back Kevin Bouie, who later went to two Super Bowls with the St. Louis Rams.

Unfortunately, Blaze and Pell had graduated before the Blue Devils could win the championship. Pell had gone off to play ball for the Air Force. But Blaze had surprised everyone by turning down his scholarship to Troy State and enrolling instead as a student at the University of Central Florida. After a life steeped in the game, he chose to walk away.

"I'd been playing since I was six years old," he said. "I was done."

But as soon as he quit, he felt a hollow place. He returned home after graduation, and just like his dad, accepted a job with the Blue Devils. "Once you get away from something, you realize how much it meant to you," he said. "I had the opportunity to get back into football. Now I can't see myself not in it."

When head coach Joe Marx hired Blaze, he doubled up, pulling Don out of retirement and tapping him as strength coach. Starting in 2003, with father and son together on the Blue Devil staff, Pahokee won five more championships in six years and firmly established the Muck City reputation. In a chilling repeat of Glades Central's emotional 2006 title run, the Blue Devils clinched the 2008 championship three months after the murder of senior linebacker Norman Griffith. The winning touchdown came with fifty-five seconds remaining on the clock. After the game, when Griffith's mother wrapped her arms around Blaze after accepting her son's gold medal, the Citrus Bowl nearly lifted off the ground.

The following year, the team moved into a $9 million, five-thousand-seat stadium across the street from the high school that was named in honor of alum Anquan Boldin. It was the same year the Blue Devils sent thirteen of their twenty-two seniors to Division I programs.

Unfortunately, losing that many upperclassmen sapped the strength and experience from the Blue Devils' roster and marked the end of its glorious run. Belle Glade could brag that they "don't rebuild, they reload" whenever their coffers were full, but even the mighty Raiders once went twenty-seven years between titles. By the time the 2010 Muck Bowl arrived, the Blue Devils had won only three games all season. For the first time in a decade, they were not going to the playoffs.

Several days before the game, Don and Blaze were riding golf carts around the stadium, painting lines on the field and preparing to host the Raiders. A rumor in Belle Glade was that the Blue Devils had jinxed themselves when they built the new, fancy digs. They'd stripped the grass and removed the precious black soil underneath to lay artificial turf, then changed their minds, replacing it with topsoil. The new Bermuda grass struggled to grow and died in patches. A maintenance man with the school district said that was what Pahokee deserved for "demucking" their hallowed home ground. They'd taken away the juju.

"We're just rebuilding," said Blaze. Unlike his dad, who loved to gab, Blaze could be taciturn and easily annoyed, especially when reporters came around pestering him about his team's losing record. "We graduated twenty-two starting seniors. It's been pretty tough to get back to our normal success."

The Blue Devils' only hope, he said, was that the Raiders would play to type and come out overconfident. "But the fact is," he added, "our record is fairly accurate, which is to say we're not as good as we've been in the past. We've just gotta play our best game."

Worse, the Blue Devils star defensive back, Rontavious "Buck" Atkins, had broken his hand the previous week against University. Buck now stood outside the Blue Devils' locker room with his hand wrapped in a thick, puffy cast. As his team suited for practice, he looked dejected, out of place. Buck was a senior, off to play for the University of South Florida after graduation. Broken hand or not, he wasn't missing his last dogfight with those GC flyboys.

"People tellin me it could hurt me in the future if I make it worse," Buck said, referring to his hand, which he'd snapped on an opponent's helmet while making a tackle. "But this my last Muck Bowl. This a big game, man. Muck Bowl mean *everything*, man. That's the game everyone wanna win. If I had to sit out, I'd break down and cry."

• • •

IN BELLE GLADE, emotions ran just as high. Both Jaime and Davonte caught word that Buck had them marked. ("I'm going for Jaime," Buck had warned. "And Davonte been sayin how sorry we are. I'll be lookin for him, too.") Both sides relished the pregame smack talk as much as the game itself. The Raiders gave it back in spades.

"Buck?" Davonte asked, feigning insult. "Tell Buck the only thing he'll be lookin at's the back of my numbers."

Mario said, "I'm gonna put my helmet right in the center of that field, *bwah,* right on top of that Blue Devil head."

The Muck Bowl was like two neglected brothers squaring off in the backyard year after year. Both sides had grown up together, played little league against each other, shared the same families, hopes, and tragedies. For the Raiders, it was like playing themselves. The scrap and grit of the Pahokee boys should not be underestimated, said the coach.

"Do not look at these people's records," Hester told his team. "Do not. My senior year, they must have won two or three games the same way. We were the high-and-mighty Raiders going in there, top dogs, same deal. And they beat us. *They beat us.* Going into Muck Bowl, it's always zero-zero.

"Those kids are built of the same creed and gusto as you guys," he reminded them. "They already know you, so they aint afraid. Just know you gonna have to fight."

• • •

A CREW FROM ABC News had arrived in town for a story about the Muck Bowl. The pretty brunette reporter had given small video cameras to Davonte and Oliver and asked them to film their lives for twenty-four hours before the big match. On game day, the two weaved through the cafeteria filming the pregame meal of chicken and cornbread, then interviewed teammates in the shop room as they strapped on pads and blasted Lil Boosie.

"What you think about Muck Bowl?" they asked.

"We gon' punish, dawg."

Aside from that, there were few words spoken as the team dressed and boarded the two buses to Pahokee. With sheriff's cars escorting the convoy, the buses blew through red lights, having near misses at intersections, the driver cackling and yelling back, "I'm ya number-one bus driver, don't worry none, I get yall there!" The laugh could be mistaken as sinister, given the scowling, red-eyed Blue Devil that peered from her straw hat.

After the bus cleared the divider of canefields, it entered Pahokee along state route 715, passing between rows of majestic royal palms that lined both sides of the road. The tailgating had begun in Pahokee before noon; all along Rardin Avenue and Larrimore, men stood over hot grills wearing white tank tops smudged black with soot. Nearing the stadium, the wood smoke grew even thicker and the smell of chicken and ribs seemed to ride on an invisible vapor of booze. Crowds poured across the street from the parking lot. Once they saw the police lights, great cheers rose up from both sides of the road, along with scowls and jeers. The Raiders had arrived in enemy lands.

"I've been to Pahokee five times in my life," said Coach Fat, as the team entered the locker room. "Once to the park and four times to play. And that was enough for me."

Thousands already pressed into the bleachers of Anquan Boldin Stadium. The lights were on. The field, for all its troubles, looked electric green and inviting. A cool breeze blew off the lake.

"This is *the* Muck Bowl," Hester reminded the Raiders, who were smoldering with excitement and did not need the memo.

"*YEAH!*"

"They supposed to be rebuilding. Well, we fixin to tear this whole structure down. *We are here to tear your whole structure down.* No prisoners, guys. I wanna see some head-knockin out there tonight."

Mario then asked the coaching staff to leave the locker room so he could speak to the team himself. On the other side of the steel door, all that was heard was a roar and rumble of cleats before the Raiders hit the field.

The Blue Devils came out with arms outstretched like flying warplanes that swooped toward the Raider sideline, dropping insults. More words were exchanged, and soon both teams were out on the field, chest to chest, snapping like pit bulls on a chain and foaming for a fight. The crowd went nuts, but upon closer inspection the two sides were hardly touching. When they finally parted, all that remained was a trembling, uneasy energy.

Earlier that day at the social club in Belle Glade, Pie said the line was 35–10 in favor of the Raiders. For the first time in many years, betting on the Muck Bowl was down. "Everybody just suspects it'll be over before it begins," he said.

He was right.

For all the pomp and ceremony, the game was a blowout. Buck Atkins and the Blue Devils provided little challenge for the Raiders' tuned-up, playoff-ready squad. The Glades Central defense held Pahokee to minus fifty-seven yards rushing after the Blue Devils fumbled the ball numerous times. Seven different Raiders crossed the goal line, including Robert Way, who, in his first game as tight end, scored the Raiders' first touchdown on a nineteen-yard pass play. In the third quarter, Davonte added to his highlight reel with a one-handed swan dive in the corner of the end zone that made the score 37–0. The Blue Devils lost 58–0, making it the most lopsided game in the history of the rivalry.

When it was all over, both teams met at midfield again. This time they hugged and joked and made plans for the Christmas break. Coach Blaze walked over and addressed the maroon and gold, who were swelling with victory. "Great game, guys," he said. "I wish we'd had the team to really challenge you."

Hester praised the kids on their sportsmanship. With all eyes on the Glades, both sides had represented their schools with dignity. "Everybody wants to see the negatives brought out of all this," he said. "I'm glad to see you all brought the positives."

For another year, at least, the Raiders were Kings of the Muck. As their bus pulled out of Anquan Boldin Stadium, leaving it dark until the spring, the Raiders turned their attention to the playoffs that lay ahead. But for several boys, there was talk of other business. It was mid-November, and that could only mean one other thing: rabbit season.

CHAPTER

November was the money season, the time of year when the sugar growers began their annual harvest. From dawn until dusk, the roads were busy with trucks bearing giant yellow trailers filled with freshly cut cane. They would first appear like tiny white cyclones along the vast green horizon, kicking up a dust trail on the shale-covered roads that divided the fields. Once the trucks were on the highway, the wind whipped the dry cane leaves from the trailers like loose confetti and scattered them across the blacktop. The trucks then slowed, blinkers flashing, and turned toward the sugar mills, where thick pipes of steam poured from smokestacks throughout the day and night.

It was the time of year when Jamaican cutters had once arrived by the thousands, transforming the small towns and leaving them flush with cash and future talent. Heavy yellow machines did the harvesting now, their work all but invisible from the highways. But one thing had not changed since sugarcane was first planted in the Glades.

Before every harvest, all the fields had to burn.

Setting fire to the cane cleared away most of the leaves and under-growth and made it easier to cut. The burns were usually done in the morning, depending on the winds. If the leaves were very dry, the fires could consume a sixty-acre plot in under an hour.

In November, when harvest was in full swing, you could drive around Belle Glade and see a dozen fires burning on both sides of the horizon, evoking the image of a countryside under siege. Sometimes the smoke was white and wispy, other times inky and black. The columns snaked so far into the sky they fused with clouds, pumping them dark with soot, then continued like invasive vines across the heavens. When the burns were close to town, residents would awake each morning to find their cars covered in a blanket of ash. If the wind was right, you could be sitting at a red light on Main Street and think it was snowing.

• • •

THE ADDED BENEFIT of burning the fields was to drive out wildlife, such as mice and snakes and wild hogs that rooted in the cane rows. The smoke and flames also pushed out hordes of rabbits that would scurry for fresh air. When they reached the canebrakes, groups of boys were waiting to give chase with clubs and BB guns.

The gray "muck rabbits" were often overwhelmed by smoke and ex-haustion and easily killed. Sometimes, locals said, "they run so fast their hearts explode." But the cottontails, vigorous and quick, could cut on a dime and vanish in a second. For this reason, the cottontail became the pro-tagonist in the great myth of why kids from the muck were so damn fast.

If half the stories ever written about Glades football were about the Muck Bowl, the other half involved chasing rabbits. It had clearly become the "legend of the Glades" and divided people into two camps: those who perpetuated the myth, and those who were quick to call its bluff.

Don Thompson used to make rabbit hunting part of midseason conditioning in Pahokee. "If you couldn't get twenty rabbits, you'd have to go to the line," he said. "If you were a five-rabbit man, you were a lineman for sure. There was a pecking order."

Others were happy to see the myth fade away.

"Hunting rabbits was a way of life, a way to get food," said Ronald Cook, who'd played on the 1965 Lake Shore Bobcat team. "Rabbits don't run that far anyway. Aint like no rabbit's gonna run a twenty-yard dash so you can get some speed. It's all stop and start, stop and start."

"I never chased a rabbit a day in my life," Fred Taylor said. Neither had his son, Kelvin.

The current generation was certainly slower to embrace the sport. Greater access to food assistance meant families were less likely to resort to rabbit meat to feed their kids. And the sugar growers had started cracking down on hunters anyway, seeing them as little more than a liability. But many boys still flocked to the fires, piling into old jalopies that could move though the rutted cane roads, or riding in caravans of bicycles with plastic bread sacks stuffed into their pockets.

· · ·

ON THE SATURDAY after the Muck Bowl, a group of Raiders met at the trailer park to go run the rabbits. They included Don'Kevious, lineman Cordero Phillips, backup quarterback Jems Richemond, and defensive back Clayton Pusey. The boys piled into a Honda Civic and drove east along state route 80 toward West Palm Beach and looked for smoke and birds. When a field was burned, dark clouds of vultures often hovered over the ashes, waiting for the smoke to clear to eat the mice and rabbits consumed by the blaze.

They saw a dark column of smoke to the north and turned into the canefields, driving along a shale-covered road that rattled like a washboard under the wheels. They soon realized the burn was too far in, so they kept driving, the guys saying stuff like, "Look over there, they sparkin there? Where them vultures flyin?"

A Spanish-speaking guy driving a tractor said four fields were being cut about a mile away, so they drove there, even deeper, to where the road disappeared and gave way to soft black muck. The tires began to sink, and rocks scraped the undercarriage. They could drive no farther. They spotted a slow-moving flock of vultures in the distance and got out to walk. The cane on both sides of the road was nine feet high and thick, impenetrable. The boys rummaged on the roadside for cane poles to use as clubs. After thirty minutes of walking the green wall, they came to a clearing and took off running.

In the distance were six giant harvesters working a freshly burned field. The cutters seemed to inhale entire rows of cane, chewing them to pieces and shooting the remnants into a rear catch. Another machine followed closely behind and turned the soil. The giant blades and tires churned up a cloud of black smoke and dust into which Don'Kevious and Cordero disappeared. Barely visible through the haze were dozens of rabbits, suddenly exposed and running for cover.

The boys ran with their backs bent, hands poised and ready to pounce. These weren't cottontails, so they were slower. Don'Kevious flung his cane pole to the ground, only to have the rabbit narrowly escape. Cordero emerged from the haze holding a dead rabbit by the back legs. It was then that two white pickups rumbled over and screeched to a halt.

The man behind the wheel motioned violently for them to leave. Not wishing to do so, Don'Kevious ran over to the cab and tried to plead his case, but the man was angry.

"What are ya doing?" he said in a thick Jamaican accent. "Ya can't be here wit all dese machines. Yall be trespassing on Okeelana prop-erty. I'm callin da sheriff now."

The thought of getting arrested for trespassing at the outset of playoffs stood the boys up straight, and they agreed to leave. They first moved to a neighboring field where they were hidden by the tall cane and separated from the machines by a shallow canal. The boys hoped the commotion would flush some rabbits into the water, where they'd be easy pickings. But they soon realized that could take hours. The sun was high and they'd left their water in the car.

While they stood there, Don'Kevious took Cordero's rabbit, gripped it by the head, and pushed the innards out its anus. He shook them loose into a shimmering pile on the dirt.

"Damn, man!" screamed Jems, hopping away. "You got it on me. It's all wet."

They headed back down the road, looking for more vultures and signs of sparking fields. As they walked along the canal, enormous flocks of white egrets flushed from the water's edge and sought safer ground, their contrast against the black soil an exquisite portrait of nature. Giant plumes of butterflies, the color of buttercups, exploded from the tall grass. Don'Kevious spotted a baby alligator against the bank and threw a rock to flush it loose. It shot into the water, leaving a long wake behind its tail. They walked and walked, the dirt and ash exploding against their footsteps like moon dust.

The gator got the boys thinking: What would you do if one was chasing you?

"All you gotta do is zigzag. That gator can't catch ya."

"Man, I jump in that bitch's mouth."

"I be runnin a 4.2 forty if a gator behind me."

"You be rollin, *bwah.*"

CHAPTER

17

The Raiders arrived at Monday practice with the burden of the regular season discarded on the road behind them, shucked among the stat games, close calls, and defeats that had little relevance to what lay ahead. There was one single objective now, an obligation to their coaches, to the woebegone Glades, and to themselves: to chase down the Cocoa Tigers and beat them in state.

"It's all about gettin that ring now, fellas," Coach King told them. "All about that ring."

Cocoa had ended the regular season undefeated, giving the Tigers three straight seasons without a loss. They were set to play Orlando Jones on Friday at home in the 2A regional quarterfinal, a game everyone expected them to win.

Glades Central's first matchup was also at home, against Cardinal Gibbons, a private Catholic school in Fort Lauderdale with a 6–4 record.

The game would be a rematch of the previous season's first round, which the Raiders easily won 27–3. As the coaches saw in their Sunday film meeting, the Chiefs' defensive line still appeared big, but lacked speed. "Just straight bull rushin," Hester said. "But they can stop the run."

The Raider coaching staff had been making adjustments. Robert Way would still double at tight end. And Gator, the best offensive lineman, would double on defense to protect against the Chiefs' running game. For the slow-adjusting OL, play calls—Bunch, Trip Right, Trip Left, Fake 24 Dive, and so on—had been simplified toward the end of the regular season and honed for speed. Gator had also been working with Salt, Cubby, and others on how to use their hands more effectively, mainly by tricking their opponents into committing their weight, then throwing them off balance.

Going into the playoffs, natural athleticism could no longer carry the Raiders, who remained largely out of shape. The quarterback, in addition to the shooting pain he felt every time he threw the ball, still experienced occasional headaches as a result of the concussion, both of which he kept secret from the coaching staff. His weight also remained an issue. On a recent trip to Burger King for lunch, Mario had ordered like a linebacker, packing down a Triple Whopper, super-sized fries, a large soda, and an ice cream.

"I'm full as a bitch," he'd groaned after putting it all away.

Hester had never wavered in his support for Mario, but couldn't help sighing one afternoon at the sight of the quarterback's sagging belly. "I mean, with his kind of fire, imagine what he could do if he were in top shape."

For Mario and the Raiders, football practice was about to become harder, the runs longer, and "my bad" would no longer be acceptable. If Hester had his way, the boys would go to bed that week with every muscle sore and haunted by the little things.

• • •

AFTER FILM, THE boys ran their normal laps, followed by cone sprints. After two sets, many were wilted and could hardly breathe. Coaches Fat and Randy ordered them back on the line.

"Do not be afraid to get better. Do not be afraid to be faster!" Fat screamed at the boys, a few of whom appeared on the verge of vomiting.

The clocks had readjusted to standard time, meaning the sun was setting sooner. But instead of going home, the team moved to the adjacent baseball field and the coaches threw on the lights. Under a game-night glow that drew hordes of hungry mosquitoes, the boys continued to run.

"It's football season now, *bwah,*" Randy shouted, his hands on his hips. "There's boys in the rest of Palm Beach County who aint got practice tonight. Them boys are at home right now watching *Wheel of Fortune.* They probably went to the locker room after class, then remembered, 'Damn, we done lost.'

"But *we* got practice. We may not have practice after Friday. Then again, we may be the only team in the county that *do have* practice. That's right, *bwah,* smell that soot from the canefields. Feel that chill in the air. This when football season *really* begins."

After a grueling night of running and two-minute drills, Hester gathered his team with a wild dance in his eyes. He bent down low, leaned in, and began to whisper.

Shhhh. Shhhhh. The players hushed the others, then crowded around their coach, who had that sly grin they so loved.

"Here's what I want," he said, just above a murmur, "so listen up. I need this said properly now. I need that 'HA-HA-HA.' I need that said properly. Like you laughin at somebody. Say it after me:

"We gon' hit 'em in the mouth."

HA-HA-HA.

"We gon' hit 'em in the head."

HA-HA-HA.

"We gon' hit 'em so hard."

HA-HA-HA.

"They gon' wish they was dead."

HA-HA-HA.

"GON' HIT 'EM IN THE MOUTH!"

HA! HA! HA!

"GON' HIT 'EM IN THE HEAD!"

HA! HA! HA!

"GON' HIT 'EM SO HARD!"

The chant rose to a screeching climax and the boys could no longer contain themselves. They exploded from the huddle and took off running across the baseball diamond, shouting and doing backflips under the lights. When they finally settled down, the team gathered for what could be their last football practice of the year, and, for some seniors, for the rest of their lives. They put their hands together and said it on three:

"PLAYOFFS PLAYOFFS PLAYOFFS!"

• • •

AFTER EVERYONE HAD gone home that evening, Coach Andrew Mann walked across campus, switched on the lights over Effie C. Grear Field, and prepared it for play. He was a big man, a former Raider who'd suited two sons of his own in maroon and gold and now coached the offensive line. He was forty-six now, yet when he laughed, usually at one of Q's dirty jokes, those giant shoulders would begin to roll and the years would fall from his face. He was a true muckstepper; his eighty-six-year-old mother, Eddie Mae, could remember when Okeechobee rolled her dikes and swallowed the town in the hurricane of 1928.

As head of field maintenance, Coach Mann had a ritual of his own. He began by trimming the grass, feeling the wheels of the riding mower sink into the spongy soil. But before he continued with the painstaking work of painting the lines, he stood at the edge of the field, no audience save the night birds that hunted in the lights, and he prayed. He asked the Good

Lord to bless the lines he was about to draw, that they'd guide his Raiders in an honorable game, one with no injuries or harm. Then, with the big business out of the way, and because he *was* a true muckstepper, Coach Mann asked for the victory.

The next morning, looked down upon from the press box, the field appeared as pristine as a birthday cake. A gust of wind shook the row of royal palms behind the visitors' stands and carried the smell of burning cane. Flurries of ash spiraled through the air, leaving a light dusting. In the distance, beyond the trees and across the highway, wide plumes of smoke rose from the fields, blackening the bulbous clouds that hung in high relief against a blue sky.

It was around this time that Lester Finney arrived to add the finishing touch: painting the Raider head on the fifty-yard line. Finney was a local artist and musician who ran a youth program on Avenue A. He'd also been a Raider in December 1974 when Glades Central fans rioted on the field at Chaminade and put four policemen in the hospital. After the incident, Finney's face was plastered across the *Belle Glade Herald* with the headline A CRYING SHAME. ("It's a crying shame when high school students like Lester Finney are disgraced by the actions of their elders at a football game," the editorial read.)

Standing at midfield, Finney—wearing a straw hat and a T-shirt that accentuated his sinewy, muscled body—free-handed the image of a Raider using Coach Mann's paint machine and a hand nozzle. Finney's Raider was once the official face of the team, he said, until former coach Willie Snead came in and replaced it with the current stock image. The new Raider had whiter features—almost Spanish-looking—and appeared more friendly. "A cartoon character," said Finney, more *Pirates of the Caribbean* than Mucktown Destroyer.

Finney's Raider was black with a wide nose. He had a wild, bushy beard, a gold ring in his ear, and a tomcat look in his eye. "That's the Raider that's gonna hurt somebody," he said with a smile. "This one's from the hood." Within an hour, the fourteen-foot mascot was staring up from midfield at the heavens—just as the cane fires reached the highway and blotted out the sun.

When the school bell rang, the team congregated around the flagpole for the pregame prayer. The boys locked elbows and became quiet. Eyes closed, head bowed, Pastor Dez lifted them up to the God of the Glades in another plea for triumph.

"Father, give them eagle eyes tonight," he prayed. "Make them strong like lions and swift like gazelles. Brace them with the same power that you used to roll back the mighty Red Sea, the power that gave Joshua the victory over Jericho. We ask that the defense might be as a wall, and that the offense might be fierce and powerful, and that our opponents won't be able to stand before us. They will come to us with a sword and a spear, but we will overrun them in the name of the Lord."

• • •

THE RAIDER HOME field was a fortress in late November. In postseason play, the Raiders were 29–1 at home. Of course, one of those playoff victories had come the previous year against the same Cardinal Gibbons Chiefs who now stepped off the bus just before dusk.

To the kids who didn't know, there appeared to be a brief moment of revelation as they breathed the soot-filled air and adjusted to the red, spooky light from a land afire under the setting sun: *So this is the Muck, huh?* The ones who already knew simply stared ahead and walked to the lockers, trying not to acknowledge the gang of Raiders eyeballing them from the sidewalk.

Fans filed into the stands of Effie C. Grear Field and crowded the fenceline, moving to the anthem that blasted from the speakers: *"First down to the touchdown . . . Everybody knows: RAIDERS!"*

The crowd cheered the Raiders as they bounced onto the field from the shop room. On the sideline, Hester lathered them up with his playoff-ready chant, so loud the fans were laughing *HA-HA-HA*. The team then paused to observe the national anthem. As always, when the silk-voiced soprano up in the press box belted the lines *"O'er the land of the freee, and the home of the . . ."* the boys lifted their helmets high and cried, *"RAIDERS!"*

. . .

THE CHIEFS, WEARING all-white jerseys with red trim and lettering, lost the coin toss and kicked to Glades Central. The Gibbons coaches were no doubt harboring some hope that the Raiders would be weakened without their six-foot-six superstar receiver, who was nowhere to be seen. But the pliant Glades Central offense quickly demonstrated its ability to fill empty shoes. His name was Davonte Allen.

It was Davonte whom Hester set in motion on the first call of the game: 989 Rolls-Royce. The deep go route had become Jet's signature airmail with the question *"Can yall run?"*

The pass from Mario, whose eye blacks bore the name of his dead mother, sailed thirty yards downfield and landed in the crook of Davonte's arm. The next play, Baker crashed through the line for twenty-seven more yards and the crowd chanted, *"Move them sticks!"*

Now, on the Chiefs' forty, Mario rolled out of the pocket and threw the ball on the run before getting slammed out of bounds. Davonte was already standing in the end zone. He leaped just as a defender clipped his thigh and spun him upside down, landing hard on his shoulder with the ball still in his hands. But his pain was for nothing; the touchdown was called back because the Raiders had jumped offsides.

On the very next drive, however, Davonte shot across the middle with two white jerseys on his tail, then dove across the goal line to meet a thirty-seven-yard bullet in midflight.

Raiders up 7–0.

The Glades Central defense was watertight from the start, quickly shutting down the Chiefs' go-to running back, Denzel Wimberly, and forcing Gibbons to punt on its first two possessions. Coach Tony, the Raider defensive coordinator, pulled the trigger on blitz after blitz, sending a swarm of maroon jerseys into the face of quarterback Chase Bender. After having been suffocated under double coverage most of the season, Robert Way took his vengeance tonight. He sacked Bender so hard in the first quarter that even the bloodthirsty mucksteppers in the stands had to wince. Before the night was over, Bender would go down seven times.

At the start of the second quarter, Jaime took a punt return and started home. But as he sliced up the sideline, the ball bounced loose from his hands. The Chiefs defensive back Dan Fitzpatrick picked it up and raced fifty yards for an easy touchdown to tie the game. But Jaime was quick to redeem his sloppiness. As soon as the Raiders had the ball again, Mario hit him on a short route for a fifty-one-yard play into Chiefs territory. The next snap, he found Oliver on a twenty-yard strike into the end zone.

After the extra point, the Raiders led 14–7.

There was something unusual happening to the short, fat quarterback. The panic and impatience, the *fear* that had once gripped him as soon as the ball touched his hands, no longer was there. No imaginary ghosts haunted his blindside, spooking him into the open. For the first time against an admirable defense, he felt relaxed.

And he knew why: his line was holding. After months, his boys up front—Brandon, Corey, Salt, and Gator—were finally giving him the game he'd always wanted. For once, there was rhythm. They were in sync. Here tonight on the hallowed muck, the quarterback could finally show his town that he was worthy of their tradition. Tonight, he was *man of tha city*.

Anything seemed possible. After the touchdown, LeBlanc made a spectacular, one-handed tilt-a-whirl interception with both feet kissing the grass before his body flew out of bounds, the very kind of play that sent boys from Belle Glade to college. Back on the field, Davonte told his quarterback, "Throw it as far as you can. Wherever you put it, I'll get it."

Hester nodded from the sidelines: 989 Rolls-Royce. From the Raider forty-seven, Mario took the long snap, cocked his arm with two short steps, and launched the ball. Davonte was already halfway to the goal and racing to beat his man. Just as he broke away, he craned his head and saw the ball as it twisted under the lights, precisely on course. It dropped into his arms at the five, and Davonte trotted into the end zone. A fifty-yard bomb. The stands went wild.

"It's pretty, aint it?" Jet said, smiling. "That's the best pass he's thrown all season."

The quarterback rode the high all the way through the fourth quarter, throwing for over three hundred yards to eliminate Cardinal Gibbons 28–14 and take his team one week closer to a rematch with Cocoa. Up north, the Tigers had done their part, narrowly beating Orlando Jones 14–9.

Later that night, Mario went home and turned on his computer. Jeff Greer's recap of the game was already up on the *Post*'s website, the whole article dedicated to the quarterback's great transformation:

"The former linebacker gets so pumped up for big games that sometimes he forgets that he now plays a position that requires a steady hand," Greer wrote. "But playing in his first playoff game as a quarterback, Rowley was as cool as ice, throwing three first-half touchdowns. . . . The Raiders will live and die with [his] arm this season."

"It's playoff time," Mario told Greer, the arm in question feeling as though it were attached by a metal spike. "My attitude switches to a whole new mode now."

18

R ound two of the playoffs took Glades Central on the road. On the Friday after Thanksgiving, the Raiders traveled south to Fort Lauderdale to face American Heritage–Plantation, the private academy whose sister school in Delray Beach had nearly beaten them at home in October.

Despite their shaky 7–4 record, the Patriots had one of the most talked-about players in Broward County, a fourteen-year-old Haitian running back named Sony Michel. For weeks the Raiders had been hearing about the great Michel, the six-foot, two-hundred-pound freshman prodigy who ran a 4.3 forty and smashed through lines of scrimmage like Bo Jackson.

"If a safety gets on Sony in the secondary," his coach Byron Walker once said, "there's going to be a wreck."

Michel had recently racked up 350 yards in a game against Chaminade. He was one of several backs in Florida, along with Glades Day's Kelvin

Taylor, who were giving legitimate chase to Emmitt Smith's all-time rushing record. Michel had a slight advantage over Smith: American Heritage was K–12, so he'd played varsity the previous year, as an *eighth-grader*—running for 1,825 yards and twenty touchdowns (Smith, by comparison, had run three hundred fewer yards as a freshman at Escambia High with just as many TDs). But the Raiders had faced Michel that same year in the playoffs and eliminated the Patriots 46–20 to advance to the semifinals.

Even so, coaches from opposing squads, when jawing with Glades Central staff after games, couldn't help but offer words of warning: "Watch out," said one assistant from Boynton Beach, "'cause that boy a *man*. That boy will run the stretch all night, and if you aint got him locked up by the time he passes that line of scrimmage, *he gone*."

To which the coaches replied: seen it, done it. But regardless, all week they prepared for the stretch. They also prepared for Michel's brother Marken, a flyboy receiver and defensive back. They'd even practiced on Thanksgiving Day, meeting in the early-morning chill for three hours of walk-throughs before going home for turkey and sweet potato pie. Looking to squeeze in some extra conditioning, Don'Kevious and Jaja had even found a burning canefield and killed some rabbits.

Despite the team's apparent readiness, an unavoidable statistic still haunted Hester: the Raiders carried the stink of a losing record in playoff games on the road after Thanksgiving. Those numbers included Hester's first season, when they'd lost the regional finals at Miami Pace. Superstitious as Hester was, it gnawed at him: through his entire Thanksgiving dinner, on the bus ride south through the canefields and sawgrass prairie, up Broward Boulevard and into the locker room at American Heritage.

"This is a test we haven't passed in a while," he told his team. "On the road during this time of the year, we got to understand what we're facing. That's a big monkey on our backs and we got to get it off. *This* is the statement game. Everybody will know after tonight what kind of football team we are."

And just to illustrate the power of bad juju, he reminded everyone that the previous week, Jaime had chosen to break the rules and stand out. He'd worn black socks instead of the uniform white, then suffered a grievous fumble that led to a Gibbons touchdown.

"We still got some guys who don't wanna follow the norm," Hester said. "Look at the type of game this cat had last week wearing the black socks. *Look at his game.*"

The playoffs seemed to bring out the old crow in everyone. Now, before each game, about twenty Raiders lined up to get patted down by Coach Sherm. The six-foot-seven coach would stand the boys in front of him, then pound his clenched fists violently atop their shoulder pads like two cannonballs rolling off a house. A glow of barbaric ecstasy would wash over their faces. The beating "settled" the pads, they said, like tenderizing a tough piece of meat. But it was also rooted in superstition.

"Every time Sherm pats me down," Davonte said, "I score a touchdown."

At American Heritage, there was also coincidence at play, and it certainly wasn't lost on the old-timers. Byron Walker, the Patriot head coach, was a muckstepper from way back. He'd coached the Glades Day Gators for sixteen years and led them to three state titles. Before that, Walker had been the Glades Central quarterback who'd led the Raiders to their second championship in 1972.

Even more of a coincidence was that during the Raiders' first title run in 1971—under Pearl Williams, Wayne Stanley, and Mark Newman—Walker had been a paunchy linebacker. When he came aboard his senior year as starting QB of the mighty GC Raiders, the town had mocked and doubted him, saying he was too fat, too short. But Coach Al Werneke hadn't budged. "You're our quarterback," he'd told Walker. "Now that's the end of it."

As Glades Central began its pregame warm-ups, Walker looked out across the field at the Raider captain in the number 1 jersey and smiled. "Yep," he said, "Mario reminds me a lot of myself."

The Patriots' field sat adjacent to the pristine American Heritage campus, its buildings uniform red brick and surrounded by tall trees. Tuition was upward of $22,954 for high school seniors—the per capita income in Belle Glade was just $14,018—with students drawn largely from the wealthy gated communities nearby.

After nightfall, the weather was crisp, not a breeze to be found. The planes beginning their descent into nearby Fort Lauderdale–Hollywood airport appeared as blinking stars above. "It's a great night for football," said Hester.

Coach Fat provided inspiration. "You give anything on this planet life, they gonna fight for life," he said. "And when you give them life, you also give them strength. Now let's go step on their mutherfuckin throats."

"Pursue piranha-style," Coach Tony told his defense. "If we pursue, everybody's gonna eat. Make them feel that pain all night."

. . .

IT WAS MARIO and Davonte who dealt the first blow. On the opening drive, the two connected on a forty-yard pass; the receiver scooped it up at his ankles, then jogged into the end zone.

Glades Central 7, American Heritage 0.

But as soon as the Patriots had the ball, it was all Sony Michel.

Play after play, the running back made the Raider line look more like guppies than flesh-eating piranhas. He would average eight yards a carry and not encounter trouble until he reached the open air, where Boobie and Page were waiting. It was Page who hit Michel on that first drive, so hard the bleachers recoiled when the boy's helmet slapped the cold mud. But still he got up and celebrated, raising both arms to the crowd like a mini King James. He got the Patriots far enough downfield for an easy field goal, putting American Heritage on the boards.

The Patriot defense, for its part, sealed every gap and eliminated Glades Central's running game. The heavy pressure also forced mistakes and penalties that hobbled the Raiders throughout the first half: little things such as holding, false starts, illegal blocks, and an ineligible-player-downfield penalty that erased a touchdown.

The Raider Nation was not pleased. And since the American Heritage field had no track, the bleachers were within spitting distance of Hester and the bench. They heard it all:

"Get yall head in the game, man!"

"O-line coach, that line is standin straight up! They standin up, Coach!"

"The middle wide open, Jet. Open yo' eyes. The middle wide open!"

Halfway through the second quarter, Likely pulled down an interception that put Glades Central inside the Patriot thirty. Two plays later, Mario hit Oliver on a seven-yard route in the end zone to put the Raiders up 14–3.

American Heritage responded with another field goal after Michel single-handedly drove downfield, taking five- and ten-yard chunks out of the Raider defense before Boobie nailed him to the grass. Coach Randy winced when he heard the hit, then said, "That bitch won't be gettin outta bed tomorrow."

Before the half, the score still 14–6, the Raiders were forced to punt after a drive stalled in their own territory. Before Jaime could kick the ball, he looked up and found three defenders racing toward him. He froze, then flung the ball to the nearest maroon jersey—Don'Kevious—who caught it like a hot potato and took off running for the first down. The next play, Jaime took a short pass and ran it thirty yards for the touchdown. Raiders led 21–6.

"That's the way to be great, baby!" Mario shouted into the manic crowd as he paced the sideline after the play. *"That's the way to be great!"*

After the half, Michel snatched away the Raiders' cushion with a quick forty-yard touchdown to make the score 21–13. At the fourth-quarter whistle, American Heritage was within one possession of tying the game.

The Raider Nation grew eerily quiet after the Patriots forced Glades Central to punt, then drove down the field once again. Just when it seemed as if they would score—the quarterback gave Michel a needed rest and called for the pass—Likely appeared once again out of nowhere and stole the ball from midair.

The crowd took to its feet as Mario returned to try to seal the game. On his first play, the defense blitzed and pushed him from the pocket toward the sideline. Just as he crossed out of bounds, a defender rocketed toward him headfirst and speared him in the helmet.

The quarterback's body crumpled onto the grass as he lost consciousness. He lay on his back in the mud, his eyes moving in different directions. Coaches huddled close while the team doctor held up his fingers, shouting, *"How many do you see? How many do you see?"* From the stands, you could hear the collective gasp.

"Get up, Mario!" someone screamed.

"Come on, baby!"

The panic grew worse as he hobbled to the bench. Davis then entered the game and threw a bullet up the middle without a maroon jersey in sight. The ball was nearly picked and Hester lost his mind. *"Do not throw the ball up the middle, Greg,"* he screamed.

The Raiders were forced to kick. But the Patriots could not manage a first down and sent out their special team. The center snapped the ball, and then—chaos, followed by jumping and screaming on the field. Boobie blocked the punt! The Raiders recovered the ball on the Heritage thirty and started tasting blood.

* * *

IT WAS A call of duty too great for the dazed quarterback to resist. When the Raider offense took the field, Mario limped off the bench and into the huddle to the rippling applause of his fans. But he was not okay. His mind swam in a woozy sea. Everything in his vision was doubled. Looking downfield was like gazing into a fun-house mirror. So blind and befuddled, he didn't even bother to pass, just lowered his shoulder and smashed his way twenty yards to the ten—setting up the field goal that would seal the Patriots' fate.

"That's when it got away from us," Coach Walker said. "We just couldn't recover after that."

The Raiders went on to win, 31–19.

CHAPTER

19

It was nearly midnight before Jonteria and Theresa Williams got home from the game, and two o'clock before Jonteria could shower and wind down enough to sleep. She was back up at six the next morning for an eight-hour shift behind the cash register, but too excited to be tired. The ladies who came through her line were met with that smile and the big news behind it:

"I got accepted to Florida State!" Jonteria told them, all but dancing on her aching feet.

The message had arrived the day before Thanksgiving. The school had sent her a letter with its decision. But the acceptance had hinged on her enrollment in the Center for Academic Retention and Enhancement (CARE), designed to assist disadvantaged students.

"One of my ACT reading scores was under their minimum," she said, annoyed. "It's a program for low-income families to help you finish your college career. They don't want you dropping out. The program gives us study groups and mentors just to make sure you make it."

The low reading score had come on a test she'd taken midway through her junior year. Since then, she'd taken the ACT two more times and performed better.

"But if I submitted those, I wouldn't qualify because my scores are too high," she said. And what if college was really hard and she needed the tutors? As much as it pained her to do so, she'd swallow her pride and stay in the program.

"But that's even if I decide to go to Florida State," she said.

She and Theresa planned to drive to Tallahassee in February for a campus tour. By then she'd have more information about financial aid and scholarships. There were just too many balls up in the air right now to make a decision.

She'd texted Vincent as soon as she'd received the letter. "I thought you were going to FAU," he wrote back. "I don't know why he cares," she said, sitting at home on the living-room sofa, dressed in white shorts and pink socks. "He'll be okay wherever I go. He wants me to be home with Mom. How do you think I feel? He's all the way in Virginia. I told him that he's just afraid because I'm going to Tally, the big city. But he just brushes it off."

She laughed, then added, "We text every day. He didn't get my text yesterday. I said 'Hey,' and he didn't text back. He said he tried to send something but I didn't get it. That dorm room, I swear. So now at the end of the text messages, I send the time. He's not getting it till the next day. Maybe it's his new phone. Whatever it is, they need to fix it."

Vincent's mother had passed away during his senior year, thus severing his strongest tie with Belle Glade. Now, with football and living out of state, he came home less and less. Vincent had not returned for Thanksgiving, had not been there to feast on the jambalaya with shrimp and sausage that Jonteria had cooked, along with her mom's curried chicken and grandmother's collard greens, ribs, and sweet potato bread. "Mom says my seasoning is better than Zatarain's," she said. "It was *good*."

But Vincent would be home in mid-December to spend Christmas with his aunt Peggy. His arrival was just two weeks away. He and Jonteria had not seen each other in seven months, since the previous May. At the time, Jonteria had been so busy with final exams, college classes, cheerleading, and work that she'd had to cancel some of their dates and hardly saw him. It had bothered her ever since. For this visit, she'd been working double time to make sure her schedule was clear. She wanted to make the visit special, nothing less than perfect.

"I'm going to take him out for his birthday," she said. "I want to take him somewhere nice. We like to go to Applebee's."

But her dream place was the Seafood Bar restaurant at The Breakers, the 140-acre beachfront hotel and resort in Palm Beach. She'd attended a scholarship banquet there with Jessica Benette and her cousin Donalle, who was the third-ranked scholar at the school. Jessica had won the award, but it hardly mattered. Jonteria had been spellbound.

"It's the richest place," she said, imagining it now. "The window is right there by the beach. It looks like the water is going to come right in. It's *gorgeous*. The thought of being able to sit there and relax, and to be able to afford it—that's what I want someday. I hope I get to go there again."

Of course, there was that place that occupied the other end of her dreamworld, the University of Miami. But unlike The Breakers, there was a danger now that the university would remain just a fantasy, a dream that got away.

What had happened was this: After paying the rent, car payments, phone, and grocery bills, plus the added expense of the holidays, Jonteria and Theresa had scraped the bare bottom of their bank account. Jonteria had received fee waivers for her applications to FAU and Florida State, but not for Miami. The application fee was sixty dollars and they simply did not have it.

Sixty dollars. Certainly she could borrow sixty dollars from friends or teachers. She could ask her boss at the grocery store or even Dr. Grear, who loved Jonteria like her own blood. And if that didn't work, certainly she would be justified in taking one of the boys' football helmets and walking the fenceline at practice, or into the lobby of U.S. Sugar or Duda & Sons or any of the handful of firms whose fortunes had blossomed from that soil, to put forward her worthy case, to present to them one of those rare moments to quietly redeem their place on the land, to plant the small seed that bore the righteous fruit.

But she didn't, because she knew that if she applied to the University of Miami, she would most likely be accepted. She had no guarantee, though, that she would receive any of the scholarship money for which she applied. And because her mother had vowed those many years ago to deliver the dreams of her daughter, Jonteria knew Theresa would bury herself to make the tuition, which was now $36,000 per year.

For her, it would be too devastating to have to throw away an acceptance letter. So one night, sitting alone in her room, Jonteria simply let go of the dream. She would not apply.

• • •

SIX HOURS NORTH in Tallahassee, Kelvin Benjamin looked bored. The receiver sat slumped at a small table in the Seminole locker room tucked deep in the bowels of Doak Campbell Stadium, staring vacantly at a large-screen television. It was rivalry weekend in college football, two days after Thanksgiving, and Florida State was hosting the enemy Gators later that afternoon.

Benjamin was taking his "official visit" and had been in town since Wednesday, attending practice, shadowing the team as they prepared for the big game, even crashing with Greg Dent, his former teammate on the Raiders and one of the Seminoles' promising young receivers.

All of this had been arranged by Coach Dawsey and Big Mike, who now sat across the table with his wife, Melanie, and their two children. Mike and

Melanie owned a second home just outside Tally and spent Thanksgiving up north during rivalry week. On Thursday they'd fed KB his turkey and souse (a form of headcheese) and given him back to the Seminoles. The weekend visit was Mike's last-ditch effort to thwart the Gators and give his alma mater the gift of a future first-rounder.

The lieutenant was dressed in his khaki PBC sheriff's uniform, which earlier that morning had exhibited incredible power in slicing through stadium security, even negotiating an otherwise impossible parking spot three streets away.

"They been lovin on him all week," said Mike. "Look at him. He's worn out."

They'd roused KB out of bed at Dent's place around nine that morning. Dent and another teammate lived in Burt Reynolds Hall, the dormitory which had housed football players since the 1980s and was named after one of the 'Noles' most legendary boosters. Take-out containers were stacked against the wall. The carpet was worn and ratty, and the bathroom was a science experiment. A typical dude's place.

Like many college teams, most of the Seminoles stayed in a hotel the night before games in order to review film and keep out of trouble. They were still being quarantined by the time KB and everyone reached the stadium.

The locker room where they sat doubled as a shrine to Seminole greatness throughout the decades: glass cases displaying the jerseys and cleats of heroes past, players such as Deion Sanders and Heisman-winning quarterbacks Chris Weinke and Charlie Ward, both of whom had led the team to national titles.

Freshmen and redshirts who didn't suit up—and therefore did not stay in the hotel with the rest of the team—passed through the room, as did a handful of other high school recruits on hand for their visit. But KB did not acknowledge them, didn't even look up. When told about the Raiders' amazing victory the night before against American Heritage, his eyes became wide for a second before he looked away, not even asking questions.

It wasn't until a Seminole equipment man appeared in the locker room with a stack of towels that Benjamin came alive.

"Man, this guy's gonna have his own case in here someday," Mike told him. "He'll be a first-round pick, too."

"Yeah," the equipment man said. "I suited him out when he was here whippin' butt in that seven-on-seven."

Benjamin beamed. "These coaches still talkin about that," he said. "That's when they first started noticin me."

The praise was like a fix. Once it reached the bloodstream, the body and mind could function. One could tell the Seminoles had been feeding him the drug all week.

"Jimbo's a good coach," KB said. "He likes to throw, but they don't got a good line. They good at blocking but can't go out for the pass. He's lookin to get that tool, and that's why they want me.

"Receivers they pick turn out to be sorry," he added. "Just 'cause they good in high school don't mean they good in college."

A coach entered the room and said the day's events were about to begin. The recruits would be treated to a short film, he said, then get a chance to walk the field during warm-ups. Benjamin rounded a hallway and was soon joined by dozens of other players and their parents. He towered over all of them and immediately caused a stir—a giant among boys, and with his own police escort!

"Wanna see the best receiver in our county?" a player wearing a jersey from Dwyer High School in Palm Beach Gardens said.

"Who that?" his friend said.

"Back there, in the sweat suit."

"*Dang.*"

A large black man, perhaps a coach or a father, then approached.

"You a *receiver*?" he asked, his eyes wide.

"Yeah."

"Hey." He turned to the crowd. "Yall ever see a receiver that big?"

The players and their families were guided into a large meeting room with a projector screen. When KB entered, one of the coaches hosting the event led him to a front-row seat and slapped his leg. A young and pretty student escort passed out 3-D glasses and the film began. It was a dizzying montage of Seminole highlights spliced with Coach Fisher's rousing locker-room speeches, all in three-dimensional splendor and accompanied by a thundering soundtrack that featured the rush of jet engines, clashing light sabers, and beats by Eminem and Jay-Z.

> *It's based off toughness. It's based off effort. It's based off discipline. It's based off pride. That's what you live by every day. And that will carry you through everything in your life. . . .*
>
> *Here's the kick. . . . He's got the distance. . . . It's gone! It's gone! Florida State wins in the last second. . . .*
>
> *You create championship behavior. Championship habits. Know what that's called? That's called Florida State football. That's called Florida State football. . . .*
>
> *Inside handoff . . . It's Thompson. . . . Thompson to the fifty . . . Thompson to the forty-five . . . forty . . . he could go . . . he might go . . . he will go . . . all the way. Touchdown Florida State!*

The film ended with timpani drums pounding out the rapturous anthem of the National Football League, as if the message could not be more clear. All that seemed left was for Bobby Bowden himself to step off his bronze pedestal out front and come crashing through the wall. When the lights came on, there wasn't a person in the room, young or old, who didn't want to suit up that second and go pancake a Gator.

As everyone stood up to leave, the coach who'd seated KB directed one of the smiling blondes to personally escort the prized recruit onto the field.

"This guy here's a nightmare for any opposing team," he told her, then looked at Big Mike. "I've been doing this for thirty years, and he may be the best I've ever seen."

More than eighty thousand fans packed the stadium by the time KB entered the field. The news of his visit had spread across the blogosphere. Boosters and diehards knew him by sight. Once they saw him, many began to shout from the lower sections.

"*How GC do last night?*" yelled one.

Others screamed his name and gave him a tomahawk chop in salute.

A fat guy appeared on the sidelines and grabbed his arm. "We need you, bro."

A gorgeous, light-skinned escort then approached and gave him her number. KB's gold teeth sparkled as he watched her walk away.

"People wanna know you," he said, grinning. "People you don't even know wanna be seen with you 'cause they think you gonna be a star."

When both the Seminoles and Gators had taken the field for warm-ups, KB stopped and scanned the opposite sideline, looking for someone.

"Coach Z called and talked to me last night," he said. "He just some-how knew I was here. You can't hide nothing from these recruiters. They know everything."

The Gator assistant coach who'd been courting KB for two years had implored the receiver not to "drink the punch" of Florida State, KB said. The phone conversation had lasted two hours. Now, on the sideline, KB fixed his gaze, looking for Azzanni or, better, for Urban Meyer.

"I just want them to see me," he said, then laughed.

If Coach Z was afraid of Benjamin drinking the Seminole punch, his team certainly didn't help matters that night. With Tebow and the champi-onship squad now graduated and gone, the Florida offense looked raw and out of sync. Up in the stands with the other recruits, KB saw all he needed to see. Florida rarely passed the ball. In fact, quarterback John Brantley only appeared out of the wildcat formation every third down to attempt a pass. At the half, Florida had only thrown for thirty yards, compared to 167 by FSU quarterback E. J. Manuel.

Florida State went on to win the game 31–7, the first victory over their archrivals in six years. As the clock hit zero, the Seminole players took a victory lap around the stadium, hoisting the head of a stuffed gator. Later, Benjamin joined receivers Dent and Bert Reed for a night of heavy clubbing. "We *need* you here, bro," they too implored.

On Monday, Coach Z sent the following e-mail:

Dear Kelvin,

It's all about people. We've been on you since junior year. Where was FSU? Listen, I know you had a good time at FSU, but recruiting is a process. I'm trying to make my plans to see you on Tuesday. Are we still on? I hope so. I think you made up your mind already from one visit, and one good atmosphere, and that would be a mistake. Give me and Florida a chance. Trust me, you won't be sorry. I'll prove that this is a better fit. They beat us one time in the past six years. Don't get caught up in that. Please hit me back. I'm gonna drive down tonight. Remember big-time players make big-time places. Go Gators!

The following afternoon, Coach Z appeared on the Glades Central practice field. He told Hester and others he'd come to look at Jaime, Likely, and Davonte. But everyone knew he was in Belle Glade to talk with KB, to try to salvage whatever allegiance he thought he'd gained. Standing on the sidelines with Coach JD, he could not conceal his frustration.

"The Seminoles have their tentacles all in my boy," he said. "They're all over him. What's worse is that this town is crawling with them. Once they come down here, it's gonna be a block party."

He told JD that as he drove south, a trip he hoped wouldn't end with him losing the best recruit of his career, the big-time player for the big-time place, he'd phoned his wife—the woman who'd followed him from Bowling Green to Central Michigan and now to Gainesville.

"You know what she told me," he said, the lines finally relaxing from his face. "She said, 'Sometimes the greatest players don't always turn out to be the greatest players.'"

The words provided comfort, but still, knowing that KB was questionable, Azzanni was out to get the second best, and that was Davonte. "What kind of player is he?" he asked JD, who, sensing the line of his question, laid it on thick about the receiver. Azzanni also grilled Robert Way.

"Who's better at receiver, Davonte or Jaime?" he asked him. "Who's the best overall athlete? Don't sit on the fence, Robert. You can tell me."

Before practice was over, Coach Z slipped into the darkness and drove to KB's house. He stayed for spaghetti and appealed to Benjamin and his family. He was careful not to bash the Seminoles. Instead, he employed the strategy Meyer had taught him long before when it came to winning a recruit: Stick with the facts. And the facts spoke for themselves. Florida was in the SEC, the greatest conference in college football. And until recently, they'd beaten Florida State six years in a row. He also added that in the most recent NFL draft, seven Gators had been chosen in the first three rounds.

After three hours, Benjamin assured Coach Z he was still undecided. Getting back into his truck, Azzanni was doubtful, but not defeated.

"I felt like we'd certainly taken a step back," he said. "But by no means did I think I'd lost him."

CHAPTER

20

The win over American Heritage had earned the Raiders a trip to the state semifinals game, putting them only one date away from the ever-desired rematch with Cocoa, who'd also won the previous week and were very much alive.

For the first time in two years, the Cocoa Tigers were traveling for a postseason game—this time to the state's northern border to meet the Madison County Cowboys, the fierce defensive squad that had fallen to the Raiders in the 1998 state championship. Even the name of their stadium, Boot Hill, sounded ominous.

Although the Cowboys were undefeated and executing their signature swarm defense that had carried them to five state title games, there was a psychic understanding among the coaches and players in Belle Glade that Cocoa would prevail. It was how the ending had always been written, they felt—the two teams meeting once again on the cold and empty plain.

In fact, the entire postseason schedule had become an exact replica of last year's run: Cardinal Gibbons, followed by American Heritage. And now, once again, the Raiders would face Robinson High School in Tampa as the last obstacle before reaching the Citrus Bowl. Hester would not even acknowledge the coincidence, never once brought it up in practice or in meetings with his coaches. On his ever-sensitive radar of superstitious activity, this was bleeding red off the scale.

Like Cocoa, the Raiders would also be traveling—this time across the state to Robinson's home turf. In last year's semifinals game, the Raiders had embarrassed the Fighting Knights 33–0 on Effie C. Grear Field. But Hester knew the Raiders would be facing an entirely different team this year, one bent on revenge behind the support of its own fans. The Knights were coming in with a 10–2 record and running Glade Central's same spread offense. They'd scatter the defense with receivers Frankie Williams and Ruben Gonzalez, who'd combined for fourteen touchdowns that season, then slice the soft middle with their running back, J. J. Hubbard.

Hubbard was nimble and downright slippery. Only five foot eight, he weaved and shimmied through defenses like a small deer before streaking across the open field. He was the Class 2A leading scorer, with twenty-seven touchdowns on 1,450 yards, averaging a first down with every carry. He'd killed Tampa Jesuit the previous week with 177 yards and two TDs, not including a seventy-yard burst to the end zone that was called back on a penalty.

"When I see daylight," he'd told a reporter, "all I think is touchdown."

But for its part, Glades Central was coming in ranked one of the fastest defenses in the state, allowing opponents just nine points a game with five shutout victories. In their last meeting with Tampa Robinson, the Raiders had allowed the Knights only twenty-eight total yards, not only stopping Hubbard but crushing his running game for negative fifty.

Even so, you could never overestimate a scorned team who sought redemption at home. "Trust me, guys," Hester warned his squad that week, "these people want this badder than yall can understand. They want this. We need to make sure they don't get it. We need to bring that grit from the Glades."

. . .

GRIT WAS ABOUT all the quarterback had left in his bag. After Mario had been knocked unconscious in the game against American Heritage, he'd faked his way into being let back in the game. Just to be safe, the team trainer had ordered Mario to the doctor to check for a concussion. Mario didn't go, yet told everyone the doctor had cleared him to play. "What's the point?" he said later. "All he's gonna do is tell me something I don't wanna hear."

Hester remembered Mario being cleared on the sideline. Regardless, for several days, Mario practiced despite blinding headaches. The concussion was helped a bit by an early-winter storm that blotted out the sun and eased the pain. But the damp, cold weather just made his shoulder hurt worse.

On Friday, after lunch and prayers, the Raiders boarded two charter buses and hooked north around the lake, through the fields of burning cane and orange groves of LaBelle, then west toward the Gulf, where the wind whipped against the window and turned the glass crystal-cold. A winter chill was settling over the state. Hester sat in the front seat suffering through a cold, his first in a decade. His eyes were puffy. He couldn't breathe. His whole delicate constitution was under siege.

As they drove, the coach was also handed some unfortunate news.

Earlier in the day, administrators at Cocoa High School confirmed they had just suspended Tiger running back Chevelle Buie. No reasons had been given, but rumors were quickly spreading. Whatever Buie had done, he would not be playing that night against Madison County.

Immediately the thought was, *Could Cocoa win at Boot Hill without their superstar?* Playing at home, the Cowboys were already the favorites. Even

worse, people were saying Buie could be suspended for the rest of the semester. It was Buie who'd sunk the Raiders with two touchdowns in the
state finals. And now the much-anticipated rematch was suddenly thrown
in jeopardy. The news cast a fog of disappointment over the team. No one
wanted to win a championship with an asterisk.

The weather was freezing by the time the bus pulled into Robinson
High School. While Hester watched the teams warm up before kickoff,
he saw something else that sank his mood even lower, something downright insulting. The Knights were practicing with only three down linemen
while stacking the secondary with linebackers and DBs to anticipate the
pass. Running such a formation implied that the Raiders were only one-
dimensional. Since he was already in a foul mood, seeing that sent Hester
over the edge.

"Typically, you know what I like to come out and do," he told his team
as they gathered before the whistle. "Nine-eighty-fuckin-nine. But I aint
doin that tonight. I looked out there and saw these cats runnin a three-man
front. That irks the heck out of me. Think about that shit. *A three-man front.*
Three guys on five? I mean, I took that personally. They tryin to tell me my
dawgs aint got that kind of fight in 'em. Yall about to send the message to
whoever we play next week that three men aint gonna work. We gonna hit
these boys in they goddamn mouths tonight."

"*All night!*" Mario shouted.

"They think we comin out there to pass. Our intent aint by air, aint by
sea, it's by any means necessary to hurt them."

"*Come on, baby,*" the quarterback cried. "*I'm goin to O-Town.*"

"We gone too far for this story to end," the coach said, now scanning
the eyes. "We all know it's gonna get written either way. So how's the story
gonna be told? Who gonna be the hero this week? Which guy will it be?"

The team grouped in pairs, slid their helmets on, then sprinted down
the long sidewalk. They burst through the concession scrum, parting a sea
of parents and teenagers with painted faces and balloons, singing a military
cadence with Boobie's warbled voice leading the charge:

Mama, mama can't you see
Mama, mama can't you see
What Glades Central doin to me
What Glades Central doin to me
I used to drive a Cad-il-lac
I used to drive a Cad-il-lac
Now I'm beggin for a snack
Now I'm beggin for a snack

During the last stanza of "The Star-Spangled Banner," the capacity crowd began to hiss when the squad ceremoniously held their helmets high and shouted *RAIDERS!,* all but drowning out the singer.

The Knights, wearing all-black uniforms, set the tone immediately by executing a perfect onside kick and recovering the ball on the Raider forty-seven. Two seamless plays later, Frankie Williams took a handoff from quarterback Blake Rice and zipped thirty-eight yards into the end zone, beating Robert Way and the entire Glades Central secondary.

When the Robinson defense trotted onto the field, they were so tall Mario had trouble seeing the field over their heads. But it hardly mattered tonight. As the Knights lined up in their three-man front, the coach had just the answer.

Robinson, meet Aaron Baker.

Before Hester had released the Raiders onto the field, he'd laid out his strategy for the three-man front. "We goin 23 Load," he said, "and we gonna load it till they can't carry it no more. So yall better bag your teeth, squeeze your nuts. Do whatever you gotta do, goddamnit, 'cause these people gettin up out of this three-man front."

It was a staple rushing play where the guards pulled left or right and the back shot the opposite gap. And Aaron Baker, at five foot eleven and two hundred pounds, was the load the Knights never saw coming.

All season long, the sophomore halfback had been the great *if only.* Both his parents were dead, leaving him to stay with relatives in the gang-addled trailer park near the school. He floated with thugs and brimmed with ready violence. The previous season he'd been in constant trouble with teachers and his grades were horrible. Coaches had all privately braced themselves for the phone call saying he was either dead or in jail. As much as he hated doing so, Hester had been forced to kick him off the team, hoping to send a message. Baker was a classic case, a jitterbug time bomb headed for zero.

But with a mature, strapping physique and legs like timbers, he also had the potential to be a special athlete who succeeded beyond the Glades. After the game in Dallas, when Coach Randy had made both Baker and Page a season-long project, getting them out of Belle Glade and just being a friend, Baker began to thrive. So much that he even made the honor roll. In practice, he began to listen and learn: "Don't stop pumping your feet, Aaron," they told him. "Don't run with your eyes closed, Aaron!"

Most of the season, Randy had rotated Baker with Likely, Page, and Neville Brown, leaving in whoever got hot. But the past few games, the coaches had started building their postseason rushing attack specifically around Baker and Likely. Likely, who played both directions, had been the ace in the blowout against Suncoast, running over a hundred yards for two touchdowns. But tonight, one victory from O-Town, Baker was stepping into the light.

The vertical runner went headlong into the Robinson defense with a confidence and power never before seen. In three plays he drove the team to midfield to set up a pair of quick strikes to Jaime and Oliver for the touchdown.

Running off the field, Baker appeared as surprised as anyone. *"It's working, it's working,"* he shouted to Hester and Randy. *"The pumping of my feet!"*

Baker's coming-out performance proved the perfect opening for a flashy scatback such as Hubbard. Two plays into Robinson's drive, the Knights were poised on the Raider twenty-three. Rice flipped Hubbard a shovel pass and the disappearing act began. As he crossed the line of scrimmage, he came face-to-face with Robert Way, faked to his right, and blew past, flying down the sideline headed for the end zone. As Hubbard crossed the five-yard line, three steps from glory, Way—having sprinted nearly twenty yards in pursuit—suddenly pounced on him from behind and smashed the ball from his hands. It took a bounce before Way could throw his body atop it and secure the fumble.

It would be Hubbard's longest run of the game. After that, the show belonged to Baker. The running attack provided a much-needed respite for the battered Mario, who'd been in no shape for forty-eight minutes of run-and-gun football. The inclement weather had grounded the flyboys, anyway. The wind coming off the bay was bitter and turned the football as hard as ice. The leather had no give, and Mario's hands were suddenly too small to get a grip.

Denied by air, the Raiders went by train, and Baker's engines were steaming hot. He lowered his shoulder carry after carry, and moved the Raiders across the plain. Halfway through the second quarter, he broke two tackles and hit the open field for forty yards, dragging two black jerseys across the goal line. That made the score 21–7, and the Knights could never rally.

Just like the previous meeting, the Raider defense stifled Robinson's fight for life. They walled off the Knights' receivers and intercepted them twice. Play after play, they stormed the offensive line, and sandbagged the quarterback five times. Two of those sacks came courtesy of Way, who flattened Rice so hard before the second half that Way's own face mask was crushed like a beer can. One of the coaches later had to use a hammer and a pair of pliers to straighten it back.

Hubbard would finish the game with only four carries over four yards. Meanwhile, Baker had the game of his life, finishing with 142 yards, two touchdowns, and the undying knowledge that he'd given his team a second chance against Cocoa. Before the whistle ended the game, giving the Raiders the 35–10 win, word spread that the Tigers had scraped out a narrow victory at Boot Hill, defeating Madison County by the score of 17–15. Even without Buie, Cocoa had prevailed.

The rematch was on.

"Straight gutsy effort," Hester told his squad as they gathered in the end zone. "We got that ticket to the dance. That girl said yes. And when we get her to the dance . . ." He left the sentence open for the boys to bark and howl.

Just then, Ruben Gonzalez, the Knights receiver, crashed through the huddle and stood huffing in the middle. A wide stream of blood dripped from his bottom lip and painted his teeth and chin. He looked insane. He'd been crying.

"Yall take that shit, dawg, yall *take that shit.*"

He was all messy adrenaline, but the boys in the huddle were rapt. He was talking about Cocoa.

"Last year yall lost. For real, take that shit. Yall beat me and I wanted that shit bad. For real. *Go get that shit, dawg.*"

"We got ya, bro," the boys said, then applauded their fallen opponent.

Hester squeezed the receiver's shoulder as he left. "We appreciate that," he told him. "What that cat's tryin to say is that if they lose, they wanna lose to the champions. What we got ahead of us is Cocoa, baby. This is what we wanted. This is what they wanted. They got us. Those kids are the champions and that means we have to dethrone them. We have to go to Orlando and take it. Monday, we go back to work."

CHAPTER

21

The Raiders' return to the state championship sent a jolt of excitement through the school campus that week, helped in part by some other encouraging news. The state had just released the new school grades, and Glades Central, for the first time since opening its doors, had scored a C.

For most schools, such a grade would not be cause for celebration, but in Belle Glade it was monumental. A passing school grade sent a ripple of optimism throughout the embattled community: property values could rise as a result, businesses could be lured, residents might think twice before packing up and moving to the coast.

The minute the news was conveyed, a collective hallelujah erupted through the halls of the administrative building. Vice-Principal Angela Moore, who'd driven that school bus through the migrant quarter picking up kids on test days and ironing their clothes, raced to the school's

PA system and made the grand announcement, at one point becoming so emotional she broke into song.

"It *IS* a good morning, in fact," said Ms. Rudean Butts as she answered the school switchboard. "Glades Central is now a C school." The news was not lost on anyone who called.

"We knew it could be done," said Anderson, emerging from his office looking like a man who'd just enjoyed the best sleep of his life. "This truly demonstrates the progress students can make once they get to Glades Central. The monkey is finally climbing off our backs."

There was a small caveat, the principal said. For the first time, the state had determined the schools' grades by considering more than just FCAT scores. The school's graduation rate, students' overall success in AP classes, and their scores on SAT and ACT exams now factored into the grading process. But when it came to the FCAT, Anderson's students still struggled, especially with reading scores. They also needed to find a better way to advance the group of kids most at risk. In fact, the sluggish rate of improvement in the school's bottom 25 percent had narrowly kept Glades Central from earning a B grade.

"There's still more to do," he said. "But this sends the message to our teachers and students that their sacrifice and effort have not been in vain."

• • •

THE RAIDERS WOULD not be the only team from Belle Glade traveling to Orlando. Glades Day had beaten Victory Christian Academy 45–27 in the Class 1B semifinals for a championship game in the Citrus Bowl to be played on Friday. Mucksteppers from across the Glades would soon be on the move.

The cold snap that had blown in the previous week now dropped temperatures into the low thirties. The wind off Lake Okeechobee was damp and settled in the bones. As the Raiders prepared for the biggest test of their young careers, many practiced while numb in their fingers and toes. Most spent the majority of the time with their hands tucked down their crotches to keep warm. Mario clenched his teeth and said nothing.

The freezing temperatures were also ravaging crops throughout the Glades. The big farms from Moore Haven down to Belle Glade began sending fleets of helicopters zipping low across their fields of beans and corn to keep the frost from settling. It was a decades-old practice. The blades pushed down warmer air that hovered some forty feet off the ground, where the difference in temperature could be as much as ten degrees. But there were risks in flying low and often before the sun. On December 8, three choppers went down in the freezing fields near Pahokee, all in the same morning.

Along with the cold, the month of December ushered in college recruiters by the dozen. Now permitted to visit schools, they arrived from programs far and wide: Buffalo, Kansas, Iowa State, Syracuse, and Toledo, just to name a few. But the big news that second week was that Urban Meyer was stepping down as the University of Florida's head coach, throwing into question the future of every kid from Jacksonville down to Naples who'd already given the Gators his commitment. Weeks earlier, the Miami Hurricanes had fired coach Randy Shannon with the same results. After Davonte got hot in November, Miami—his dream school—made an informal offer. But in the days after Shannon's exit, the calls stopped coming. The recruiting coaches, too, had been sacked, their words of honor meaningless once the swinging doors hit them on the way out.

Benjamin knew that Meyer's imminent departure would certainly throw Coach Z's future into question. His decision seemed easier now. In the days afterward, a Seminoles cap remained perched upon his head, yet he gave nothing away.

The nation's eighth-ranked receiver still told reporters he was undecided. I'd like to see who's replacing Meyer, he mused. Perhaps I'll give LSU a second look, he told the *Post*. He even scheduled an official visit to West Virginia, stirring up the pot even more, then failed to board the plane, saying he was sick.

"I'll probably hold a press conference," he finally said one afternoon.

After months of waiting and anticipation, Mario secured a college trip. Coach Field, the recruiting coordinator at Hampton University, had been watching from the stands the previous week against American Heritage. He'd seen Mario rise from the dead like Lazarus and pound his way downfield to set up the field goal that secured the victory. Afterward, he'd arranged to fly the quarterback to tour their campus and athletic facilities once the season was over. Now among the Chosen Ones, Mario could be heard at practice saying, "I can't *wait* to take that visit, *bwah*."

Davonte and Robert Way had recently returned from their official visit to Marshall, transfixed. In November 1970, the Thundering Herd lost thirty-seven members of its varsity team and eight coaches in a tragic plane crash, an event that still rallied the town of Huntington. It was even the subject of a Hollywood film, *We Are Marshall*, which Way had watched twice on YouTube before leaving.

In Huntington, the two boys socialized with the team and watched a game; then JaJuan Seider had taken them around town. For Way, it was like football heaven and cast Belle Glade into a harsh new perspective.

"That whole town is green," he said, referring to the school colors. "Everything surrounds that team. We'd be eating in a restaurant and people would come up to us and say, 'Yall football players?' and we'd say, 'No, recruits,' and they'd still shake our hands and say, 'Welcome, hope you can come.'

"I mean, even when the Herd made mistakes on the field, the community backed the team no matter what."

He could only imagine.

During those weeks, most of the recruiters came to see Davonte and Way. Others came to eyeball the various goods on display with hopes of getting an overlooked sleeper. For the most part, their demeanor was peculiar. The culture of scandal and punishment in college football now dictated their every move. Most were polite but cagey with coaches and skittish around reporters, with whom they were forbidden to speak about potential recruits under NCAA rules. And because they weren't allowed to speak with players until the season's end, they tried their best to remain inconspicuous. They hugged the sidelines like Secret Service men, mostly in silence, scribbled things on clipboards, then climbed back into their rental cars and drove away.

Some recruiters didn't try to hide their disdain for the region, even while feeding from its trough. Former Tennessee coach Lane Kiffin had upset many in the Glades two years before when he'd said this about Pahokee: "There ain't a gas station that works. Nobody's got enough money to even have shoes or a shirt on."

A recruiter from Illinois was just as shameless as he stood on the sidelines at Glades Central. He was good-looking, like Joaquin Phoenix, and seemed proud of himself for having paddled so deep into the heart of darkness.

"So are all these guys involved in crime, or what?" he asked a reporter, and smirked.

Then, later, "You go into their houses and stuff? I bet they all look like shit inside."

When he heard the answer was negative, that most were actually pretty nice, he looked embarrassed and quickly changed the subject. Later he said he was hoping to lure away a defensive lineman.

If the presence of recruiters on the sidelines incited anxiety or excitement, the Raiders never showed it. Recruiters had simply become part of the late-season landscape, like cane trailers on the highway or the ash that settled each morning on windshields. And despite the enormous dominion the university men possessed over their futures—for they were the rainmakers of the Glades—surprisingly little was even said about them once they were gone. Either they'd already called you or they had not. For the ones who had not been called, the smart ones anyway, all you could do was give a hundred percent when the men entered your orbit and hope to hear something before February. Talking loud about it with your boys only made you look stupid when the call never came. Or that was the thought, anyway.

But on this particular week, all attention was toward O-Town. Starting Monday, Purvis and several teammates gathered for daily prayer, asking God for guidance and clarity. Jaime would awake each night around 3:00 a.m. from dreams of already playing the game; the lights and sounds of crashing bodies left his heart racing too fast for sleep.

Each day after school, both Mario and Way would sit at home and replay film of last year's championship. They searched for the soft spots in the Tiger line, studied how the secondary stacked up against the pass. Mainly, though, they watched to see themselves lose—to feel that helpless panic again and again as the Tiger lead expanded and the clock ratcheted down to nothing. For Mario, it brought back that emptiness as he watched Cocoa celebrate and the conviction that came, so pure in his guts, that he would walk that field again.

"I'll bring us here," he'd told his coach.

For the Glades Central coaches, the preparation focused on pushing Cocoa out of its comfort zone: shutting down their highly efficient running game and making them pass. Compared to the modern red-gun attack of the Raiders, the Tiger offense was an homage to the old breed, a thin but effective playbook of "wing-T" and "power-I" formations.

Coach John Wilkinson would run it until you couldn't stand it. Wilkinson trusted his rushing attack so much that his quarterback had only executed one pass all postseason.

A key component to stopping the rush was stopping Chevelle Buie— who at that point was still the great unknown. It was still unclear if the running back would be playing on Saturday in Orlando, and Cocoa officials were saying nothing on the matter.

By then, the rumors in Belle Glade about Buie had become absurdly colorful. One had the player brandishing a gun. Someone else on the team said Buie's only crime was that he'd been caught skipping school.

"Nah, dawg," a teammate interrupted. "He got caught skippin school *and* stealin a car. For real, bro."

With no clear information, all the Raiders could do was practice and prepare for the young man whose legs had beaten them the previous season. Thoughts of crushing Buie and the Tigers were what woke them up in the mornings and put them to bed at night.

"Buie's ass needs to play," Hester said that week. "He's part of their team. That's the kid who did it to us. If he aint there, then who do we defeat? He's that diamond-encrusted egg they got in that basket. And we comin to take everything in it. Buie needs to be there."

• • •

ON THURSDAY AFTERNOON, 150 miles north of Belle Glade, a gray and turbulent sky churned over the town of Cocoa. The town was centered in the storied "Space Coast," just across the Indian River lagoon from Cape Canaveral, the Kennedy Space Center, and the powdery sands of Cocoa Beach. The arrival of the space industry in the 1960s had quadrupled Cocoa's population, which continued to grow to more than sixteen thousand residents.

But in the past decade, as ambitions of space exploration have diminished, many of the high-paying jobs have moved elsewhere. Cocoa now had the highest poverty rate in Brevard County, at 27 percent, and the lowest number of college-educated residents. And like Glades Central, the high school had been a perennial low performer. In 2006, four administrators had to be removed for rigging the school's FCAT results.

After school the Tigers hit the practice field at Cocoa Municipal Stadium, located directly across from campus. A heavy drizzle began to fall, pushed sideways by a bitter Atlantic wind that whistled through the rafters. On the field, many of the boys wore spirit jerseys underneath their pads that read, COMPLETE THE MISSION. LET'S RIDE TIGERS. There was no sign of Buie.

Athletic director Chuck Goldfarb appeared in a golf cart and got out. He was an older man, tanned and loquacious, the kind who seemed more at home selling oceanfront developments than running a sports program at a scrappy central Florida high school. As the Tigers ran through their drills, he guessed the town was not dissimilar to Belle Glade: too few jobs, too much temptation, and a narrow, stunted worldview. "We have a hard time getting kids to want to leave Cocoa," he said. "They don't care to know anything beyond this place."

Goldfarb came to Cocoa twelve years ago after having won two championships as baseball coach at the regional powerhouse Merritt Island, just nine miles across the river toward Cape Canaveral. When he arrived, the Tiger football team had one of the worst records in the region; in four years they'd won only six games, and they had just one playoff victory in their entire history. Only one coach on the squad had ever played college ball, and two others had never suited up in their lives.

"I fired them all," Goldfarb said.

Even worse, the Tigers were sharing a home field with their rival, Rockledge High School, giving the team no sense of ownership. So Goldfarb worked with the city to build a $3.5 million stadium, then went looking for a new coach. In 2002 he hired one of the best: Gerald Odom, his old friend who'd won back-to-back state titles at Merritt Island in '78 and '79 and was already one of the winningest coaches in the history of Florida high school football.

Known for both his tough discipline and compassion, Odom took a squad of mostly black, no-name teenagers, many of them from broken homes and vulnerable to trouble, and chiseled them into competitors.

"I don't understand what they're saying half the time," the sixty-two-year-old coach told a reporter shortly after arriving. "As long as they understand what I'm saying, though, we're okay."

In 2003, Odom got the Tigers to 9–2 and met Glades Central in the regional semifinals, held in Cocoa. The undefeated Raiders were rolling toward their fourth title in six years and, as usual, were brimming with celebrity. Their all-star quarterback, Omar Haugabook, was the state's leading passer and would later embark on a stellar career at Troy. The Raider first-team all-state wide receiver, Albert Dukes, would later sign with Ohio State.

But on this night, Odom's squad of anonymous storm troopers flew out of the gate and kicked the mighty Raiders off their feet. It was an epic fight, with the lead changing five times throughout the night. Haugabook was sacked eight times for losses of eighty-three yards, yet still managed to throw for four hundred yards and four touchdowns. He even ran for one himself.

In what would become the team's signature style, Cocoa had rallied in the final minutes to execute the fatal plays that mattered most: a fake bootleg fumblerooski that set up the leading touchdown, followed by a forty-three-yard breakaway run that sealed the game. The Tigers went on to eliminate the Raiders 45–35.

After Odom resigned two years later, his methodical style and philosophy were carried over by Wilkinson, his former assistant and disciple. Wilkinson had played offensive guard under Odom at Merritt Island and, after graduating from UF, had come aboard as his offensive coordinator. He'd then followed the coach to New Smyrna Beach, where Odom had transformed the program, and then finally to Cocoa.

"Johnny is just a highly intelligent person, and that transposes to football," said Goldfarb. "Our kids believe in our coaches. We've got the same bad influences as Belle Glade and elsewhere, but our kids have bought into our program and staff."

That much was clear. Unlike the Raiders, the Tigers practiced mostly in silence. There was no evidence of showboating, no smack talking, no small fires that erupted to derail the schedule. As the offense ran series of old-style sweep plays, bootlegs, and flea flickers, even the B-squad stood attentive along the sidelines. Even more striking was the presence of only six assistant coaches on the field—as opposed to Glades Central's twelve—each of them locked into his own assignment. There were no jokes, no passing around porn on smartphones, no idlers on the sidelines with vague and dubious titles. There in the cold rain, the scene on the field was almost militaristic, a place where ego and tomfoolery, even passion, had been drilled out of the atmosphere.

And in this absence, there was still no sign of Buie. Goldfarb shook his head at the mention of the running back's name, then called over Wilkinson.

"Buie's not going to play," he said.

When the coach arrived, neither he nor Goldfarb would say what Buie had done, only that he would not be suiting up in Orlando.

"The team will be great without him," said the coach, who wore a goatee and still carried the stocky build of a lineman. "They know he made a mistake and they'll do it for him. Buie gets a lot of attention, but we have a lot of talented kids on this team. We'll see some kids stepping up."

The next day, both the Florida High School Athletic Association and the Brevard County school board cleared Buie to play, saying they were satisfied with his punishment. But it was the head coach who made the final decision, and the ultimate gamble, to go a step further and bench his marquee player in the biggest game of the season.

As Wilkinson described it to the local paper, he drove over to Buie's house and told him "eye to eye." No matter how much he loved Buie as a kid, he said, and no matter how much the team and Tiger Nation thought they needed Buie to play, there was a larger message to deliver.

"There's consequences to rules," Wilkinson said. "Nobody is above the program."

CHAPTER

As much as Hester wanted Buie on the field, he knew better than to believe his absence made Cocoa a weaker team. Just from studying film, he knew the Tigers had three other players in their backfield who were capable of feats equal to or greater than Buie's, boys who'd sunk opponents that season on their own.

If anything, Hester knew that Buie's absence could only sharpen his teammates' resolve and, most important, that Cocoa played best when they were down. He'd learned that from watching them beat the Raiders.

But there were other intangible factors, things for which he could not prepare. There was Cocoa's thirty-seven-game winning streak, now the longest in the state. There was also the fact that all postseason, the Tigers had survived three of the best teams in Florida despite having trouble scoring, and having committed a number of near-fatal turnovers. Even Goldfarb said the Tigers should have lost to Orlando Jones "by four touchdowns." But still, the team had always caught breaks and found a way to win.

Superstitious as Hester was, he dared not give voice to what kept turning in his mind: the Tigers were playing lucky. And that, above all else, was what worried him the most.

It had been an exhausting week. By now the Raiders had practiced for every possible scenario and honed every conceivable key to victory: the OL blocking Cocoa's swarming pass rush; shutting down their sweep running plays and ensuring the linebackers and ends didn't get trapped inside; forcing the five-man front by running the ball into their faces, then pulverizing defensive back Rick Rivers and their secondary with crossing routes and deep passes.

"That DB is soft against receivers," Hester said of Rivers during film. "We're gonna go at him all night."

All week the coaches had stayed late watching film, arguing over strategy and tweaking the schedule. On Thursday evening after practice was over, they gathered in the film room to get out of the cold and ate sausages pulled hot off a parking-lot grill. Coach King, who'd seen a lot of great Raider teams fall over the years, pulled up a chair and looked at every coach in the room.

"I've been around a long time, fellas," he said. "And I think these guys are ready. In my mind, we done won this thing."

For Hester, it was too early to know. He didn't see it on Friday afternoon when the team gathered for one last walk-through before leaving. Despite looking dressed for the big dance, with maroon polos and pressed khakis, shoes polished, hair freshly cut with uniform tags across the backs of their skulls that read, simply, STATE BOUND '10—it was the Old Raiders who'd appeared, dragging ass through their drills, clowning instead of following instruction, still freelancing out in the void. If only they could have seen the way the Tigers had looked in the cold, driving rain.

The coach let out a sigh. "It's too late for you to change because of who you are," he said. "And that's the only thing I'm disappointed about."

• • •

BUT SOMETHING MUST have occurred on the three-hour bus ride to Orlando, perhaps a slow but sobering register of the kind of battle that awaited. Along the way, the team learned that Glades Day had just beaten Warner Christian in the 1B championship held in the Citrus Bowl, giving the Gators seven titles, one more than both the Raiders and the Pahokee Blue Devils. Taylor had scored the winning touchdown, one of five that afternoon.

The added pressure seemed to purge the boyish energy and align each player into a state of deep reflection. That night in the hotel, the cell phones and gameboards were surrendered and turned off. The hallways were silent. Lying two to a bed, the Raiders went to sleep and played their final game in their dreams.

Boobie found himself standing near midfield. There were lights all around, then loud voices. Screaming. It was Purvis and Buie. They were in some kind of argument and Buie was crying. *Why was Buie crying? Where is everyone? Purv, man, come on. We gotta get our stuff on and play.* Suddenly the team was lined up on either side, looking at him. Through the row of face masks, he saw their eyes were wide and wanting. He saw the ball perched upon the white line, ready for the kickoff. Boobie took his steps, felt the leather smack his foot just as someone pounded on the door of his room. He shot straight up in bed, looked over at Jaja, who was still asleep beside him. *Holy shit.*

"Jaja, wake up," he shouted. "We at state, *bwah!*"

It was the dream that Boobie shared as the team filed into a small conference room that morning after breakfast. Hester had called a casual meeting in order to review last-minute changes, to keep the minds fresh and bodies busy before the four o'clock bus. But the gathering soon turned into something else entirely.

Hester started by reviewing a few route patterns with his receivers; then his coaches asked to address the room. Most delivered rah-rah speeches about the great magnitude of the event, of the boys' duty to their downtrodden town, to the Raider program, and to all the men who'd ever worn the maroon and gold.

"Take a look back and see how much you guys have improved from March until now," said Coach JD, cutting closer to bone. "Some of you guys have made a complete turnaround, both mentally and physically. The skills are there, the teaching is there. All you gotta do is believe that it's inside of you."

The quarterback then stood up.

"Yall boys know that after that Skyline game, all the criticism came: how I'm too short, too fat, too slow. How we aint ever gonna have a winning season. You know, that hurt me inside. They said we couldn't get past the first round of the playoffs. You know why? They said that 'cause of me. They don't think I have the ability to carry my team on my back. But I've told yall from day one that I'd get us back to the promised land. Last year, after we lost, I just sat on that field and stared at the scoreboard. I told Coach Hester that we'd be back. And I be damned, we back.

"I took all the criticism for yall, *bwah*," he said, his voice rising from his gut. "Yall feel me? I put my recruiting in jeopardy for yall. But we here now. So let's go and win this shit."

The room erupted with applause, and Hester rose and addressed his captain, repeating what he'd told Mario, the team, and the town all season long.

"Coaches on the team talkin about you. Players talkin about you. I tell them what I told you. I'm the coach and you the guy. *You the guy.*

"You wanna replace him? Who we gonna replace him with? Who else is better suited to lead us than him? We got capable quarterbacks that could do *okay*, but they don't give us the best chance to win. Mario, you always said I got your back. Well, homeboy, I got yours."

The exchange between the coach and the captain seemed to tap an emotional reservoir in each boy that lay guarded under lock and key. Before Hester could sit down, Courtney Porter stood and asked to speak.

Porter was a reserve defensive back, an ambitious student with dreams of college and becoming a math teacher. He'd come a long way from Jacksonville, where, as a boy, his father had sold crack to a procession of addicts that moved through their house day and night. Courtney's grandmother in South Bay had finally taken him after one of the junkies extinguished a cigarette on his chest. "I just remember them wiping off the blood," he once said. "After that, I learned to watch my back." He'd been four at the time.

Porter now stood among his teammates and addressed Hester. "I aint ever had a pops in my life," he said. "He's been in jail trying to raise me from the mail, and it's never worked. But over these three years you've been with me, Coach, you've been like a pop to me. Just you, Coach."

Tears were already running down Hester's face as he walked toward Porter and embraced him. A man hugging a boy who needed to be hugged, who needed to know that a man's love could be healing and real. And when it was over, Hester briefly excused himself from the room.

As he composed himself in the hallway, he realized what was happening. It had snuck up on him like a heart attack, made him weep like a child. After three years of struggling to win them over, persuading them to trust and to believe in themselves and the program, to allow themselves to be loved, he was finally breaking through. It occurred to him that no matter what the scoreboard said later that night, no matter the wins or losses on the season, the ranking in the national press, inside that small room, the Raiders were already winning their greatest victory.

Standing in the doorway of what could be their greatest day, surrounded by the safety of four walls and teammates who'd bonded as family, one that did not lie, cheat, or walk away, many of the boys let their emotions run.

They stood one by one and gave their testimony, let go some pain. They spoke of failures, disappointments, and regrets, and, at the same time, described a feeling of pride in themselves they'd never before experienced.

"I got kicked off the team last year," said Baker. "But Coach Randy came to me every day this season, talkin to me about what I needed to do in school and stuff. Boobie kept tellin me good work and to keep my grades up. So I made an effort. First nine weeks, I didn't get into trouble, no talking back to teachers. My first report card I had As and Bs and one D. I hung it on the fridge like a kid. My sister even gave me money. And every game I worked hard and I listened, and it worked. Last year I cried, but this year we're back. We in state."

Seniors confessed to having cried the whole night, fearing what lay ahead when the sun rose tomorrow.

"The last time I cried I was in like seventh grade," said Oliver, "but I cried last night. It's my last time to play football with yall, and I love yall. And when coach calls a running play, I'm gonna be blocking my ass off."

"Ever since I got to Glades Central," said Page, "football has been like a light, like an everlasting light compared to what I've been through in my life. This has been a journey I never imagined. I just feel like I'm living a dream right now."

What had started in the quarterback still pushed to be free, and after some time, he stood, trembling all over. For the first time in his life, he spoke openly about his parents.

He shared his father's dream of having a son win a championship ring, how his brothers had been unable to deliver that gift. How life as he knew it had lost all purpose once his father died, and it was only because of his sister, his coach, and the brothers in the room that he now found reason to live and be great. But it was no rousing homily, no message to inspire or stir the team into battle. Rather, it was a boy staring down from the peak of his young life and wanting nothing more than to share it with his mom and his dad.

"I just wanna tell yall, *bwah,* if you got a mama, just love her," he said, his voice strained and weakened from tears. "I got to look at my mama and daddy in a picture every day, and it hurts me to death. I just want yall to know that there aint nobody like your mama. There aint nobody like your mama 'cause when she gone, she aint ever coming back."

He could lead his team as promised, carry them to their crowded hour, yet what he said now suggested that he could never fully savor its reward, for there would always be an emptiness inside of him, one he would always keep searching to fill.

The captain sat down, buckled under the weight of his grief. And for one of the last times in his life, his Raiders put their hands together and assured him, "You got us."

• • •

THE TEAM BOARDED the bus at four o'clock, cloaked in a confidence that wrapped them like new skin. Never before had they felt such an accord, such union of mind and purpose.

They said little as the bus rounded West Church Street and the Citrus Bowl came into view, looming colossal, every bit as intimidating as the occasion. As the afternoon sun began to fade in the sky, the stadium glowed from within, as if brimming with treasure. The early game was still in progress, a triple-overtime thriller between Davie-University School and Ocala Trinity Catholic for the 2B title. Minutes after the bus pulled into the lot, University failed on a two-point conversion to lose the game 56–55. The running back who'd been stopped inches from the goal line had remained on the turf and wept.

Through the windows of the bus, the Raiders watched University exit the stadium like the walking wounded. They steadied themselves on parents and girlfriends, their faces drawn and their eyes dim, swollen, and red. When the Raiders took over their locker room, it still hummed with sweat and the off-gassing of adrenaline.

Second-place medals littered the floor and greeted the team like dead, bloated animals. Baker stepped around one and eyed it with disgust. "Don't want no silver," he said to himself, then looked up. "Silver don't buy you shit in Belle Glade."

The boys found their lockers and began to dress with a strange, pressing urgency. Above the door leading to the field, a giant digital clock ticked down the minutes and seconds until kickoff. Its bright neon numbers seemed to lord over the room like a moon pulling tide, speeding time and the beat of the heart, drawing everyone toward the door and into uncertainty.

"Tighten up. Let's go!" shouted Coach JD, blasting his whistle for warm-ups.

The team hurried through the door and onto the field, then slowed to a jog to drink it all in. Under a crisp, dark sky, the lights of the Citrus Bowl were radiant and white and illuminated every object like a dream of heaven. The turf glowed electric green and seemed to stretch a thousand yards. Cameras were everywhere as Fox Sports Florida prepared to beam the broadcast across the Sunshine State.

Up in the visitors' stands, the mucksteppers were already several thousand strong and still arriving. The lights and distance from the field blurred their features into a patchwork of the Glades: dark skin and maroon mixed with the green and gold of the Glades Day whites. When the Raiders appeared in sight, they let out a collective roar.

The Cocoa Tigers entered the field as the Raiders began their drills. They wore slick, all-black uniforms with numbers and cleats punctuated in bright neon orange, a combination that evoked an image of speed. Up high in the opposite stands, the Tiger Nation formed a matching sea of black and orange and rumbled to life, waving tiger paws and already chanting *"THREE-PEAT-THREE-PEAT."*

At the sight of Glades Central at the far end, the Tigers let out a battle cry and began to run. They stopped at midfield, and, in a rare display of bravado, raised their helmets in victory, letting it be known the champions had arrived.

Back in the locker room, the clock reeled off the seconds and stirred the room into a frenzy. But in the far corner, the quarterback appeared impervious to the pull of its current. He sat in a metal chair outside his locker, wrists and cleats immaculately wrapped in tape, his body battered and tired.

His head was still not right. The headaches still visited him—ribbons of pain that shot across his temples and popped out of his eyes—but they came with less frequency now. He also seemed thinner. For once the quarterback's gut no longer spilled from under his flak vest, and his face appeared wan. He leaned forward in his chair, fingers locked, and stared at the floor. As banged up as Mario was, he'd never felt more ready to play football in his life.

Just like the quarterback, Davonte was playing hurt. That week, he'd managed to find the only hole in the Raider practice field and twisted his ankle. It had swollen up and sent pain shooting up his leg when he'd tried to walk on it. He sat out for two days, and, on Grandma Nora's orders, soaked the ankle in warm water and Epsom salts until his toes shriveled and turned gray. It was still tender when the trainer wrapped it with tape, but after a dose of ibuprofen and a few seconds under the bracing lights, he could have run all the way to Belle Glade and back.

Sitting there waiting to begin, the receiver calmed his mind by picturing the ring on the shelf next to his old Bible. There it was, the power and the glory. Deacon Julius could no doubt find a sermon in that one. He focused on the ring until it was clear in his mind, until the light began to sparkle off its crown of diamonds. And once he had the ring, he imagined two.

With only minutes left until kickoff, Hester stood before his team one last time. He'd been studying the faces, he said, and there were still some in the room who were not ready, some who still did not understand.

"We're not just happy to be here," said the coach. "We're here to win. Nothing else. We are here to win."

He took a show of hands: Who was ready to walk through that door and take it from the champions? The response was staggered. "Yall who put your hand up first," he said, "you got some scared ones with you. You got to show them that it's okay. Show the ones who are a little scared that it's okay. Show 'em how to fight. Show them the way."

The clock signaled it was time to go. The Raiders lined up according to number, with Mario standing at the lead. As the announcer called their names, they ran through the door and into the light.

• • •

IN TERMS OF size, the Cocoa defense could have been Muck City boys in different dress: small, agile, and liquid fast. Anchored by the linebacker Antonio Wallace and Rick Rivers in the secondary, they'd held opponents to an average of just six points per game. No team had scored on them in the first quarter. To add ornament to their menace, the defense had even named themselves the Dark Side. They hung together outside of school, dressed in black whenever possible, even lobbied the Tiger band to learn "The Imperial Death March," the theme music for Darth Vader.

On the Raiders' first snap, they turned on the dark.

Mario dropped back in the shotgun while four receivers flew out of the gate. He saw Davonte on a short route up the right side, and slung the ball. But from out of nowhere, a black jersey sealed the hole and swatted it down. The message was sent.

A false-start penalty pushed the Raiders back five yards, and then Baker rushed into nowhere, leaving Mario with third and long.

He shouted to the Dark Side, *"No three-peats tonight!"* then took the snap. He found Oliver wide open on the very same route and made the Tigers pay. The catch was good for twenty yards and the first down.

The next play, Baker ran once again into a wall as linebacker Grady Redding hit the halfback at full speed in the gap. The sound of helmet meeting bone echoed through the stadium and raised up a howl. Baker shook it off and walked to the backfield to reload.

Seeing the pattern, the defense then gave Mario a three-man front, daring him to go deep. He teased them instead, lobbing a short floater up the left side for Jaime that gave the Raiders a fresh set of downs and carried them across midfield. The mucksteppers cried, *"MOVE THEM STICKS!"*

In the days before the game, Rick Rivers must have caught word that he was a soft target. Indeed, the defensive back—whom Hester identified as the crack in the Dark Side through which the flyboys would sail—kept his brown locks braided with bright orange beads. They poked through from underneath his helmet, swayed whenever he ran, and complemented the orange Tiger trim of his jersey. The six-foot-one cornerback may have given up the pass in the miraculous win over Orlando Jones, but tonight, with the cameras rolling, pretty boy Rivers was snapping.

On the next play, he remained one step ahead of the Raider offensive line as Mario dropped back and found Davonte five yards upfield. As soon as the ball touched Davonte's hands, Rivers appeared from shallow space and drove the receiver into the backfield for a loss of three yards.

On the sideline, Hester was livid. *"Goddamnit, Jaime!"* he shouted. Jaime had been playing the inside receiver. When Rivers had torn past, he'd barely put up his arm to block. Once again, the little things.

On third down and eight, Mario's pass to Burgess sailed over the receiver's head and was blown incomplete. On their first drive of the game, the Raiders were forced to punt it away.

As the offense ran onto the sideline, they felt the giant hands of Benjamin slap the tops of their helmets. "Yall get that, *bwah,*" he said.

The receiver wore his Raider jersey over a garnet Seminoles sweatshirt, along with a pair of massive headphones wrapped around his neck. And like Buie, the other deposed superstar on the opposite side of the field, KB watched his team with a jumble of emotions.

The six weeks spent away from football had left him to focus on his college decision and linger in the rhapsody, but it had also left him mentally drained. Reporters were constantly calling. Coach Z still phoned once a week, determined as always, even as the floor seemed to slip from beneath him. And it seemed that everywhere Kelvin went in Belle Glade, someone else had an opinion about his future. Often he just stayed home with his girlfriend, Mika, or sought tutoring after school. Because of his time spent in jail, Kelvin was having to retake ten classes in order to meet NCAA requirements. All of the schoolwork and commotion had at least kept his mind off not playing for the Raiders. In a weird way, it had also given him a peace about his senior season.

"In a way I'm happy I aint out there," he'd said earlier that week, "'cause most of them cats had settled on just being behind me and stuff. Especially Davonte. I knew he had more potential, but he wasn't giving his all 'cause I was out there. I was getting the recognition. Most of the people coming to the games wasn't watching those guys. Now it's good because they can see them. Now it's not just about me."

It was a selfless acknowledgment from a player whose eyes were cast toward greater glory. But the truth remained that here under the lights of the Citrus Bowl, before God and the Glades, the receiver would have given just about anything to suit up and go out a champion.

• • •

THE TIGER OFFENSE sprinted onto the field led by the diminutive quarterback Latravious Campbell. In the huddle, he was so short that his teammates had to crouch slightly to hear the play. But the Cocoa offense required no gunslinger to fire downrange, but rather a levelheaded technician to set the earthmovers in motion. And tonight, Campbell had an assortment in his bay, not the least of whom was Chevelle Buie's replacement, Antwan Lee.

Coming off the bench to substitute for a national top-ten running back, Lee was a five-ten, 170-pound sophomore with only 145 yards to his name. But he'd pulled his weight against Madison County the previous week, running for a touchdown and sixty-eight yards, enough to convince Wilkinson to give him the cherished start in the finals. "He proved himself when his number was called," the coach said.

Jaime's punt had pinned Cocoa on their own five-yard line. With Lee lining up deep in the end zone behind Campbell, the Tigers went to work. The fullback had a head of steam as he hit the Raider line and moved them four yards into safer territory. Campbell then faked a toss and set up a trap. The defense parted as running back Devonte Jones raced through the middle gap for the first down. The next play, the Tigers' parade of hardware was finally complete as Tarean Folston introduced himself with a four-yard hammerstep to move the ball to the twenty-five.

The Raider defense received their new callers by slamming the door in their faces and forcing them to punt. But Robert Way, his nerves firing in overdrive, overshot his block attempt and tackled the punter, Cody White. Way cursed himself as he got up and saw the yellow flag glowing on the turf beside him. The penalty gave the Tigers the first down and sent memories of the previous year rushing like an ominous wind through the stands. But, luckily for the Raiders, the Tigers had yet to settle down themselves. A pair of penalties erased two commanding runs by Folston and Jones, stranding the offense in their own territory and forcing them to punt again.

Two of the best defenses in the state quickly found their groove and managed the tempo into the second quarter, each denying the other mere inches of ground on fourth-down attempts. With seven minutes left in the half, Mario found a crack in the Dark Side.

The drive started out in shambles. The Raider defense had once again forced the punt, and White's kick had put Glades Central back at their own sixteen. On the first play, no Raider receivers bothered to block on a screen pass to Jaime, leaving a wide-open lane for a surging Tra Cadore. The linebacker wrapped Jaime at the line of scrimmage and deposited his body on the Raider ten. The next snap, Jeffery Philibert could not hold his man, and the Tigers swarmed the hole and buried Mario on the three.

It was third down and twenty-three when Mario waded halfway into his own end zone and called for the snap. A fevered howl rose from the stands and lifted into the dark night. One half of the stadium cried for two points and his blood; the other just hoped to shoo the ghosts that caused their boy to scramble and be cut down in the weeds.

But instead of running scared, the quarterback hung in the pocket. He fingered the ball and let his eyes roll over the gaps. Calm. Breathing. Alone. Everything seemed to fall away, and for the first time, the middle revealed itself.

For months he'd been listening to Hester shout *"Check down! Check down!,"* reminding him of the underneath receiver running the hot route across the middle. Mario had never been comfortable with the middle, partly because he'd always had trouble seeing over the line. And without fail, Monday film would find Hester pointing out the receivers running free in the shallows, usually while Mario scrambled and launched it deep.

"All you have to do is find the defender," Hester would say. "And if you can find him, the middle is yours. The receiver will be there. Just trust yourself." Instead, Mario had always played it safe and looked for the outside man.

"It's just a confidence thing," Hester said. "As soon as he finds his confidence, he'll see the field."

Now on third and long, wading in the lake of fire of his own end zone, the quarterback saw the middle. And cutting right across it was Burgess. He fired the ball with such velocity that it jerked the six-foot receiver backward, as if he'd latched hold of a rocket. The pass was good for thirty yards, the hardest he'd thrown all season. Two plays later, he found the middle again and hit Jaime for another first down.

But as Mario had stepped back to throw, Redding pounded through an open crease and rounded his right side. The quarterback had seen him coming, but it was too late. As he released the ball, the linebacker speared him in the ribs just below the shoulder blade and knocked him off his feet. Blood rushed to his ears as he landed on his stomach, clawing the turf and gasping for breath. He flopped onto his back, ripping at the flak vest that squeezed his lungs with the terrible weight of the blue-black sky above.

No air! No air!

Several coaches rushed out and lifted the vest, just as Mario's lungs filled enough to gag—then came . . . short . . . stuttered . . . life-sustaining breaths. After a minute, the coaches pulled Mario to his feet and the stadium erupted. The Jumbotron had shown it all.

The quarterback sat out for one play—a handoff to Baker from Davis that went two yards—before toeing the white line, wanting back in. As he trotted to the huddle, he looked toward Redding and smiled. The Raiders lined up at midfield, four receivers loaded on the wings.

"We 'bout to turn this shit up," the quarterback said, and took the snap.

The play call was "sally," in which all four receivers run a quick slant. Mario aimed for Davonte. Ten yards upfield, the receiver planted and twirled to make the catch—just as Rick Rivers flew into its path. The ball zipped right through the cornerback's glove, missing by an inch, and into Davonte's hands. Rivers fell as Davonte tore down the sideline, dodging one, then two defenders who dove for his legs. He was finally knocked out of bounds, but not before stretching his body like a piece of putty to get the ball over the pylon.

"*Let's ride, baby!*" he screamed, as Jaime lifted him into the air. "*Let's ride!*"

But the officials blew the whistle and ruled him out of bounds at the one-yard line—even as Fox's instant replay, broadcast on the Jumbotron above, clearly showed him catching the corner.

A handoff to Baker then got nowhere. A pass to Burgess was tipped and nearly intercepted. So Mario, after driving ninety-seven yards and taking the hardest hit of his life, hiked the ball from the shotgun, lowered his shoulder, and ran it through himself.

Touchdown!

Marvin's extra point gave the Raiders a 7–0 lead, which they took into the half.

• • •

THE BOYS HURRIED into the locker room, feeling high and buzzing all over. They could feel it: they *had* them. The defense had held the Tigers to just fifty-seven yards, denied the open field, and, just before the whistle, even forced a rare turnover when Boobie broadsided Lee like a train. Still, the Tigers were the best, most dangerous team any of them had ever seen— even without Chevelle Buie.

But so were the Raiders, especially right now, grooving in the tailwind of their captain. They would follow him anywhere.

"This is our last twenty-four minutes," Mario said, pacing the room. "Make it our best. Make the last twenty-four minutes our best!"

"Defense, if they don't score, we win. Plain and simple," Hester said. "Offense, we got to keep going, baby. We got to finish those blocks and keep making plays. Let's go clean this up right now. *Right now.* This is *our* half. We got to shut these people down."

"Be smart," he warned as the clock pulled them out the door. "'Cause it's gonna be hard for these guys to get something big on us, and they know this. It'll have to be some kind of trick."

The team pressed around their quarterback, raised their hands, and said it on three:

"FINISH! FINISH! FINISH!"

• • •

IF THERE WAS one thing the Tigers had in spades, it was tricks. Lethal combinations of simple plays they could employ with devastating precision. But as they lined up to receive the kickoff, there were no tricks in their bag. They didn't need them.

Boobie's squib kick tumbled across midfield to the thirty-two, forcing Antwan Lee to spin and give chase as a pack of Raiders closed in. From the middle lane, Boobie watched the fullback grab hold of the ball and followed the momentum of his body, cutting right to meet him when he turned back around. The teammate to Boobie's left abandoned his lane and followed his lead. A split second later, Lee—playing only in his second start of the season, all of 145 yards to his name—fooled everyone by reversing course and wheeling the other way. There in front of him was a gaping path straight to glory. Sixty-nine yards. No one even came close to catching him.

As Lee zipped past and pranced into the end zone, Hester was dumbfounded. He'd seen Boobie misjudge the takeoff, but who was that running next to him, the kid who left his lane? He turned to Sam, the special teams coach, and together they said the same thing: "Where is Jaja?"

"Where the fuck is Jaja?"

They both spun around to find Jaja, the all-star linebacker, second-leading tackler, special teams enforcer who'd never allowed a breakaway, sitting by himself on the bench—a look of pure horror across his face.

Besides being the most disciplined player on the team, Jaja was also a really nice guy. So nice that during halftime, one of his buddies—a kid fresh up from JV—had bemoaned not getting any click-clack during the biggest game of the season. So, without informing Hester or Sam, Jaja pulled himself from the game and gave the kid his lane, and it was that kid who had missed the tackle to give the Tigers the tie. In their most critical hour, it was Jaja who'd gone rogue, who'd put himself above the program. And for Hester, it was a confounding, almost heartbreaking twist of irony.

• • •

HALFWAY DOWN THE SIDELINE, Jonteria couldn't breathe.

She was allergic to dyes, and without thinking, she'd let one of the cheerleaders paint her face with a glitter pen. Toward the end of the half, she'd felt her throat begin to close, then panicked. Luckily, one of the mothers had reached into her purse and pulled out a packet of Benadryl, which stopped the reaction. Except now, just before kickoff, the medicine had gone straight to her head. She felt groggy as she faced the crowd. The sea of bodies rippled under the lights, which themselves kept bouncing when she tried to jump. Jonteria let her mind wander.

Not surprisingly, her attention drifted toward the many things on her to-do list. Right now at the very top was the Gates Millennium Scholars application, which was due in three weeks. It was by far her biggest pursuit, her number in the Academic Jackpot million. If she was among the lucky one thousand scholars—chosen nationwide from a pool of tens of thousands of applicants—it would pay for every day of school until she began a residency. *Everything*. No worries no more. But it also required *eight* separate essay questions.

She'd hoped to write some of them before Vincent's arrival, now just several days away. It had been seven long months since they'd last seen one another, and Jonteria wanted nothing to keep them apart. No homework, no club meetings or practice, no obsessing over her career. She wanted him to know she was capable of letting go. She could chill.

Today was also Vincent's birthday. Jonteria had texted him before the game but didn't tell him about her surprise. She was taking him out to Applebee's, since that's where he liked to eat. She was excited. But wouldn't it be better, she thought, if Vincent came home and they dressed up and drove to The Breakers? She wanted him to see the ocean from that dining room, hear the clatter of silverware and the murmur of pleasant conversation. She wanted Vincent to notice how the waves broke against the beach behind her, how the soft light kissed her skin and made her eyes dance. *This is why I work so hard,* she would say. *Vincent, this is where I belong.*

She was about to say something else when the crowd jolted her awake. Women seated in the front seats suddenly threw their hands to their faces and men began to curse. Jonteria turned to see Antwan Lee racing past for the score. *Oh dear.* She turned to her squad and shouted, *"Get 'em up."* It was time to calm the crowd. Jonteria shook off her grogginess and swung into the routine.

"We got spirit . . . deep down inside. . . . We roll up, we fold out, and call it Raider pride. . . ."

• • •

ON THEIR NEXT possession, Mario and the offense answered Lee's touchdown with an eighty-five-yard push downfield. Using a combination of chipping runs and short pass plays, they thwarted the Tigers' relentless rush attack and found themselves perched at the Cocoa five. But the Dark Side held.

Facing fourth down and four, Hester had to make a critical decision: whether or not to kick a field goal. He knew that Marvin was not strong under heavy pressure, the line was chronically weak, and he felt Cocoa's special teams had come dangerously close to blocking the extra point after the touchdown. After discussing with his coaches, Hester made the call: The Raiders would go for six instead. If they didn't make it, at least the defense would have Campbell digging out of his own end zone.

After hearing the call, Mario dropped back and slung it to Oliver on a slant, only to have Tiger safety DeMario Gilmore swat the pass incomplete. The Raiders lost the ball and the three points. But when the Tigers took over, Boobie and the defense managed to hold them to nine yards and force the punt. The gamble had paid off for now.

The Raiders took over at midfield with the momentum firmly on their side. The defending champs were thrashing in their cage. With only fourteen minutes left to play, the Raiders needed the kill shot.

Just one more touchdown, thought Mario. *And fast.*

But two plays later, the Glades Central drive came to a terrifying halt. Once again, the Tigers blitzed and flushed Mario from the pocket. He took off running down the middle of the field, and just inches from the first down, he felt his leg seize with pain. As he dove to the turf to protect himself, all he could think was, *My hamstring. I just tore my hamstring.*

The pain was diamond-sharp and took his breath away. He quickly realized it was only a cramp, but he'd never experienced one like this. With Oliver's help, the quarterback hobbled to the bench, then collapsed in frantic breaths. The muscle in his leg was clenched up and angry, pulling off the bone. His whole body was in revolt.

The quarterback choked down a mouthful of salt and cursed the food the ADs had been serving them all trip. No lean meats, no pastas, no fruits or vegetables. Just greasy chicken and gravy mashed potatoes that hardened in his veins now like sabotage. He tried to walk but fell. Looking up, Mario saw Davis trotting out to take his place.

The power of his moment was slipping from his grasp.

Desperate, he began screaming at his leg.

COME ON! TIGHTEN UP! TIGHTEN UP! COME ON! COMEOOOOON!

Soon he was punching it with all his strength, pounding his battered fist into his calf, begging it—*COMEOOON!!*—to awaken and realize the magnitude of 1:14 in the third quarter in a game that could, if only, work to fill that impossible hole in his heart.

Come on. Yeah. Straight. The muscle finally let go, began to give like an old rusty spring. The salts got him on his feet. He winced through the pain and limped back onto the field.

While Mario was writhing on the bench, Baker had given him a gift. On a third-down-and-one handoff from Davis, he'd rifled through a hole created by Boobie and Corey Graham, juked right, then beat two defenders for twenty-two yards.

Save for three quick offensive snaps that went nowhere, the Cocoa defense had been dragged up and down the field the entire third quarter. They were looking tired, less invincible. By the time Mario returned, the Raiders were at their twelve and going for the knockout. Again, Hester sent Baker straight into their face, headfirst through a wall of black jerseys for a gain of nine. Once at the five, Hester brought out the wrecking ball. Mario took the snap and handed off to Boobie, who leaped over the pile and bounded into the end zone.

Touchdown Raiders!

But if the Cocoa defense had to go down, they were going down swinging. As Marvin booted the extra point, the Raider line separated, allowing Rick Rivers to jump the open gap and bat the ball to the ground. A gasp rose from the Raider stands. Not because Cocoa blocked the point and now had the ball. But because Cocoa had the ball—*and life!*

Raiders 13, Cocoa 7.

• • •

WE NEED A FUMBLE. We need a fumble.

As the fourth quarter began ticking down, this was the plea uttered softly along the Glades Central sidelines, invoked like silent prayer.

Come on, get us a fumble!

Praying for fumbles only seemed reasonable, especially since the Cocoa offense had only sixty-six total yards and one turnover already. But perhaps three titles in a row for one coach was in fact the prayer too big to ask. Two was a respectable number. In Brevard County, two had made Gerald Odom a legend, and two was certainly enough for Johnny Wilkinson.

Hester wanted just one. Just one championship for his twenty-five years in the game, and especially one as a Glades Central Raider. The fact that he'd never won a ring was the little-talked-about disappointment of his life, his lingering sadness. Throughout college and a decade in the league, he'd never been with a team that contained "those perfect pieces" and, at the same time, that precise chemistry between players and coaches that rendered them unstoppable. The closest he'd ever come was his junior year as a Raider, when he'd stood alone in the end zone waiting for the ball.

As a pro, his biggest window for a Super Bowl had been the Colts. The years in Indianapolis were Hester's prime, when all of his own pieces had come together and he could flow. It was where he'd also built lasting friendships and enjoyed the love of a town, one where fans still remembered the minutiae of his career nearly twenty years after he was gone.

But the Colts had never possessed the right pieces to win. And before long, Jessie's body started giving out. He began slowing down and getting caught, started taking hits to the head. Lena still shuddered at the memory of him lying unconscious in the end zone after being flattened by the Chiefs' Kevin Ross (whom Hester had juked for a touchdown five years earlier as a Raider). Or the call she got from teammate Clarence Verdin after a Monday-night game saying Jessie was in the hospital. He'd started convulsing on the team plane, so dehydrated that every muscle in his body, even his tongue, had locked up and dropped him in the aisle.

After being waived by Indy in 1994, Hester signed with the Rams. By then, his body had grown tired and football had become more of a job. Monday mornings hurt worse than ever, and Wednesday practice filled him with dread. In November 1995, while playing in New Orleans, Hester's catching streak finally ended at eighty-six games, the third-longest streak of active NFL receivers behind Art Monk, Jerry Rice, and Keith Byars.

Soon Hester was needing shots in his lower back just to play, then more in his foot for his plantar fasciitis. He ended up missing five of the last six games of the 1995 season due to a deep-thigh contusion. In April 1996, when the Rams needed to free up their salary cap, they cut Hester loose.

Midway through the season, Hester was back home in Wellington and still suffering from foot pain, when he got a call from Ron Wolf. Wolf had drafted Hester in Los Angeles and was now GM for the Green Bay Packers.

"Jessie, we need a receiver," he said.

"Ron, I can't run."

Still, Hester told Wolf to give him two weeks to heal, to figure something out. But the next day, the Packers signed Andre Rison and won a Super Bowl that season.

"My pro career just came down to what-ifs," Hester said. "In the end, my body just broke down on me and I had to come to grips with that. Some things are meant to be. Certain things are just destined."

.   .   .

STANDING ON THE sideline with the fourth quarter under way, his Raiders up by six, Hester battled the urge to imagine that his luck was about to change. The fourth quarter was Cocoa's witching hour, and something told Hester they'd yet to unveil their most potent magic.

Wilkinson had said as much himself. Before the half, he'd told the on-field reporter for Fox Sports, "Our problem is we're not playing Cocoa football." Everyone knew what he meant by Cocoa football, and it wasn't a fluke seventy-yard kickoff return to tie the game. What was missing was that mechanical, coldhearted execution for which the Tigers were known.

Down 13–7, Campbell and the Tigers came out like a gang of accountants and quickly went to work. On the first snap, it was Campbell to Folston, who swept right and was cut down by Boobie for a gain of four. Next, Campbell pitched to Lee, who swept left and into the arms of Jaja for a gain of two. The Tigers were still working the same clinical rotation the Raider linebackers had memorized and contained all night.

Which was exactly what Wilkinson wanted them to think. Drawing them close, he sprang the trap.

On third and four from their own forty-two, Campbell faked to Lee on another sweep, then rolled out of the pocket. And then—for only the second time in eighteen quarters of play—he threw a pass. It was to Jones, who was wide open in the flat. By the time the Raider secondary could adjust, Jones was across midfield to the thirty-six. The Tiger crowd leapt to their feet, for they saw the dark lightning in the distance and knew what was rolling in.

The pass play rocked the Raiders' equilibrium and the Tigers continued to pound. Folston for two. Jones for six. Jones again on fourth and one for a fresh set of lives. In the thick of the drive, the cameras closed in on Campbell's face to reveal a placid calm, the long stare of a young man who'd already played the game and was relaxing by the pool.

On first down, Campbell gave it to Folston for another three yards, before Jones blasted a hole to the Raider nine. Two plays later, Jones met Boobie at the goal line and forced his way inside, tying the game.

The kicker, Cody Bell, ran out to attempt the extra point.

It was Bell who had carried his team to their first state title game in 2008 on a fifty-two-yard field goal in the semifinals. In the championship game against Tallahassee Godby, Bell missed *all four field goals* he attempted. The game ended with the score tied 0–0—the first time that had ever happened in Florida state finals history. It was Godby who scored first in overtime, but the extra point was blocked. Backed into a corner, the Tigers fought downfield for the tying touchdown, then placed their bets once again on the conflicted legs of Cody Bell. His extra point was true.

Now, two years later, on the same stretch of field, Bell's kick sailed through the center of the uprights.

The Tigers took the lead 14–13.

·   ·   ·

MARIO WATCHED THE kick from the sideline and felt a quickening, as if the earth had suddenly gained speed. He looked up at the clock. It read five minutes and fifty-four seconds. It was as if his whole life and its parade of heartbreak were suddenly distilled into this tiny teacup of time. He had six minutes to right so many things: to bring home the ring to rest near his father's photo, to quiet the ghosts and for once shed the mark of the piteous orphan. Six minutes to become immortal, at last beloved. The man of the city.

Six minutes was enough to win. The quarterback strapped on his helmet and ran back onto the field.

From their own twenty-yard line, the Raiders came out throwing fire. Mario launched his first pass up the right side, hitting Jaime for a gain of eleven and the first down.

That's right, baby! That's how to be great!

His heart pounded in his ears. The rush of the moment seemed to lift his rubbery legs and carry him downfield, his body all but floating to the fresh set of sticks.

Mario looked toward Hester on the sidelines.

"Cadillac! Cadillac!" the coach shouted.

It was a fifteen-yard dig route on the left side for Davonte. Mario lined up in shotgun and shouted the snap. That's when everything fell apart.

Not a second after Mario touched the ball, Tyrell Denson appeared on his left side, charging at full speed. There was no time to react. The defensive end wrapped Mario's waist and flung him to the turf. Mario instantly sprang to his feet in a rage. From the corner of his eye, he'd watched Densen fly past *two* of his linemen. Neither player had done anything to stop him.

Mario ran toward them, his arms raised in a panic. The clock was hammering down. This was not the time to forget assignments. *"What's goin on?"* he shouted, then saw something in their faces that scared him to death.

"Don't give up on me," he said, then pleaded, *"Don't you give up on me now!!"*

Later, Hester would contend that the quarterback had misread his teammates' expressions. They had not given up on their captain, he said. Rather, they were not made of the same stuff. They did not have that fight raging inside, that impossible hole to fill. Unlike Mario, they just didn't need to win.

The sack pushed the Raiders back eight yards, and then it happened again. The Tigers blitzed with three defenders, who busted through the line with ease. All three linemen hit Mario at the same time and drove his flailing body deep into the backfield.

The Cocoa crowd were on their feet, hysterical. The momentum had shifted. The Raiders had given the Tigers life. And once they had life, they rarely let it go.

On third down and thirty-two, Hester called a 989 Rolls-Royce. Davonte went into motion up the left side as Cocoa once again brought the rush. As Mario dropped back to pass, Ferguson broke free and slapped his arm just as he let go of the ball. It hung in the air, spiraling in the lights across midfield, and almost made the distance. Davonte ran it down like an out-fielder staring into the sun, then found himself in a frenzy of black jerseys. The ball came down into the arms of Datarius Allen, the Tiger safety.

With four minutes left in the game, Cocoa began chewing the clock and letting it bleed. On the sidelines, Hester waited for the big play. The defense had been performing miracles all season. It was only a matter of time, he thought. *Who's it gonna be? In the final chapter, who's gonna make the big play?* But the only big play came from Page, who accidentally grabbed a face mask. The penalty pushed Cocoa deeper into Raider territory. Boobie and the defense managed to hold the Tigers to third down and three. But with 2:39 left, Folston fought loose on the right side and seized the first down.

The coaches knew.

"That did it," said Sam.

Hester shook his head. "Yeah."

On the sideline, the Raiders watched with blank expressions as Campbell took a knee at 1:34 to run the clock down. As the crowd chanted, *"THREE-PEAT! THREE-PEAT!"* a lone voice could be heard over the din.

It was the quarterback, standing halfway on the field, still clutching his helmet.

"Do something!" he shouted. *"Do something!"*

. . .

THE TIGERS RUSHED the field in triumph. Many fell to the ground, released from the burden of work, and laughed in one another's arms. They behaved the way true champions did, by raising the sword and passing the credit. Wilkinson, drenched in a victory bath from the Cocoa water jugs, walked the field whispering something to his small son, whom he held in his arms.

Glades Central, once again the losers, did not fall and weep. Instead they stood in stunned disbelief, then discarded their helmets on the turf like tools they'd never use again. By the time the officials erected two platforms for an awards ceremony, most of the Raider Nation had found the exits. But about a hundred stayed behind, among them gamblers who'd just lost thousands. And when Jessie Hester was announced as the coach of the second-place Raiders, they rose to their feet and booed him. Later, as Hester walked off the field toward the locker room, an older man chased him down along the railing, raised his arm, and called him a piece of shit.

For them, nothing was good enough.

As the players packed their bags in silence, more silver medals found their way to the floor. One belonged to the quarterback, who'd bent down and taken his prize like a sickness. Mario had left immediately following the ceremony with Gail and his sisters, his only consolation being that he'd done everything in his power to win.

As the team readied to load the bus, Hester sat alone on the opposite side of the locker room. Elbows on his knees, he stared vacantly at the floor. Minutes passed. Seniors left with parents without saying goodbye. No one dared disturb him. As the room emptied, one could hear the sounds of shouting and loud music. On the other side of the wall, the Tigers were celebrating.

"I've just been sitting here listening to it," he said, not looking up. "I just want to hear what it sounds like."

He'd been rewinding every play in his mind, searching for an answer: Should they have kicked the field goal? Was it Jaja's absence on the return? At some point he realized that none of that even mattered. The premonition he'd felt before the game had been correct. Except Cocoa was more than just a team playing lucky. They were a team of destiny. And teams of destiny could not be defeated.

Destiny once had its place in the muck, but those days may have passed. Sitting there now, the coach doubted they would ever return again. Not to a town that devoured its own, a town that had lost its way. Destiny had no place where dark forces were free to roam.

EPILOGUE

Six days later, Jessie Hester was fired.

School principal Anthony Anderson delivered the news the Friday before Christmas break in a meeting with athletic director Edwin James that lasted less than five minutes. The principal did not mention the loss in Orlando, or the group of angry fans who'd crowded his office that week demanding a change. The coach who'd returned home to give something back, whose record was 36–4 with two state championship appearances, was being fired over grades.

"We are grateful for the three years that Mr. Hester spent with our football program at Glades Central," Anderson said later in a statement. "As we move forward to connect the bridge of academics with our athletic program, we have decided to move in a different direction."

Despite widespread outrage over play calls during the Cocoa game, particularly Hester's decision not to kick the field goal, the news of his firing stunned and angered parents and fans. Many saw academics as a veiled excuse for not bringing home the title. In the days that followed, they flooded the comments section of the *Post* story, lamenting the loss of a role model and mentor. They also criticized a culture that valued winning over all else and routinely tore down its heroes.

"For the past three years with Hester, he has made them not only believe in themselves, but each other as a team," one parent wrote.

"What kind of message does this send to our kids?" asked another.

Hester's players were equally shocked by the news.

"I can't understand it," said Robert Way. "He was the best coach I ever had. No one ever motivated me like him. We all looked up to him."

"I thought we should have kicked the field goal," said Davonte. "But that was no reason to fire him."

Others were not surprised. "That's how they do you in Belle Glade," Mario said. "Nothin's changed."

• • •

FOR MARIO, the crushing loss and firing of his mentor made the ground he walked on seem all the more poisonous. He ached to leave Belle Glade, and his official visit to Hampton University in late January appeared to be his only option.

The week before flying to Virginia, Mario was selected starting quarterback in an all-star game for local seniors, held in Boca Raton. The game would be his last time to wear his Raider helmet and offered a chance to at least go out a winner.

After six weeks of rest, the quarterback's shoulder was feeling better and his headaches were gone. But the time off had also added pounds. "Damn, Mario's big," his sister Jamekia said, watching from the bleachers as her brother squeezed into his flak vest and pads. She turned to Canisa and Aunt Gail. "Look at him. *He's fat.*"

Gail said that ever since the loss in Orlando, Mario had been calling a lot, needing a boost. "He keeps saying, 'I need to get out of here, I just can't wait,'" said Gail, who wore a wool shawl and purple scarf to keep out the cold wind. "He told me as long as the two of us can talk every day, he'll be okay. We just need to keep him positive."

She sighed and added, "He never got counseling. People gave him material things, but they never filled that emotional void."

Despite his added weight, Mario gave the crowd another tireless and riveting performance. As captain of the American team, he passed for 140 yards against the Nationals, ran for one touchdown, and threw two more—one of them to his trusted receiver Jaqavein Oliver. The other came in the last seconds of the fourth quarter. With American down 20–13, Mario hit Dwyer wideout Shawn McClaine for a thirty-nine-yard score, but the two-point conversion failed just as the clock struck zero. Once again, the quarterback found himself one point shy of victory.

The crowd in Boca couldn't have cared less; they whooped and cheered as Mario was awarded his team's MVP. Standing at the far end of the bleachers was Hester, who slipped out just before the ceremony.

A few days later, Mario traveled to Hampton and received his much-awaited official treatment: campus and facility tours, a hotel room and restaurant dinners, beautiful chaperones, assurance of a role as middle linebacker—and, more important, a vision of a new home. Upon leaving, Coach Field said they'd be in touch with the details of the offer. Mario was ecstatic.

"Hampton's on point!" he announced on his Facebook page. An unfettered joy seemed to radiate from his beaming profile photo.

The trip came just in time for Signing Day, held the following Wednesday. And just in time for Mario's name to be printed on a large placard along with the other Raiders signing to Division I programs that afternoon: KB, Davonte, and Robert Way.

Mario awoke that morning and dressed for school, throwing on his maroon polo and pressed khakis. The ceremony and visions of college life filled his thoughts and made him miss his parents even more. But as he drove to campus, he received a text message from Coach Field. After talking to head coach Donovan Rose, he said, the Pirates could only extend a partial scholarship of $14,000. Full tuition was around $27,000, and Mario knew the difference was impossible to cover. He quickly considered taking out a loan, then realized the true meaning behind Field's text. Hampton did not really want him. Not only did they not want him, but the coaches couldn't even bother making a phone call to tell him so themselves.

Mario's mind spun out. He sat in his car in the school parking lot, flattened by the news and ashamed to go inside. He called Canisa and told her what happened. The sound of his voice made her worry, so she called Gail. When Gail rang Mario minutes later, she repeated what she'd been telling him since Mary and James died, ever since she'd wrapped him up trembling in her arms.

"God has something planned for you," she said. "You have purpose. You were put on this earth for a reason."

They made plans for Mario to come stay with her in Fort Lauderdale that weekend, to get a change of scenery and go to church on Sunday. Mario always felt better after hanging up with Auntie Gail. Because if he could not hear his mother's voice, then Gail's was the next closest thing.

• • •

MARIO DID NOT appear at the Signing Day ceremony at four o'clock with the rest of his team. The auditorium was packed with students and family. People had heard what had happened to the quarterback and were already whispering. But that news was suddenly superseded when Hester walked through the doors. He'd told his boys he would watch them sign, and despite his bitterness and confusion over his dismissal, he'd swallowed his pride and kept his word. It was odd how he suddenly seemed out of place, like a character from a previous story who'd walked into another book. He heard about Mario and dropped his head, the gesture expressing the worry that most everyone now felt.

Signing Day commenced with jubilation but few surprises. Benjamin stepped up to the podium, which was festooned with maroon and gold balloons. He thanked God and his coaches. "And with that," he said, whipping on a Seminoles cap, "I'd like to further my education at Florida State." Both Robert Way and Davonte announced they were joining the Marshall Thundering Herd. All three players then posed for photos with Hester. But

the joyous mood quickly turned ugly. As people walked out the doors minutes later, they passed the former head coach engaged in a seething argument with Anderson.

Mario finished the school week in a mild panic. Watching his boys in
their college caps filled him with both sorrow and desperation. He would
now join Oliver, Page, Purvis, and the other seniors navigating their way
into a DII or junior college, whoever would have them. Hester called and
assured him, "We're gonna find you a home." But still, Mario feared he
would have to go it alone.

The thing with Hampton upset Gail. She was still hot when she called
Canisa Friday morning. "How can those coaches not even call him?"
she said.

But Gail was never one to lie down. "The power of life and death is in
the tongue," she always told her niece. "Speak life and you will speak things
true."

She'd spoken life to Mary's doctors at the hospital those many years
ago ("My sister is gonna walk outta here!"), and now Gail was speaking life
to Mario's uncertain future.

"Just because one person passed him up," she said now, "doesn't mean
someone else won't come and get him."

Canisa and Gail spoke on the phone nearly every day, usually for an
hour or so. But for some reason Friday was a marathon. The two of them
jawed well into the afternoon, covering just about everything. Gail said
she was having dreams, the way she did, but more of them recently. She
was dreaming of her mother and father, both of whom had passed. A few
nights after Mario's all-star game, she'd even seen her sister Mary. "The
dream was about her and my mom," Gail said, "but I still haven't been able
to put it together."

For Canisa, talking with Gail was effortless, like having a conversation
with herself and her mother at the same time. They even talked again at
nine thirty that evening. Gail was already in bed, and she sounded tired

and maybe a little sick. She wanted to know if Canisa and Mario were still coming to stay the night tomorrow for church on Sunday. Canisa told her, "Yes, we'll be there. I'll call you in the morning."

But that night, alone at home, Gail died in her sleep.

Her goddaughter Ginell found her body the next evening, still under the covers. Her hands were clasped under her chin. "Like an angel," said Canisa. The family suspected she had suffered a heart attack.

Canisa heard the news as she prepared to drive to Gail's house. She'd started doing laundry that morning and completely forgotten to call as she'd promised. Then her cousin Carmen rang and said, "Have you talked to my mom? I've been trying her all day." *Strange,* Canisa thought, *Gail always answers her phone.* Something instantly felt wrong, as though the temperature had dropped. Canisa dialed and dialed and only got Gail's voice mail. She began to pray, *Please God don't let anything happen to my auntie. She's all I got left.* Her cousin called back and said Ginell had a key and was on her way over. The next thing Canisa heard was that they'd found Gail's body. She dropped the phone and began to scream.

Mario was at a classmate's house for debutante practice, along with Les'Unique and several of his Raider teammates. He took the call outside from his nephew William Likely. "Get home," Will said. "They found Auntie Gail. She's dead." Mario repeated the news to Les'Unique but he refused to believe it himself. "We're going to her house tonight," he kept saying. As Les'Unique stood by, crying, Mario frantically paced the yard and dialed his auntie's number.

"She's gonna answer," he said, trying again and again. *"I know she's gonna answer."*

They buried Gail at Foreverglades in the same crypt as Mary and James. After that day, Mario felt as if he would drown. He drifted for weeks, snagged on the painful debris that Gail's passing shook loose. Often he'd find himself just driving, past Pahokee and around the lake, then back to Belle Glade, up one street and down the next. He started spending time with older friends, "doing things I shouldn't do," he said. People were worried, especially Hester.

"We cannot let that boy slip away," he said.

By late spring, Mario began to resurface. That resilience he'd developed as a kid helped him regain focus and concentrate on graduating and, more important, getting out of Belle Glade. He'd managed to keep his grades strong, enough that Florida A&M offered Mario an academic scholarship. But, still wanting to play football, he passed on the opportunity to consider other options. The only other interest came from a junior college near Chicago. Then finally, in July, Mario got a call from North Carolina Central University in Durham.

Henry Frazier III, the Eagles' head coach, wasn't interested at first in the chubby, undersized kid he saw on film. But one of his assistants who'd met Mario kept pressing. "This guy's a player, Coach," he said. "This kid can *play*."

They brought Mario up for a visit. One conversation changed Frazier's mind. "There was just something about him," he said. "He exudes confidence. I went against all the recruiting checkpoints. I knew we had to get him on this team."

Frazier ended up redshirting the entire freshman class. Even on the scout team, Mario kept standing out. "He just started emerging, like the voice of the class," he said. "This is when I started paying close attention."

Frazier told a story about a midseason game when the Eagles were getting pulverized by Morgan State. At halftime, the score was 42–3. Frazier was so upset that he took a seat outside the locker room, put his head down, and tried to gather himself before going inside.

"Suddenly I felt this hand on my shoulder," he said. "It was Mario. He kind of grabbed me and stood me up, looked at me, and said, 'Coach, keep your head up. Keep your head up, Coach.' Then he said, 'I promise you this won't happen when my class is playing.' Here was this freshman who'd been there two months. But I *believed* him. I kind of brushed myself off, made some adjustments, and went out and coached the second half."

The Eagles still lost the game, but after that day, Frazier understood what he had on his team. "What he did was almost heaven-sent," he said. "He uplifted me."

Entering the 2012 season, the NCCU staff were scrambling to figure out where to play Mario. The tight ends coach wanted him, but so did the linebackers coach.

"We're gonna let it play out," said Frazier. "But I do know this: he's a leader. He has a tremendous amount of confidence and I'm looking forward to coaching him these next four years."

• • •

THE UNIVERSITY OF FLORIDA hired Will Muschamp to be their new head coach on the Saturday the Raiders lost in Orlando. The following week, the Gators released Coach Z and, with him, any real hopes of winning Kelvin Benjamin. As Azzanni said, every good recruiter knows you can never take a break on a big target like Benjamin. Each day you left him alone, the more he tended to drift. By the time Aubrey Hill took over as UF's receivers coach and got his bearings, Benjamin was lost in enemy territory.

Not long afterward, Coach Fisher pulled KB aside during a final visit to Tallahassee. "Many of the other recruits are asking when you're gonna commit," he said. The coach needed an answer.

"There are moments when you know a decision is good or bad," said KB. "You can feel it inside you. And at that moment it felt really good. I said yes, and when I did, everyone started jumpin up and down."

Minutes later, he said, coaches had him phoning other top prospects with the news. "I'm goin to State," he told them. "Yall might as well jump on the bandwagon."

Many of them did, giving Fisher the number-one recruiting class in the nation, according to ESPN. That class also included Rashad Greene, a receiver from Fort Lauderdale's St. Thomas Aquinas who had just helped lead his team to back-to-back state championships. Ranked number twenty in the nation, Greene didn't possess the freakish physique that caused grown men to swoon, but he was an artful route runner and incredibly fast. And with a 3.5 GPA, Greene was also dependable. In addition to Greene, of course, the Seminoles' lengthy depth chart included seven returning receivers. Benjamin didn't seem fazed.

"Coaches think I can win the Biletnikoff Award," he said, referring to the prestigious trophy given each year by the Tallahassee Quarterback Club Foundation to the nation's best college receiver. Past winners included Randy Moss, Larry Fitzgerald, and Calvin Johnson.

"No one from Florida State's ever won it," he added. "I mean, they telling me I can be an All-American freshman."

Benjamin was MIA most of his last semester in Belle Glade. His free time mostly was spent retaking the last of ten core classes in order to meet NCAA requirements. He did his work after school in the computer lab, hunched over a workbook and a keyboard. By mid-May, he'd finally submitted everything and was awaiting approval.

By the week of graduation, Benjamin hadn't run over a mile in six months. Sitting at Frank and Tan's dining-room table one afternoon, the time off was showing. The once broad, muscled torso appeared flabby under his T-shirt. And the locomotive legs that had carried him this far seemed whittled and diminished. With training camp just under a month away, he was an alarming sight. Now the delusions that had once seemed so innocent were just depressing, almost painful to hear.

"Dawsey said if I can run six routes, I'm good," he said, referring to quick-cutting dig patterns across the middle, ideal for KB's mismatched size. "He said just do what I do best."

But the six route only worked if KB could separate, if his legs were nimble and strong. Wasn't he worried about reporting to camp so out of shape, about having to compete against the best recruiting class in America, against smaller and hungrier guys who would dig his eyes out to keep their jobs? Hadn't he heard a thousand times already that hard work always beat talent?

He shrugged.

"I aint worried," he said. "You know kids from the muck, we always gonna have that advantage, athletic-wise, over everyone else. I mean, I still know how to do it. I've been playing some street ball."

Later that day, KB returned to his mother's apartment on the edge of the canefield. Inside, aluminum foil covered the windows and left the living room dark and cool. Benjamin lay stretched out on the floor of the back bedroom staring up at a television screen, his mind locked in a game of Call of Duty. He was shirtless and fleshy, an image that evoked Brando's Colonel Kurtz.

He was not alone. Sitting in the dark living room was his girlfriend, Mika, all of seven months pregnant.

News of his approaching fatherhood had come out reluctantly. No one had dared mention it, not Frank, Tan, Boobie, or any of KB's teammates. In fact, KB had always deflected questions about his love life. Whenever Mika's name was mentioned, he would change the subject or go quiet and begin to brood. So, while sitting at Frank and Tan's house, he'd been asked if there was anything he would miss in Belle Glade. *Naaah*, he said. There wasn't anything, not *anything*, that he was leaving behind? He'd put his head down on the table, paused, and said Mika.

"I mean, we're having a baby," he said. Mika stood up from the plastic-covered sofa and said hello. She was petite, with long black hair and an easy smile. Her round belly poked through her shirt, and her skin appeared radiant in the dim light. She looked beautiful. And as she began to speak, the overweight, four-star receiver languishing in the next room began taking on new form.

Mika said it was a girl. She and KB had already decided on a name: Kelyiah. The baby was a blessing, she said, given what had happened earlier that year. Toward the beginning of the football season, Mika had miscarried. That pregnancy had been an accident and stunned them both. But when the child died four months later, KB had taken it especially hard.

"We were both really upset," Mika said, her quiet voice carrying a twinge of country. "This one was more planned. I just didn't think it would happen so soon."

The Boys and Girls Club, where she worked full-time as a family liaison, was giving her ten weeks of maternity leave. Afterward, she would decide how the three of them would have a life together. On top of her job, she also had plans to begin night school to finish her nursing degree. That left only weekends for trips to Tallahassee. KB had also talked about getting a car to make the drive south.

The whole idea of being a football wife made her laugh. She'd never been interested in sports or popular guys, she said, even when she was a cheerleader. (In fact, KB was only her second long-term boyfriend.) So all of the recent attention was jarring, all the reporters calling him, all the men who approached him in shopping malls and restaurants in West Palm to praise and give him advice, some just to stand and gawk.

The only part of KB's celebrity that seemed to interest Mika was seeing him through the eyes of her children at work. "All the boys want to make Raider jerseys with number 3 on them," she said, smiling. "They want to be like him. The kids look up to him. And when he comes and talks to them, it just makes their day."

She was proud that he'd climbed from such a low place to reach the cusp of his dream. And she was happy to share the rest of the journey, however far it took them. But it wasn't everything. "If he doesn't go to the league, it won't matter," she said. "I look beyond that. We have a bond that can't be broken."

Mika then turned and looked at KB from across the apartment, half a smile still on her lips. The look she gave was pure and asked for nothing. It did not strip him down to meat and bone, or see him as a prospect—the beautiful freak taking flight with wings made of money. It was as if she were seeing him through the eyes of their child, and it transformed and made him more human. He was simple parts now: a boy never equipped for the machine that loomed and beckoned, a young man dangerously close to throwing it all away. He would need them. When he left this town and discovered he was all alone, he would need them.

• • •

A MONTH LATER, Benjamin reported to training camp in Tallahassee and stepped into reality. "I was so out of shape," he said later, "I couldn't run my routes without wanting to fall down. I was tired and winded."

At the end of camp, Florida State gave KB a redshirt. Benjamin said part of the reason, besides not being in shape, was related to academics. The university would never comment. All that was certain was that KB was forced to sit out the entire 2011 season. Meanwhile, Rashad Greene had one of the most electrifying freshman debuts in recent memory, leading all receivers with seven touchdowns and nearly six hundred yards receiving. Greene was even named MVP in the Champs Sports Bowl.

During the season, rumors appeared on the blogosphere that KB was transferring from FSU to shine on a smaller stage, much as his icon Randy Moss had done after redshirting as a Seminole. But Benjamin stayed with the program, put his head down, and did his work. He emerged the following spring in the best shape of his life, carrying 240 pounds of lean muscle, loose hips, and a newfound comfort with the special weapons he possessed. Speaking to reporters, Coach Fisher praised Benjamin's work ethic and said he'd "gotten himself in really good shape now that he can control that body."

A year after leaving high school, there was a marked humility in KB's tone.

"My coaches expect me to be the player they recruited," he said. "They want me to be the best, and every day I work on that."

He then laughed, adding, "But they runnin the shit out of me."

On his phone he kept a picture of his daughter, now seven months old. "She's big and goofy like me," he said. He saw her and Mika every few weeks, with both of them making the trip. Maintaining that was hard work, he said. But as he was realizing, so was everything else in life worth keeping.

• • •

DAVONTE ALLEN and Robert Way both reported to Marshall University in Huntington and were also given redshirts. The raw muck talent they possessed needed time to be shaped and developed, the coaches felt. The same went for their bodies. As soon as they arrived, Way and Allen underwent intense weight-gain regimens, both in the weight room and the cafeteria. At the end of each meal, coaches often appeared with second plates of food. "I couldn't get up until it was finished," Way said.

Within six months, Davonte had gained forty pounds of muscle and Robert had added thirty. Like KB, Davonte felt he benefited from a season on the scout team, getting in shape, learning the Herd's playbook, plus a new language of sideline hand signals. "I saw it as an opportunity to get better," he said. "I'm not just a speed receiver anymore, but an all-around player."

JaJuan Seider, the coach who recruited him, agreed. "He's gonna have a breakout year," he said.

Davonte still spoke to his mother and Julius nearly every day on the phone and adhered to his own regimen of scripture and prayer. "Nothing has changed in terms of the way I live my life," he said, then laughed. "Except now when I go home, I don't have to mow the grass."

• • •

A SEASON on the scout team did not sit well with Robert Way, however. His tolerance hung on a much shorter fuse. He grew restless and tired of spending his days as a mere practice dummy. "It wasn't making me any better," he said. "Without being able to play, I just got miserable."

Despite falling in love with the city of Huntington upon his first visit, he now felt squeezed and suffocated by it. He described sitting around on Saturdays while the rest of the team traveled for games, nothing to do but lift weights, watch college football, and fume. "We're seeing all these other freshmen from Florida playing, so why aint we playing?" he said. "Finally I just got tired of it."

After his first semester, Way quit the team and dropped out of school. His coaches were left disappointed and sour. "He wasn't patient enough to wait his turn," said JaJuan. "That's the thing with these kids [from Belle Glade], they're entitled."

Way was now back in Belle Glade, living at home and weighing his options. After leaving Marshall, he received a full scholarship from Bethune-Cookman University in Daytona Beach. But he was holding out for a DI program, perhaps FAU or better. The boy who Coach Hester once pulled from the brink was aware how vulnerable he now seemed. Out of high school, without a job, and down on your luck—the casualty rate was high. "I'm keeping a positive attitude," he said. "Something will come up. I mean, it's got to."

• • •

FOR JONTERIA WILLIAMS, the final semester of high school began with her first broken heart. After months of anticipation, Vincent finally came home for Christmas break. Jonteria had built their whole reunion up in her mind, what she would wear, what they would do together, the goose bumps she would feel watching him laugh, being kissed.

But it was wrong from the beginning. From their first encounter, Vincent didn't really talk, didn't laugh, didn't look into her eyes and feel the same flutter. He was like a shell, a walking hologram. Jonteria knew: Vincent had fallen out of love.

"It just wasn't the same, that joy," she said. "It wasn't that happy, cheery feeling that it always used to be. I was so happy to see him and he was like, *hmmph.*" She stuck her lips out like the Grinch. "After a while, I was like, *okay.* I guess over seven months, we just grew apart."

She sat cross-legged on the living-room sofa, which faced the table of trophies, plaques, and medals. Jonteria knew how to talk about those things. Her ambition was second nature. But this crushed feeling, it could not be compartmentalized and explained the same way.

"You don't know what's gonna happen in the future, so you don't get so upset about it," she said, struggling for words. "Whatever happens, happens, right? You learn, I guess . . ."

Sitting in the next room, Theresa couldn't stand hearing it. She walked into the living room and raised her hand, signaling for her daughter to stop.

"We're leaving this subject off-limits," she said. "Because there's too many things that she needs to focus on now. So when she wants to talk about it, she'll talk about it. If a person keeps dragging it out, especially when you're having your happy moments and moving on with your life, next thing you know you're down, you're depressed."

She then turned to her daughter.

"That's the reason I try to keep you busy," she said. "I try to keep you busy so your mind is not focused there. I understand. I've been there. I was young and I've had my heart broken—not to say that's what happened to you. Whatever happens, happens. You have no control over that.

"So I wish you the best of luck. I'm not gonna pry into it. I'm not gonna dig. Whenever you want to talk to me, I'm here. *I'm here.* My dream is just for you to be happy. That's my dream. And when things come about in your life that you have to deal with, you'll know how. But you know what? Right now you're doing a pretty good job."

• • •

THREE DAYS LATER, Jonteria "committed" to Florida State. In his effort to bridge academics and athletics, Principal Anderson insisted the scholars share the stage at Signing Day with the football team. They also appeared on the program before the players, ensuring that the reporters and photographers on hand to capture KB's big moment counted *eight* scholars "goin DI," as opposed to only *three* mighty Raiders— one of the smallest Signing Days for Glades Central football in years. That afternoon, Jonteria's cousin Donalle announced he was headed to the Gators. Walkeria committed to FAU and Jessica Benette, the school valedictorian, was "continuing her education at the University of South Florida."

For Jonteria, the announcement helped to override the pain of her breakup, dispatching it under the moving wheels of her college dreams. She was going to Florida State, for now, and having made the decision, she could focus on the million little steps leading to its door. On top of her coursework at Glades Central, Jonteria had also crammed three additional college classes into her schedule in order to ease her load the following year. The cheerleaders were now in the throes of basketball season. As class salutatorian, Jonteria was painstakingly working on a speech for the graduation ceremony. And of course she still clocked twenty hours each week at Winn-Dixie to earn extra money.

Money.

When Jonteria put her head down each night, one day closer to college, all she could think about was how to pay for it. She'd started hearing back from the scholarships for which she'd applied, and the news was not encouraging. The Coca-Cola Scholars Foundation had recently sent a kind rejection letter informing Jonteria she would not be receiving their $20,000 award. The other foundations still kept their decisions locked away, depriving her of the ability to plan. The uncertainty of it all was maddening. She lived in constant dread that in the final hour she would not have enough. Student loans would not cover the full expense of Florida State, which was about $19,300 per year.

The veneer of confidence revealed a crack. "Sometimes I just get very tired," she said one afternoon, exhaling. "I just want to know what's happening. It's not like this for the football players. At least they know that everything is paid for."

A few weeks later, so consumed by doubt and the unknown, Jonteria abandoned Florida State and committed to FAU and its cheaper price tag. "If the scholarships don't work out," she said, "at least I know I'll be better covered."

Then one day in early May, Jonteria got home from school and noticed the mailbox bulging open. Inside was a giant manila envelope, its girth emanating importance. Seeing the return address made Jonteria's stomach do somersaults. She couldn't even wait to go in the house. She sat in the front seat of her car and carefully slid open the package.

"Congratulations," the letter read. "You are a Bill Gates Millennium Scholar."

Jonteria had to read the sentence again before it sank in. *She had won.*

The plan she'd hatched back as a bug-eyed seventh-grader had just hitched a ride on a rocket ship. Her undergraduate and medical school would be completely covered. All the bullying and alienation she'd endured, all of the sacrifice and hours on her feet—Bill Gates was telling her that it was worth every minute, to stand up and take a bow. Jonteria was too excited to even cry. All she could do was sit there and smile. *She had won.*

Over the next two weeks, the good news kept on coming. In addition to the Gates award, Jonteria received a Florida Bright Futures scholarship, awarded by the state, for an additional $9,000. The Walmart/Sam Walton Community Scholarship gave her an additional $3,000, while the Lions Club came in with another $4,000—all of which ensured she would not have to work her first semester and could focus on studying. Despite the Gates award, Jonteria chose to stay at FAU. She liked its nursing and medical schools, and more important, it was closer to home.

But FAU was just the backup plan. After one year, Jonteria would have enough credits to finish her bachelor's degree. At which point, armed with the confidence, and now the means, she would try to reclaim the dream she'd abandoned those many months before: she would apply to the University of Miami and pray her luck still held.

On graduation night, Jonteria took the stage inside the Glades Central gymnasium and delivered the salutatorian speech to the Class of 2011. She began by speaking on the fear that so often stymied the ambition and momentum one needed to clear the green wall of the Glades.

"Fear is an emotion that we learn over time," she told the 219 graduates. "We avoid things that the world views as bad or unacceptable in society. Fear is something that we create within ourselves. We are the only ones who are able to destroy that fear."

Her courage to take the long and running start, to go headlong into traffic and dare to be great, had not come on her own. She looked into the audience and found her mother's gaze.

"She is my heart, my soul, my love, my supporter, my number-one fan, my teacher, my counselor, and my everything," Jonteria said. "Without her, I would not have made it this far."

The room filled with applause and the crowd turned to find Theresa. Her eyes remained steady on her daughter, tears running down her face.

• • •

FOR JESSIE HESTER, there was no repeat of a storybook ending.

After hearing he was being fired over grades, Hester had thanked Anderson and James for the opportunity and walked out of the room, knowing there was another reason. His team's grades were no worse than those of kids who played baseball or basketball. James, the athletic director, was in fact the boys' basketball coach. Academics had only disguised a larger motive, he felt. The only reason he could think was that Anderson, James, and assistant AD Roosevelt "Tadpole" Blackmon must have conspired together to remove him.

"Their minds were already made up," he said, "and I felt like the loss in Orlando just gave them more ammunition. I wasn't going to stay where I wasn't wanted."

Several months later, Anderson did admit that academics wasn't the main reason he'd fired Hester. The reason, he said, was that administrators had long been frustrated with the coach and his staff. For one thing, they felt Hester and his assistants could have done a better job "marketing" their second-tier players to college recruiters. Anderson said he noticed decent players, guys who weren't deemed superstars, being allowed to languish and not grow, then being passed over after graduation.

"You just can't exploit these kids for the Friday-night lights. You have to make sure they all go to the next level," he said. "Take Mario, for instance. You've got him to this level. But what have you done for him to make sure they still have eyes on him at the position he's being recruited for? Player development wasn't there. When you have twelve coaches walking up and down the sideline, why aren't some of them doing this? As the principal, academically and otherwise, my job is to get as many of the students out of here."

When pressed further about the decision, Anderson said he'd also grown tired of the behavior and conduct of Hester's assistants. He mentioned the trip to Texas, when both Coach Q and Coach Fat had been disciplined for leaving the hotel and going clubbing the night before the game. Both were suspended for a week. He failed to mention that Blackmon had also joined the coaches, but was not punished.

Anderson said that he and his teachers had been so consumed with trying to raise the school grade, football was one of his last concerns. He'd relied largely on Blackmon to supervise the team. In that role, he said, Tadpole would routinely come to him with a litany of minor infractions:

coaches goofing on the sidelines, wearing their caps backward, playing with their phones, cursing too much.

But through another administrator, Anderson caught word of something more ugly, malignant: during the previous season, one of Jet's coaches had been sleeping with a female student. His alleged misconduct had since become gossip. Some parents approached administrators with the story. Students were also talking.

From what Blackmon was hearing in the community and relaying back to Anderson, Hester had covered it up. So one day around midseason, Anderson said, he pulled Hester aside with the information, but the coach denied knowing anything. (Hester said the conversation never took place.) The administration then launched an investigation, which stalled when students refused to reveal the girl's name.

When the season ended, Anderson decided to solve the problem by cutting off the head. "There was just too much coming in," he said. "I decided to cut ties. I cleaned house."

For his part, Hester said he didn't learn about the allegations until nearly two months after he was fired. It was one of the things he and Anderson had argued about in the auditorium after Signing Day. He said no one in the administration had ever mentioned the incident. If they had, the assistant coach would have been dismissed immediately (in Hester's defense, other assistants had been fired for much less). In fact, Anderson and James didn't even raise the subject the day they fired Jet. The only thing mentioned in the five-minute meeting was academics.

"I guarantee you if that was a real reason, they would have said it then," Hester said. "They heard about this stuff after the fact, then used it to give themselves legitimacy."

But chronology was sadly beside the point. The fact remained that Hester was gone from Glades Central—cut loose by an unforeseen irony. After three years of buffering his team against outside forces, from the streets, from bad men and their corrosive advice, and from the misery that always sought company—the family was destroyed by its trusted inner circle.

In late January, Glades Central hired Blackmon to succeed Hester as head coach of the Raiders. Tadpole was a muckstepper with NFL credentials, but had returned home the humble servant to work in the schools. The fact that Blackmon was never a first-round draft pick made him seem safe in the eyes of many fans and administrators. Tadpole had the true interests of every player in mind, said Anderson. He was someone "who understood the struggle of getting to that next level, not being a superstar."

Tadpole, it seemed, had become the anti-Jet.

As Glades Central shed its baggage, other schools clamored to pick it up. In the days after being fired, Hester fielded several job offers. Wishing to stay nearby, Jet took the head coaching job at Suncoast High, the magnet school in Riviera Beach that Glades Central had pummeled 39–0 the previous year. Going with him were coaches Sherm, Q, and many of the gang.

• • •

UNDER BLACKMON AND his new staff—which included Coach Fat, Sam King, and former Raider and Tampa Bay Buccaneer Reidel Anthony—Glades Central began the 2011 season once again ranked among the best teams in the nation. They lived up to the hype during the home opener, defeating 5A powerhouse Dwyer High in a thriller that was broadcast live on ESPN. The new squad was led by Boobie, Jaime, Jaja, Crevon LeBlanc, Baker, and Likely. And for the first time in decades, the Raiders also had a white quarterback—Tanner Redish, who transferred from Glades Day after leading the Gators to back-to-back state championships. After spending most of his career handing footballs off to Kelvin Taylor, Redish was hoping that a season with the GC flyboys would increase his chances of recruitment.

After beating Dwyer, the Raiders continued to roll undefeated, blowing out almost everyone they faced, including the struggling Suncoast Chargers. Unlike the Raiders, the kids on the Chargers' roster did not see football as their sole escape, and usually their season record showed it. They were a team of college-bound, honor-roll students whose schedules more resembled Jonteria's than Jaime Wilson's. Many also commuted from across Palm Beach County, meaning Hester would often go weeks without a full practice because half his team had either to study or catch a bus home.

The game against Glades Central was played at Effie C. Grear Field to a packed house expecting fireworks. For Hester, it was tough enough standing on the visitors' sidelines of his own alma mater, especially after what had happened. It was even harder watching his kids lose 44–3 and knowing the Raiders would've hung a hundred on him if they could. It was a classic beatdown in the muck, no different from the one the Raiders had given Suncoast the previous season. Still, Hester grew so upset that he lost his composure after the game. As Blackmon crossed the field to shake hands, Hester cursed and waved him off. A news camera captured the whole ugly exchange. "He was trying to rub it in," Hester later told a reporter, the anger still surging through his voice.

By season's end, the Raiders owned the best defense in the state of Florida. They demoralized Boynton Beach 70–7, then did the same to Pahokee the following week by beating them 70–0 in the Muck Bowl. Heading into the playoffs, Blackmon and the Raiders looked primed for a championship run to rival all others. They could do no wrong. As long as they won, it seemed, the fans thought little about Jessie the Jet and those victories he spoke about that never appeared in scoreboard lights.

That is, until the playoffs, when news broke that four Raiders were being accused of sexual assault. A freshman girl at Glades Central told administrators that four football players had pressured her to perform oral sex in a school bathroom. Two of the names she mentioned were Jaja and LeBlanc. The story surfaced during the national uproar over Penn State, where assistant football coach Jerry Sandusky was convicted of raping and fondling a number of young boys during his long tenure with the team. The school district quickly intervened at Glades Central and launched an investigation. In the meantime, all four boys were suspended from school and barred from playing football.

Without Jaja and LeBlanc in the secondary, the Raiders still steam-rolled through the first two playoff games, shutting out both Astronaut and Merritt Island. But in the semifinals, at home against Miami Norland, Boobie and the defense could no longer hold. There before God and the Glades, running back Randy "Duke" Johnson rushed for 265 yards and four touchdowns, helping Norland eliminate the mighty Raiders 29–13.

Blackmon's honeymoon was over, and you could bet the gamblers were calling for his head before the lights were even off. "Some of the guys had a really bad Christmas after that game," said Frank Williams. Other fans questioned Blackmon's ability to control his players, whose actions they felt led to the ultimate downfall of the team. But for the most part, the community remained by Tadpole's side.

The scandal and season-ending loss, however, were quickly overshadowed by a much greater tragedy. On January 2, the community awoke to the shocking news that Jimmy McMillan, the owner of the beloved Alabama-Georgia Grocery Store on MLK Boulevard, had been shot and killed in an early-morning robbery. The McMillans had operated the store since the 1940s and were one of the few remaining white families to keep roots in Belle Glade. Everyone knew and loved Jimmy. On the streets, it was a well-abided rule that the Alabama-Georgia was off-limits.

After studying the store's surveillance video, sheriff's detectives brought in a suspect who later confessed to the murder. It was Corey Graham, the former offensive lineman for the Raiders. Corey's dreams of football had ended after the team's loss against Cocoa. He had not been recruited alongside his teammates. After graduation, he'd enrolled at the local community college and remained in Belle Glade. But it was not enough to keep him anchored against the pulling tide. On the still-dark morning of January 2, while the town still slept, Corey slipped a bandanna over his face, walked into the store, and let himself be carried away.

Sadly, the tumultuous events distracted attention from one of Belle Glade's brightest moments. The week after Corey's arrest, while media attention still swirled around the murder, it was announced that Glades Central had raised its grade to a B, the highest in the school's history. Anderson and his teachers had finally managed to lift the scores of the lowest 25 percent and hopefully, in the process, establish a pattern for the coming years. The school slogan, "Committed to Winning in Academics and Athletics," no longer seemed such a joke when you walked through the halls.

For Anderson, the announcement was sweet validation after a three-year campaign to raise the status of the 96 percent. But in the process, he'd also come to accept the priorities of the community where he worked. As rewarding as the B grade was, he said, "we're never going to overtake football."

In the course of three years, the principal from Boca Raton had also received a rounded education on how the high school game worked in the Glades. A year after firing Hester and his staff, Anderson realized he may have acted too swiftly. Over time, he said, he'd discovered the rumors about Jet covering up his assistant's sexual relationship may have been fabricated—the product of certain members of the community trying to sabotage the coach out of his job.

"Out here they eat their own," Anderson said. "It's pretty cutthroat."

In hindsight, the principal acknowledged that Hester probably knew nothing about the incident. He now wished he'd conducted a more direct "intense conversation" with Jet about purging his staff before making the decision to fire him.

"It really wasn't all of his fault," he said, "even though it was on his watch."

Anderson even said if the head coaching job were to open again, he'd probably hire Hester back.

Not long after Suncoast ended its dreadful 4–6 season, Hester resigned as head coach. After one year on the job, the academic pressures facing the students were too great for him to properly lead the team, he told the *Post*. "It was just too difficult to do the things I wanted to do in that situation," he said.

The comments angered many Suncoast fans, players, and parents, many of whom filled the message board offering their stinging assessment of Jessie Hester and his brief tenure: the coach couldn't care less about kids and their education. All he wanted to do was win.

Around this time, Hester was nominated for induction into the Palm Beach County Sports Hall of Fame. It was a league that included Rickey Jackson, Fred Taylor, Ben McCoy, and other legends from the Glades. The nomination recognized Hester's contributions to the game, both his playing career and his 36–4 record coaching the Raiders to back-to-back state championship appearances.

It was an honor that would outlive any regrets of those three years back in Belle Glade, or the false start along the coast. For Hester, the induction was also free from the burden of his past: the absent father and family troubles, the scars, and the thousands of hours under the sun. But along with it came a new emptiness in his heart, where the love for a town once lived—a town with its haunted, self-defeating ways. In the long run, history would declare Jet the winner. And in doing so, it would keep safe his belief that he'd changed things for the better—that he'd won kids, not championships.

ACKNOWLEDGMENTS

Ilived in Belle Glade for much of the reporting of this book, in a small room at the Horizon Inn on Main Street, where Dilip Patel, Lilian Brown, and Lola Robinson took great care of me and always had a kind word. Weekend nights I'd often drive over to Fort Lauderdale and stay with the Berube family. Many thanks to Brian, Sheila, John, Katherine, and Elizabeth, for their generous hospitality, good food, and fellowship, and for being my family away from home.

Thanks to Donna Rose at South Plantation High School for first bringing me into the muck. Donna invited me to her school to talk about Congo, then implored me to visit another forgotten, underreported place—this one less than an hour's drive away. I'm glad I listened.

Thanks to Jessie Hester for opening his life and allowing me to become part of his team. And thanks to Jonteria Williams and the 2010 Glades Central Raiders for letting me ride along on their extraordinary journeys. It was an experience I'll always cherish. In addition, I want to thank the Raiders for taking me rabbit hunting, and for introducing me to new, fancy handshakes ("We gotta work on your coordination," Boobie concluded one day) and the slang and soundtracks of their lives (Lil Boosie's "Mind of a Maniac" and Waka Flocka Flame's "Hard in Da Paint" will forever remind me of riding in a school bus to football games).

Thanks to assistant coaches Sam King, Tony Smith, Randy Williams,

ACKNOWLEDGMENTS

Greg Hall, Greg Moreland, Santonio Thomas, Andrew Mann, Sherman Adams, Charles Walker, J. D. Patrick, Milton Swift, Melvin Lockett, Bruce Hytower, Terry Morris, Preston Vickers, and Leroy Singleton for guiding me through the history and culture, and for the many laughs and good conversations we shared. Same goes for Mike Petrarca, Dennis Knabb, Willie McDonald, and Anthony Williams.

Thanks to Frank and Tangela Williams, Christine Benjamin, Shawanna and Xavier Evans, Julius and Nora Hamilton, Delia Hamilton Powell, Theresa Williams, Canisa Rowley, and Gail Beard (may she rest in peace) for opening their homes and allowing me to write about their children. I also want to thank them for sharing their own personal stories, even when doing so proved painful.

Thanks to Anthony Anderson, Angela Moore, Melanie Bolden-Morris, Sherry Canty, and Terence Hart for allowing me into their school and classrooms and offering guidance. Thanks to Rudean Butts and Kevin Wright for greasing the wheels along the way. Thanks to Norman Harrison for game film, and to Donald "Duck" Williams and Coguy Miles for providing that delicious muck cooking after home games (as Sherm once said: "Ol' Duck can sure put the hurt on a backyard bird") and for the many other times those two men fed me. On that note, thanks to the good folks at the Banyan Tree restaurant for the coffee and sweet potato pie, and for letting me use their dining room as my satellite office. Thanks to Jeff Greer and Matt Porter at the *Palm Beach Post* for throwing me stats and insight when I needed them, and for being pals. And many thanks to my trusted readers: Kiley Lambert, Brian Berube, Christopher Berend, and Ann Mentink.

Sean Desmond and Tina Constable at Crown recognized the rich story beyond the Friday-night lights. My heartfelt thanks goes out to them and the rest of the hardworking people at Crown who made this book possible: Stephanie Knapp, Ellen Folan, Paul Lamb, Matthew Martin, and Jaqui Lebow. As always, thanks to my wonderful agent, Heather Schroder, for her years of friendship and counsel, and for always having my back. And a hundred thanks to Nicole Tourtelot at ICM for being a phone call away.